Micro Focus
CICS Option

*Developing CICS Applications
on the PC*

Computer Books from QED

Systems Development

The Complete Guide to Software Testing
Developing Client/Server Applications
Quality Assurance for Information Systems
Total Quality Management in Information Services
User-Interface Screen Design
On Time, Within Budget: Software Project
  Management Practices and Techniques
Managing Software Projects: Selecting and Using
  PC-Based Project Management Systems
From Mainframe to Workstations: Offloading
  Application Development
A Structured Approach to Systems Testing
Rapid Application Prototyping: The Storyboard
  Approach to User Requirements Analysis
Software Engineering with Formal Metrics

Information Engineering/CASE

Practical Model Management Using CASE Tools
Building the Data Warehouse
Information Systems Architecture:
  Development in the 90's
Enterprise Architecture Planning: Developing a
  Blueprint for Data, Applications, and Technology
Data Architecture: The Information Paradigm

IBM Systems Software

REXX in the TSO Environment
REXX Tools and Techniques
The MVS Primer
Cross System Product Application Development
TSO/E CLISTS: The Complete Tutorial and
  Reference Guide
MVS/JCL: Mastering Job Control Language
MVS/VSAM for the Application Programmer
Introduction to Cross System Product
CICS: A How-To for COBOL Programmers
CICS: A Guide to Performance Tuning
CICS Application and System Programming:
  Tools and Techniques
CICS: A Guide to Application Debugging

OS/2

OS/2 2.0 Workplace Shell: The User's
  Guide and Tutorial
OS/2 Presentation Manager Programming for
  COBOL Programmers
Micro Focus COBOL Workbench for the
  Application Developer

AS/400

AS/400: A Practical Guide for Programming
  and Operations
AS/400 Architecture and Applications:
  The Database Machine

VSE

VSE/SP and VSE/ESA: A Guide to Performance
  Tuning
VSE JCL and Subroutines for Application
  Programmers
DOS/VSE: CICS Systems Programming
DOS/VSE: An Introduction to the Operating System

UNIX

UNIX C Shell Desk Reference
The UNIX Industry: Evolution, Concepts,
  Architecture, Applications, and Standards

Management and Business Skills

The Disaster Recovery Plan
Controlling the Future: Managing
  Technology-Driven Change
How to Automate Your Computer Center
Mind Your Business: Managing the Impact of
  End-User Computing
Understanding Data Pattern Processing: The
  Key to Competitive Advantage

VAX/VMS

Rdb/VMS: Developing the Data Warehouse
Network Programming Under DECNet
  Phase IV and V
VAX/VMS: Mastering DCL Commands and
  Utilities

Database

Client/Server and Distributed Database Design
Third-Wave Processing: Database Machines and
  Decision Support Systems
Database Management Systems: Understanding
  and Applying Database Technology

Database — DB2

QMF: How to Use Query Management Facility
  with DB2 and SQL/DS
SQL for DB2 and SQL/DS Application Developers
DB2: the Complete Guide to Implementation
  and Use
Embedded SQL for DB2: Application Design and
  Development
DB2: Maximizing Performance in Online
  Production Systems

Database — ORACLE

ORACLE: Building High Performance
  Online Systems
How To Use ORACLE SQL*Plus

QED books are available at special quantity discounts for educational uses, premiums, and sales promotions.
Special books, book excerpts, and instructive materials can be created to meet specific needs.

This is Only a Partial Listing. For Additional Information or a Free Catalog contact
QED Publishing Group • P. O. Box 812070 • Wellesley, MA 02181-0013
Telephone: 800-343-4848 or 617-237-5656 or fax 617-235-0826

Micro Focus CICS Option

Developing CICS Applications on the PC

Clayton L. McNally, Jr.

QED Publishing Group
Boston • London • Toronto

This book is available at a special discount when ordered in bulk quantities. For information, contact Special Sales Department, QED Publishing Group, 170 Linden Street, Wellesley, MA 02181-0013 or phone 617-237-5656.

© 1993 QED Publishing Group
P.O. Box 812070
Wellesley, MA 02181-0013

QED Publishing Group is a division of QED Information Sciences, Inc.

Library of Congress Catalog Number: 93-3390
International Standard Book Number: 0-89435-460-4

Printed in the United States of America
93 94 95 10 9 8 7 6 5 4 3 2 1

Library of Congress Cataloging-In-Publication Data

McNally, Clayton L.
    Micro focus CICS option : developing CICS applications on the PC / Clayton L. McNally, Jr.
        p.   cm.
    Includes index.
    ISBN 0-89435-460-4
    1. CICS (Computer system)   2. Application software.
    3. COBOL (Computer program language)   I. Title.
    QA76.76.T45M38   1993
    005.4'3--dc20   93-3390
                                                              CIP

DEDICATION

I would like to thank Betsy, Alicia, and Jenna McNally, who continue to inspire me to reach for more in life. Success is too often measured by accomplishments and not relationships. I look at life as a wonderful learning experience, and I am proud to have three wonderful ladies to guide me.

Contents

Preface

Micro Focus CICS Option (MCO) is a highly successful tool for CICS application development and maintenance. MCO works equally well in a DOS or OS/2 environment.

Companies interested in adopting MCO are most concerned with its compatibility to the mainframe as well as the price of the system and/or the PC workstation and training costs it will entail. Instead of validating the purchase of the product, this book will provide some insight into the potential cost benefits of using MCO. Each company has to evaluate the return on the investment within the framework of its own facility.

MCO's capabilities will be defined, and there are examples to walk you through the use of the various functions. After reading this book you will have a clear understanding of MCO and its benefits. Extensive use of images will assist you in clarifying each function. As with any tool, there will be a learning curve for programmers before any increase in productivity will be evident.

This book is organized into 14 chapters and 2 appendixes.

Chapter 1: The PC/Mainframe Link covers topics relating to reducing mainframe usage and increasing programmer productivity.

Chapter 2: Application Development examines the phases of application development and the MCO functions that support each phase.

Chapter 3: MCO Overview introduces the various functions directly supported within MCO and those functions indirectly accessed by MCO.

Chapter 4: Establishing the MCO Environment examines customization of MCO and creating CICS Resource Definition Tables.

Chapter 5: Loading CICS Resource Tables examines the steps involved with defining an applications' resource needs to MCO.

Chapter 6: Developing BMS Screens examines creating BMS MAPS from scratch and maintaining imported macro files.

Chapter 7: BMS Macros, Copybooks, and Executables covers creating macro and copybook files from MAPSET/MAP definitions and then generating an executable MAP.

Chapter 8: BMS Utilities examines the utility functions supporting backup and recovery of the BMS screen databases and extracting and loading of MAPSET files.

Chapter 9: Editing and Checking CICS COBOL Programs explains the process to edit and check CICS programs with a discussion of editing programs in general. Because of MCOs interface with the Micro Focus Editor, the editor primary submenus are introduced. MCO does not support a check function, but a CICS translator is identified, followed by an examination of the Micro Focus compiler.

Chapter 10: Animating CICS COBOL Programs examines the process of invoking the emulation facility leading to the use of the Micro Focus Animator functions. Because of its importance to the debugging process, the Animator will be looked at in detail.

Chapter 11: Compiling and Running COBOL Programs discusses the Compile and Emulation Facility without Animation functions in relation to "running" an on-line program.

Chapter 12: Using TSQ and TDQ examines the use of Temporary Storage Queues and Transient Data Queues in an application program.

Chapter 13: Establishing Databases for Use in CICS Programs covers using WFL to establish a VSAM database, IMSVS86 for an IMS database, and XDB for a DB2 database.

Chapter 14: Accessing Databases from MCO CICS Programs covers sample sessions on accessing databases (VSAM, DL/I and DB2) from MCO programs.

Appendix A defines the mainframe CICS transactions provided with MCO.

Appendix B supplies BMS macro statements and options available.

The terms CICS, MCO, and CICS emulator are used throughout this book.

- CICS, by itself, refers to mainframe CICS
- MCO refers to the complete Micro Focus CICS product
- CICS emulator refers to the CICS emulator tool that comes with MCO

The PC/Mainframe Link

It was not so long ago that calculators were cranked by hand and occupied the better part of a desk top. Computers existed only in science fiction movies. But now we have computers that can be held in the palm of the hand and automatic teller machines (ATMs) that provide instant access to our financial resources.

In less than one generation, computers have thrust us into a new age. Now those science fiction movies of yesterday are the realities of today. As we move into the next century, new technology is driving us to reshape the way business is done.

Information is a corporation's most valued asset, and timely, cost-effective access to it is critical. Rapid compilation of crucial data for a constantly changing business is as important as the information gathered. The switch from mainframe to PC is essential to competition today. Applications need to be delivered in a shorter time frame and with as few defects as possible. The tools required by programmers in this area are now available for the PC environment.

This chapter examines various topics concerning the migration to the PC, the evolution of PC technology, and the reasons to migrate to the PC, which include reduced mainframe usage and improvement in productivity.

EVOLVING TECHNOLOGY

Technology is reshaping the way we perform our jobs. No longer do sophisticated computers exist only in the movies. From "Buck Rogers" to "Star Trek," computers have evolved from first conception to stretching the limits of our imaginations and routinely performing extraordinary tasks.

From the programmer's view, computers evolved from card punch input to native TSO that promised productivity improvements. While TSO eliminated a few steps and problems (cards and RJE readers), COBOL statements still had to be edited a line at a time. Productivity did increase to a small degree, but programmers still had their hands tied.

The current generation of PCs provides more CPU capacity than some of the first mainframes, with no end in sight. Computers have evolved from building-sized to room-sized to desktop to laptop and finally to palm-top machines. The PC has evolved from the simple terminal emulator to the sophisticated processors of today. PC operating systems that once supported single-thread processing (one job at a time) progressed to multi-tasking (concurrent jobs running), offering the ability to accomplish more in the same amount of time.

More and more mainframe workload is shifting to the PC. The tools now available to programmers have a significant impact on a company's bottom line. Tomorrow is truly here today. I hope this book will help you appreciate the potential benefits to your company and that you will find Micro Focus CICS Option (MCO) to be a powerful addition when developing or maintaining applications.

SHOULD WE MIGRATE TO THE PC?

There will be two areas in which to anticipate cost savings: reduced mainframe usage and increased programmer productivity.

Reduced Mainframe Usage

Mainframe expenses can be reduced when development or maintenance workloads are migrated to the PC for the actual enhancement activity to take place. By offloading development workloads, the mainframe can be more fully utilized to process the ever-growing production workload.

Migration to the PC can prevent purchases or leases of large and expensive mainframe hardware. The following results will realize potential savings:

- Reallocating mainframe test resources
- Reducing or eliminating test outages when the mainframe is down
- Potentially delaying future mainframe purchases

Increased Programmer Productivity

MCO offers the following opportunities to increase a programmer's productivity:

- Eliminates jobs waiting in compile queues
- Eliminates jobs waiting for test resources
- Provides a powerful debugging tool to speed up the testing process

Providing programmers with technology that improves their productivity will help reduce mainframe usage and deliver code faster. Programmers will have the tools to perform testing and debugging in an environment with fewer encumbrances.

PC development is now available, offering economy and improvement in productivity. CICS testing is available on a PC with a quality debugging process. Programmers can deliver higher-quality code in shorter periods of time.

Application Development

We think of project life cycles when developing an application on the mainframe. Developing applications on the PC is no different—a logical life cycle flow should be followed. The PC development environment can be broken into similar phases.

The following are the systems requirements and design steps of PC development:

- Program development (COBOL and screens)
- Application testing
- Application verification

The application development cycle shown in Figure 2.1 requires the following two additional steps to develop on a PC:

- Download files and programs to a PC before modifying the programs.
- Upload files and programs to the mainframe after modifying the programs.

This chapter examines the functions programmers will use when developing, testing, and verifying applications. It will identify the functions that support the various development cycle

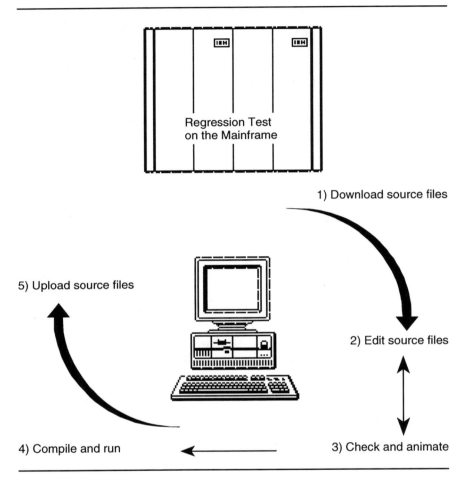

Figure 2.1.   Application development cycle on the PC.

phases. Subsequent chapters will cover the various functions in greater detail.

APPLICATION DEVELOPMENT STEPS

Developing an application on the PC requires minimal mainframe interfacing. If the application does not exist, the only interface is to migrate the code from the PC to the mainframe. If enhancements are being made to an existing application, the mainframe interface phase becomes more involved (e.g., transferring programs and files between the PC and the mainframe).

Transfer Between Mainframe and PC

Files are transferred from the mainframe to the PC (download) when changes are to be made to an existing program. After the program is modified and debugged, it is migrated back to the mainframe (upload). For programs that are modified frequently, files should reside on the PC. Items to look for when determining what to transfer to the PC are the following:

- Source code
    COBOL programs
    BMS macros
    Copybooks or include statements
- Data files
    Flat files
        Record sequential
        Line sequential
    DBMS
        DB2
            DDL statements
            DCLGEN statements
        IMS
            DBD statements
            PSB statements

When deciding what to transfer, don't forget to bring down source code for called programs that may not require changes. Common production routines are often overlooked as required items on the PC.

MCO does not provide a facility for transferring files between the mainframe and the PC, but the Micro Focus COBOL transfer facility can be used easily.

After files have been transferred to the PC, data may need to be converted from one format to another or edited to modify data values. MCO programmers can again use a tool like Micro Focus

COBOL to do this. Please refer to the book *Micro Focus COBOL Workbench for the Application Developer* (QED Publishing) for information about Micro Focus COBOL.

Program Development (COBOL and Screens)

Application programmers will spend a large portion of their time working with MCO functions that support development of an application:

- BMS screen development
- Editing COBOL programs
- Compiling COBOL programs
- Debugging COBOL programs

Figure 2.2 provides a view of how the various functions interface and where the MCO functions support the various development phases.

The Animator function can execute either .INT (checked) or .GNT (compiled) code. The animation process executes the .GNT if both the .INT and .GNT are available. It does not display lines of code on the screen if the file being executed is a .GNT file.

The Run process can also execute both .INT and .GNT files. Again, the .GNT code would be executed before the .INT file. When .INT files are executed in the Run process, they act like compiled code, and no lines of code are displayed on the screen.

BMS Screen Development. MCO provides a facility to develop or maintain BMS MAPS on the PC. BMS source files can be created on the PC or transferred down from the mainframe for processing. BMS source file editing is available through the following:

- BMS screen painter
- Native macro editing

MCO allows native macros to be loaded into the screen paint facility where programmers can complete all MAP editing. While in the screen development facility, COBOL copybooks are generated and maps can be assembled.

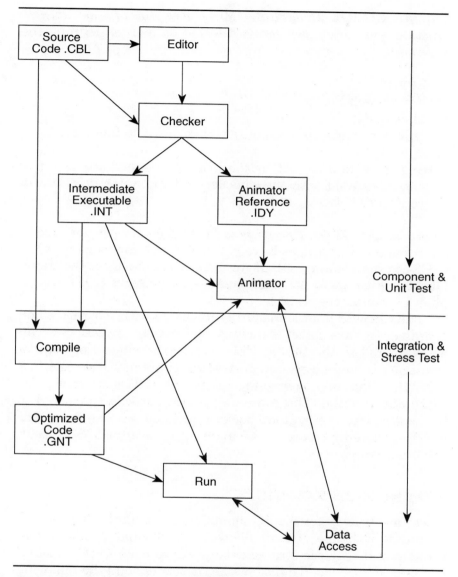

Figure 2.2.   MCO function and test integration.

Editing COBOL Programs. MCO does not provide an edit function. An editor package is selected as part of defining the environment:

- SPF/PC
- Workbench Editor
- Micro SPF
- Other (prompts for the edit package start-up file name)

Setting the default to [F2] *workbench* may be the best selection, as it is integrated with the Checker and Animator functions of Micro Focus COBOL.

Compiling COBOL Programs. MCO does not provide a compiler feature, but it does have a CICS translator to convert the CICS commands into COBOL-recognizable code. Once the translate step is complete, MCO invokes the Micro Focus COBOL compiler for syntax checking.

The Checker function is fully integrated within MCO. When syntax errors are detected during the compile process, they can be examined in the Editor. This interactive connection will be examined in more detail as part of the chapter Checking CICS COBOL Programs. Debugging programs is supported via the Animator function. The Animator is interactively connected to the editor, like the syntax checking procedures. The Animator will be covered in more detail in the Animating CICS COBOL Progams chapters.

APPLICATION TESTING

A testing strategy for the PC should not be remarkably different from that of the mainframe. We will outline what should be reasonable and realistic strategies and where each MCO function can best be utilized. Quality testing is best done in the following four major test phases:

- Component testing
- Unit testing

- Integration testing
- Stress testing

Testing in general can have a significant impact on the expense of fixing mistakes. Catching problems during unit testing is less costly than during integration testing, and catching them during integration testing is more economical than during mainframe testing. By the time coding begins, test cases should be defined, the results predicted, and the plan carefully reviewed with the customer. Not only can testing proceed immediately, but with more thorough and effective data than "doing it on the fly."

Testing COBOL Programs

MCO provides a CICS emulator that allows the execution of CICS commands and COBOL programs in a CICS region. Debugging (animating) is provided by Micro Focus COBOL.

When animating programs, data fields can be viewed and modified, and even the program's logic path can be altered. Debugging on-line CICS applications on the PC is not a complicated process. In fact, programmers should actually enjoy testing on the PC.

The Emulation Facility with Animator function of MCO should be used as part of component and unit testing, as seen in Figure 2.2. Typically, these testing phases are thought of as stand-alone testing and are well suited for testing on a PC versus a LAN.

Component Testing. Component testing is beneficial to many kinds of programs, allowing various portions of a program to be tested independently. Codes that can be tested separately include the following:

- PC DB2
- CICS logic
- COBOL logic

This method allows programmers to eliminate problems before it becomes difficult to determine what portion of the program is causing a problem. Component testing is not done often, but it should be examined in IS shops. Component testing will add some time to the early testing phase, but it saves time in the final test phase.

Unit Testing. Unit testing is a requirement that IS shops have been performing for quite some time, testing all of the pieces of a program together. Unit testing is often thought of as the phase where the majority of a program's problems are discovered. But the reality is that programs often function well during the unit test because the unit testing is not done thoroughly!

During this time the programmer involved with the coding is again intimately involved with the testing. Often, the data used in a unit test fits the programmer's view of the program's function. If a business customer is involved in the test planning, more errors are apt to be found here, rather than in a later phase where they cost more time and money to fix.

Quality unit testing should insure that the previously tested components function together. Based on data input, a set of predictable events should occur, and the unit test should validate these predictions.

Integration Testing. Integration testing is critical to successfully delivering an application. Integration implies that all of the programs of an application should function together in a predictable manner.

Integration testing on a LAN is particularly helpful when it would be cumbersome to load and store large numbers of programs on individual PCs. If done on a LAN, the executable code can be shared.

Stress Testing. Stress testing is a portion of the complete testing strategy that is rarely omitted, or it is performed with insufficient data to really stress the application. A valid stress test should consist of both (1) multiple-user access and (2) large data files.

The multi-user environment can be emulated on the PC when the test occurs on a LAN. Large data file support should be at least 90 percent of the full production file.

Running a stress test with insufficient data is not going to demonstrate any potential performance problems. As the capacity of PC drives continues to expand, it may soon be possible to perform reasonable stress testing on a PC. While a limited stress test can be performed on the PC, the mainframe is the only environment available for a true stress or regression test.

VERIFYING COBOL PROGRAMS (PROTOTYPE)

During the development cycle, programmers can complete the entire phase of coding and debugging an application as part of checking and animating. It is not necessary to verify or prototype a program prior to migrating the code to the mainframe, but there are at least two good reasons to verify it:

- Programmer verification
- Customer (user) checkout

Although verification or prototyping is an optional step in the PC development process, it might better be considered a required step. A goal of programmers and users should always be to deliver the highest-quality application in the shortest time frame possible. MCO provides both programmers and users with just that opportunity.

The Compile and Emulation Facility without Animator functions of MCO should be considered as a final checkout process during the integration and stress test phases, as seen in Figure 2.2. Compiling and running without animating will not display the source code on the screen during the execution of programs.

Programmer Verification. As the programmer debugs a program with the animator, temporary code can be inserted to correct logic errors. At the end of an animation session, the normal course of events would be to re-edit the program, re-check, and then re-animate, insuring that any temporary code is made a permanent part of the source file. Once the above steps have been successfully completed, the program can be migrated to the mainframe.

Customer (User) Checkout. Once the programmer has completed the testing phases, users can verify the application to insure the system delivers what was requested. In this manner, design requirements can be validated on the PC and potential discrepancies corrected without any mainframe interface.

SUMMARY

The process of developing on the PC begins with the transferring of source files down between the mainframe and PC. MCO provides direct or indirect access to functions that support CICS application development cycles on the PC.

3

MCO Overview

MCO is a CICS emulation product that provides programmers with the capability to code and test on-line applications on a PC. MCO does not provide programmers with sophisticated editing or debugging functions. Instead, MCO interactively interfaces with other products. This chapter examines various items that are supported *directly* by MCO:

- CICS menu presentation
- MCO functionality
- Configuration options
- Help function
- CICS environment
- BMS screen development
- CICS region

and those items *indirectly* supported by MCO:

- File management tools
- Application development and testing
- Application verification

This chapter will provide an overview of the MCO-specific functions and the functions accessed in other products. This is not to suggest that the indirectly accessed functions are less important. In fact, programmers will use these functions extensively.

CICS MENU PRESENTATION

The menu system used by MCO controls the display of all screens on the terminal, overlaying the key work area with the most recently selected function. Even with the busy nature of the screens, the continuous display of functions that led a programmer to a specific location can be useful.

When pressed, each function key will invoke a submenu, and pressing Escape returns to the choices of previous menus. MCO presents users with selections of menus, windows, and list boxes.

Menus. MCO menus present a list of PF function keys with their definitions, as shown in Figure 3.1. On menus, selecting a function is accomplished in one of two ways:

1. Position cursor to a function and press Enter, by using
   up arrow
   down arrow
   PgUp
   PgDn
   Home
   End
2. Pressing a function key

Windows. MCO windows contain one or more fields to be selected by the user. The field currently positioned on will be displayed in reverse video (see Figure 3.2). To scroll between entry fields, use one of the following keys:

- *up arrow*
- *down arrow*
- *PgUp*
- *PgDn*
- *Home*
- *End*

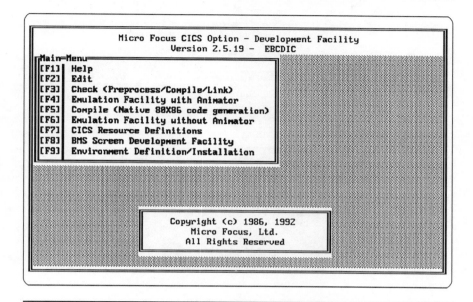

Figure 3.1.   Sample MCO function key selections.

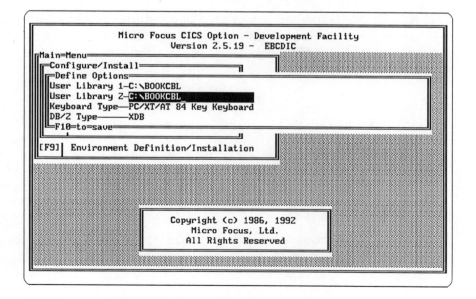

Figure 3.2.   Environment data entry submenu.

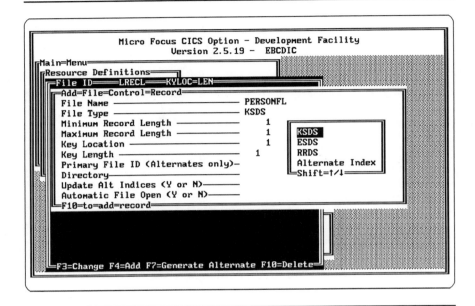

Figure 3.3.   MCO sample list box selection list.

List Boxes. MCO list boxes contain a list of items to select from and are found on various windows within the CICS functions, as shown in Figure 3.3. To scroll between list items, use one of the following key combinations:

- *Shift key/up arrow*
- *Shift key/down arrow*

Once an item has been positioned to, press Enter to select the value.

MCO FUNCTIONALITY

Mainframe programmers will find that MCO provides a powerful set of functions logically grouped into three major categories:

- File management
- Application development
- Application verification

Each of these categories contains a set of functions supporting specific aspects of a programmer's work flow, functions that map back to the logical progression of work flow when applications are developed.

File Management. File management functions are not provided by MCO. Rather, they may be accessed by invoking Micro Focus COBOL, particularly *F2=files* from the mainframe development environment menu.

The directory function is conveniently located on several menus and submenus, for example, when loading a BMS file into the painter, the directory function prompts for a file name. By placing this function on many menus, the MCO functionality is enhanced tremendously.

Application Development. To edit COBOL programs, MCO interfaces with the previously defined edit package. To compile a program for debugging, MCOs, Check (preprocess/compile/link) function prepares a program for animation. To debug a program, the Emulation Facility with Animator function executes a program displaying code on the screen.

Application Verification. To compile a program for verification, the Compile (native 80X86 code generation) function prepares a program for verification. To verify a program, the Emulation without Animator function runs a program without displaying code on the screen.

To edit or create BMS MAPS, the BMS Screen Development function should be selected to import BMS macros or use the screen painter. When editing native BMS macros, use the edit function previously mentioned.

The MCO main menu function Environment Definition/Installation supports definition of CICS resource tables, configuration of MCO, DB2 use, and which editor to access.

CONFIGURATION OPTIONS

After MCO is installed, the product can be started up from the Micro Focus COBOL MDE menu or from an operating system prompt. The banner on this menu gives the release level and the version type being invoked (ASCII or EBCDIC).

A horizontal line near the bottom of the screen is used by MCO to communicate feedback to the programmer, such as delete confirmations on some screens. To exit off of a submenu, press the Escape key (pressing Escape is also used to exit from MCO).

Directory Paths

During the install procedures, MCO establishes a directory environment for use in CICS development and testing. The following directories are supported:

- C:\MFCICS\DOCS—Directory containing information about MCO.
- C:\MFCICS\DEMO—MCO supplied demonstration programs.
- C:\MFCICS\LBR—Contains CICS library and executable files.
- C:\MFCICS\SOURCE—User source code files (.CBL).
- C:\MFCICS\TEST—Generated executable files (.INT, .GNT and .MST).
- C:\MFCICSCICS\COPY—COBOL copybooks or includes, including those generated from the BMS screen development function.
- C:\MFCICS\BMS—Native BMS macro source code.
- C:\MFCICS\CICSRDT—Contains the defined CICS Resource Definition Tables.
- C:\MFCICS\DATA—Data files used by the application.

Screen Displays

MCO allows the environment to be configured for personal taste (see Figure 3.4). Access to screen modifications is invoked from the MCO main menu by pressing [F9] *Environment Definition/ Installation* and then pressing [F4] *Configure Screen*. This window will display the various windows and message areas on the

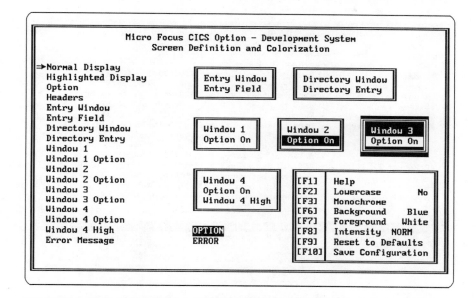

Figure 3.4.   Display of MCO customization screen.

left side of the screen and what they look like when displayed on the right side.

HELP FUNCTION

Context-sensitive Help is generated on a screen-by-screen basis, although not all screens have Help assistance. A sample Help screen is shown in Figure 3.5 displaying Help information for the MCO main menu after pressing *F1*.

The function key *F1* used to invoke Help is not displayed on all menus or submenus. Unless the *F1* is designated as used for another function, at least try the *F1*. Several screens do not display the *F1*, and yet Help information is available for them.

The on-line reference (HYHELP) feature is available when editing, using CSI, or animating a program. On-line reference is covered in the book *MicroFocus COBOL Workbench for the Application Developer*.

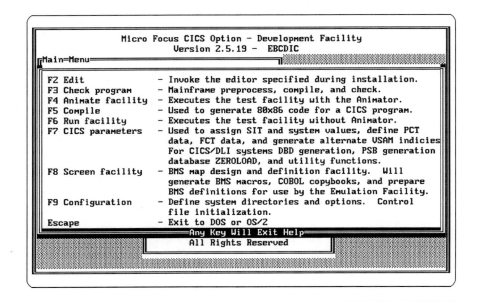

```
              Micro Focus CICS Option - Development Facility
                      Version 2.5.19 -   EBCDIC
┌Main=Menu══════════════════════════════════════════════
  F2 Edit              - Invoke the editor specified during installation.
  F3 Check program     - Mainframe preprocess, compile, and check.
  F4 Animate facility  - Executes the test facility with the Animator.
  F5 Compile           - Used to generate 80x86 code for a CICS program.
  F6 Run facility      - Executes the test facility without Animator.
  F7 CICS parameters   - Used to assign SIT and system values, define PCT
                         data, FCT data, and generate alternate VSAM indicies
                         For CICS/DLI systems DBD generation, PSB generation
                         database ZEROLOAD, and utility functions.
  F8 Screen facility   - BMS map design and definition facility.  Will
                         generate BMS macros, COBOL copybooks, and prepare
                         BMS definitions for use by the Emulation Facility.
  F9 Configuration     - Define system directories and options.  Control
                         file initialization.
  Escape               - Exit to DOS or OS/2
                       ═══Any Key Will Exit Help═══
                         All Rights Reserved
```

Figure 3.5.   MCO sample display of Help data.

CICS ENVIRONMENT

After installing MCO, the development environment needs to be configured. Configuring MCO options as shown in Figure 3.6 consists of the following:

- Identifying user libraries
- Identifying the keyboard type
- Selecting an edit tool
- Choosing a DB2 emulation product
- Defining screen colors
- Establishing CICS resource tables

Establishing the MCO environment does not load any of the CICS Resource Definition Tables (RDT). At this time, only the tables required for CICS to function are defined.

For programmers to test, VSAM files need to be defined on

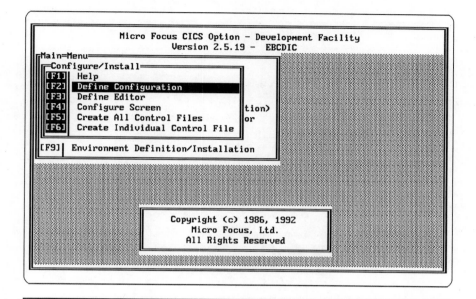

```
              Micro Focus CICS Option - Development Facility
                      Version 2.5.19 -  EBCDIC
 ┌Main=Menu═══════════════════════════════════
 │ ┌Configure/Install══════════════════════════
 │ │[F1]  Help
 │ │[F2]  Define Configuration
 │ │[F3]  Define Editor
 │ │[F4]  Configure Screen                tion)
 │ │[F5]  Create All Control Files        or
 │ │[F6]  Create Individual Control File

 │ │[F9]  Environment Definition/Installation



                    ┌──────────────────────────────┐
                    │   Copyright (c) 1986, 1992    │
                    │       Micro Focus, Ltd.       │
                    │      All Rights Reserved      │
                    └──────────────────────────────┘
```

Figure 3.6.   CICS environment definition submenu.

the File Control Table (FCT) and transaction code/program relationships to the Program Control Table (PCT). Additional entries to other CICS tables can be made as necessary.

BMS SCREEN DEVELOPMENT

BMS MAPS can be developed either by using the screen painter or coding native macros. The screen development facility seen in Figure 3.7 consists of the following:

- MAPSET definitions
- MAP definitions
- Field definitions
- Generations and Conversions
- MAP utilities

Embedded in the MAP function, the screen painter is invoked when either (1) adding a new MAP, or (2) selecting free-form

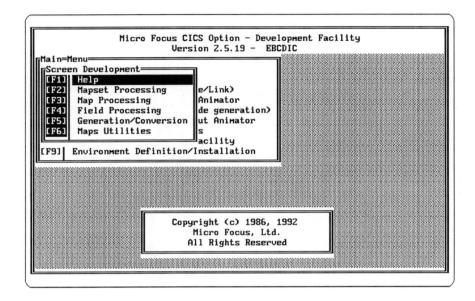

Figure 3.7. CICS screen development submenu.

screen paint. Native BMS macros can be imported into the paint feature after the macros are downloaded from the mainframe. BMS macros can also be edited directly without using the paint facility by accessing the edit function from the main menu.

The generate/conversion function supports importing and exporting BMS macros, generating COBOL copybooks, and BMS macro datasets.

The utility function allows programmers to generate a test (executable) definition for the MAPSET, much like an assemble on the mainframe. The BMS mapset data can be backed up and recovered as part of the utilities provided.

CICS REGION

The cornerstone of the MCO product is the CICS emulation facility. The emulator allows the running of CICS programs on the PC. Once started, the emulator treats the PC like a 3270 terminal connected to mainframe CICS.

The biggest difference between MCO and the mainframe is that MCO does not support multi-tasking. Only one region and one program are executing at one time.

The emulator can be started to run with or without the animator. Once invoked, the CICS region is entered into as shown in Figure 3.8. On-line application debugging is a pleasure with MCO; programmers will find the capability of MCO quite robust.

FILE MANAGEMENT TOOLS

MCO does not provide any file handling functions. For that, the Micro Focus COBOL file facility is recommended. What follows here is a brief examination of some Micro Focus COBOL file features that can be useful in preparing files for CICS emulation. Micro Focus COBOL provides the developer with six file utilities:

- File transfer
- Source conversion

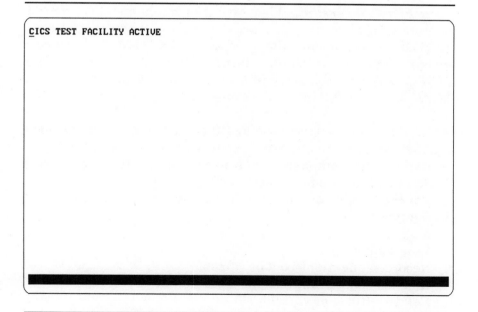

Figure 3.8.   CICS region initial screen.

- File conversion
- Data file editor
- File comparison
- Hex edit

Only the first four will be discussed here. For extended definitions, see *MicroFocus COBOL Workbench for the Application Developer*.

File Transfer. File transfer allows source files to be migrated between the mainframe and the PC. File conversions are necessary to convert the transferred file to a VSAM file format for processing in MCO.

Source Code Conversion. When working with source code that contains embedded hex values, the code should be transferred as data files and then converted. These embedded hex characters (nontext characters) should not be converted through the normal transfer process. The convert utility will insure the integrity of any embedded hex characters.

Data File Conversion. When trying to emulate a CICS VSAM environment, file conversions are a certainty. When emulating a CICS DB2 environment, other products (XDB, Database Manager) are required to prepare the data files for CICS use. When emulating a CICS DL/I database environment, accessing a product such as IMSVS86 will facilitate the accessing of DL/I databases.

WFL. Files may be processed in either ASCII or EBCDIC mode and may be converted from one mode to another or from one type to another. To accomplish these conversions, use the Micro Focus Workbench File Loader utility (WFL).

For the VSAM environment, Micro Focus (3.0) supports seven PC file types:

- Line sequential
- Record sequential (fixed or variable)
- Indexed sequential (fixed or variable)
- Relative (fixed or variable)
- VRECGEN

- Mainframe report format
- PC print format

For testing application programs in MCO, programmers will need to convert files to either KSDS, ESDS, or RRDS and then to define Alternate Indexes if needed. Figure 3.9 reflects input into a WFL conversion from a record-sequential file to an indexed-sequential fixed-length (KSDS) file. No mask is required as the records do not contain COMP-3 fields.

Data File Editing. MCO does not provide a data file editing tool. Instead, use the Micro Focus COBOL data file editor (DFED). It displays either ASCII or EBCDIC files in full screen based on the record length (record sequential) supplied at load time or the value on the header record (indexed file).

Records can be displayed as formatted (single record display, packed fields displayed as character values) by using a structure

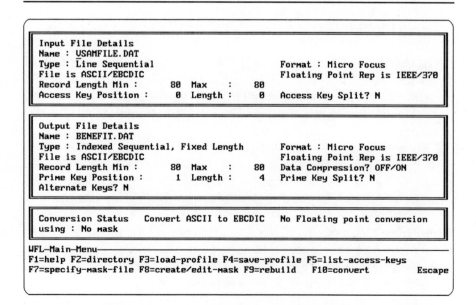

```
 Input File Details
 Name : USAMFILE.DAT
 Type : Line Sequential              Format : Micro Focus
 File is ASCII/EBCDIC                 Floating Point Rep is IEEE/370
 Record Length Min :     80  Max   :    80
 Access Key Position :    0  Length :    0   Access Key Split? N

 Output File Details
 Name : BENEFIT.DAT
 Type : Indexed Sequential, Fixed Length    Format : Micro Focus
 File is ASCII/EBCDIC                 Floating Point Rep is IEEE/370
 Record Length Min :     80  Max   :    80   Data Compression? OFF/ON
 Prime Key Position :     1  Length :     4   Prime Key Split? N
 Alternate Keys? N

 Conversion Status   Convert ASCII to EBCDIC    No Floating point conversion
 using : No mask

WFL-Main-Menu
F1=help F2=directory F3=load-profile F4=save-profile F5=list-access-keys
F7=specify-mask-file F8=create/edit-mask F9=rebuild    F10=convert       Escape
```

Figure 3.9.   File conversion utility (WFL).

file created from a clean checked program. All supported file types can be modified; records can even be inserted into or deleted from the file.

APPLICATION DEVELOPMENT/TESTING

MCO does not provide an edit function. It links to the previously selected edit package and uses the selected editor for program development. It also does not provide tools for testing application programs, but offers an emulation function that allows the execution of programs in a CICS-like region. The emulation process is invoked using the Emulation Facility with Animator as the testing tool.

Debugging Aids

When using the Micro Focus Animator, some debugging aids can be toggled on from MCO:

- CSI
- STRUCT
- ANALYZE

CSI. CSI (COBOL Source Information) allows the querying of fields and procedure division routines to better understand how a program is constructed. Using CSI during program construction can be very useful in locating unused data items (DEADDATA) or unexecutable procedure routines (UNEXEC).

To use CSI from MCO, press [*F10*] *Directives* on the check screen and type in the directive CSI, which will create a file called program name.CSI, whether or not the program had syntax errors. CSI files can be used in the Editor and in the Animator.

Structure Charts. To use STRUCT from MCO, press [*F10*] *Directives* on the check screen and type in the directive STRUCT. The structure directive displays a structure chart of the program. A clean check is required to generate the chart.

Analyze. To use ANALYZE from MCO, press [*F10*] *Directives* on the check screen and type in the directive ANALYZE. The analyze directive displays the number of times each line of code is executed when animating a program. After execution, it may seem that lines of code can be deleted if they have not been accessed according to the analyzer, but before deleting any code, consider two reasons why statements may not have been executed:

- Insufficient test data to execute specific routines
- Missing "perform or go to" statements

APPLICATION VERIFICATION

MCO does not provide tools for verifying application programs. It provides an emulation function that allows the execution of programs in a CICS-like region. The emulation process is invoked by selecting the Emulation Facility without Animator function.

SUMMARY

MCO offers mainframe programmers a set of functions that are enhanced by the access to Micro Focus COBOL. MCO integrates with other software (DB2 and IMS) to further emulate the mainframe environment.

At this time the examination has been just brief enough to pique interest in using this tool. MCO is well worth using and is enhanced when used in conjunction with Micro Focus COBOL. As identified in this chapter, several functions used by MCO are actually resident in Micro Focus COBOL.

Establishing the MCO Environment

Prior to any development activity, the MCO environment must be established. This chapter examines the detailed process of defining various resources to MCO:

1. terminal configuration
2. products supported
3. edit tool to use
4. screen configuration
5. CICS resources

ENVIRONMENT DEFINITIONS

CICS (mainframe or PC) must know what resources will be used by an application. CICS resources are defined to MCO once. The actual Resource Definition Tables (RDT) can be established in many directories. By doing this, programmers can develop two or more applications on a PC and maintain different resources for each. In order to take advantage of this, programmers have to lay the groundwork for specific resource tables.

DEFINE CONFIGURATIONS

The first area that MCO needs to have configured is the definition of the terminal and other products to interface with (see Figure 4.1). Pressing [*F9*] *Environment Definition/Selection* from the MCO main menu invokes the Configure/Install submenu.

No specific order is required when defining the environment:

- Identify user libraries
- Select keyboard type
- Select edit software
- Identify SQL software

User Libraries. MCO provides basic directory paths used when editing or animating programs. It also supports two additional user libraries that are not defined in the AUTOEXEC.BAT or CONFIG.SYS files. Two user libraries can be defined as shown in

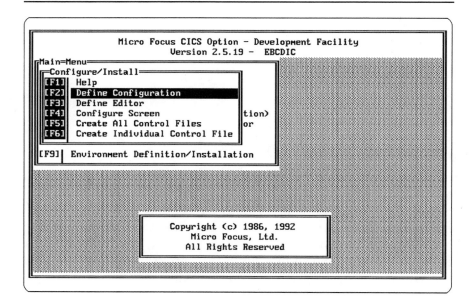

Figure 4.1.   MCO configuration submenu.

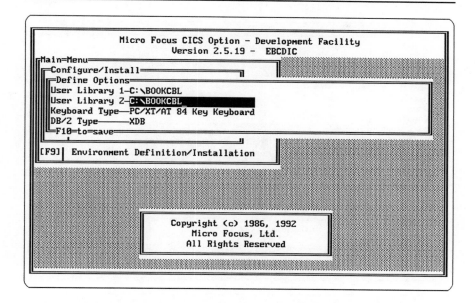

Figure 4.2. Identifying user libraries.

Figure 4.2 by typing in the PATH/directory, and are used to locate directories containing other data files and programs. Press [*F2*] *Define Configuration*:

- User Library 1—
- User Library 2—

The same library can be specified for both user libraries. More often, each user library will point to a different subdirectory.

Keyboard Type. Selecting one keyboard type is required to provide function key support, particularly if the use of *PF11* and *PF12* is required (see Figure 4.3). Keyboard configuration is selected from the MCO main menu by pressing [*F9*] and then pressing [*F2*] *Define Configuration*.

The list box presents two keyboard selections when either [*F2*] or [*F3*] is pressed:

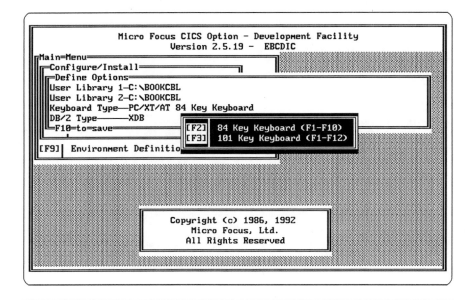

```
            Micro Focus CICS Option - Development Facility
                    Version 2.5.19 -  EBCDIC
┌Main=Menu══════════════════════════════════════════════
│ ┌Configure/Install════════════════════════════════┐
│ │ ┌Define Options═══════════════════════════════
│ │ │User Library 1-C:\BOOKCBL
│ │ │User Library 2-C:\BOOKCBL
│ │ │Keyboard Type─PC/XT/AT 84 Key Keyboard
│ │ │DB/2 Type──────XDB
│ │ └─F10=to=save══════════════╔═════════════════════════════╗
│ │                            ║[F2]  84 Key Keyboard (F1-F10)║
│ [F9]│ Environment Definitio  ║[F3]  101 Key Keyboard (F1-F12)║
                               ╚═════════════════════════════╝



                    ┌─────────────────────────────┐
                    │    Copyright (c) 1986, 1992  │
                    │       Micro Focus, Ltd.      │
                    │      All Rights Reserved     │
                    └─────────────────────────────┘
```

Figure 4.3.   Selecting the keyboard type (84/101).

- 84-key keyboard
  Supports function keys F1 through F10
- 101-key keyboard
  Supports function keys F1 through F12

keyboard mapping

MCO provides standard mapping of some keys, whether it's an 84 or 101 keyboard:

327x	PC equivalent
Clear	Ctrl + Home
Del	Del
Erase EOF	Ctrl + End
Erase Unprotected	Ctrl + PgDn

327x	PC equivalent
ENTER	Ctrl + ENTER or numeric keypad plus sign
Home	Home
Insert	Ins
PA1	Alt + 1
PA2	Alt + 2
PA3	Alt + 3
Reset	Escape
Return	

The standard configuration on a 101 keyboard is

PF1 through *PF12*	equals	*F1*	through *F12*	
PF13 through *PF24*	equals	*Alt + F1*	through *Alt + F12*	

The standard configuration on an 84 keyboard is

PF1 through *PF10*	equals	*F1*	through *F10*	
PF11 through *PF20*	equals	*Alt + F1*	through *Alt + F10*	
PF21 through *PF24*	equals	*Ctrl + F1*	through *Ctrl + F4*	

Define Editor. Select an edit package by pressing [*F9*] from the MCO main menu. The list of edit software MCO interfaces with is presented in Figure 4.4. Press [*F3*] *Define Editor*.

Once the Select Editor menu is opened, the user selects an editor by pressing the appropriate PF key:

- [*F1*] *SPF/PC*
- [*F2*] *Workbench Editor*
- [*F3*] *Micro SPF*
- [*F4*] *Other*

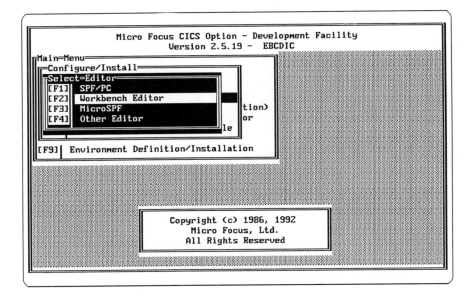

```
        Micro Focus CICS Option - Development Facility
                 Version 2.5.19 -  EBCDIC
┌Main=Menu
 ┌Configure/Install
  ┌Select=Editor
   [F1]  SPF/PC
   [F2]  Workbench Editor
   [F3]  MicroSPF                              tion)
   [F4]  Other Editor                           or
                                               le

   [F9]  Environment Definition/Installation




              Copyright (c) 1986, 1992
                 Micro Focus, Ltd.
                 All Rights Reserved
```

Figure 4.4.   Selecting an edit software package.

other editor

MCO allows the selection of other than the default edit software packages by typing in the command used to start the edit package. First select [F4] from the Select Editor menu (see Figure 4.5). Type in the executable file name for the edit software, and press Enter to accept the value.

DB2 Type. MCO interfaces with SQL preprocessors when checking a program and during animation of a program to access the DB2 data files. At this time, three SQL software products can be selected, as shown in Figure 4.6, from the MCO main menu. Press [F9], and then press [F2] *Define Configuration*.

The list box presents three DB/2 software tools to select from and a fourth option of no SQL interface:

- [F2] *NONE* (no DB/2 interface)
- [F3] *XDB*

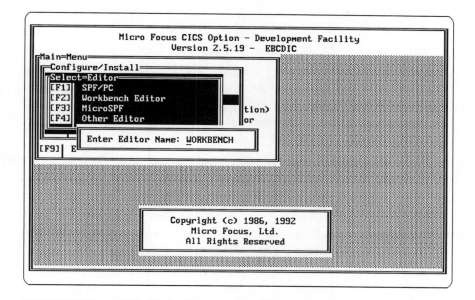

Figure 4.5.   Selecting another edit package.

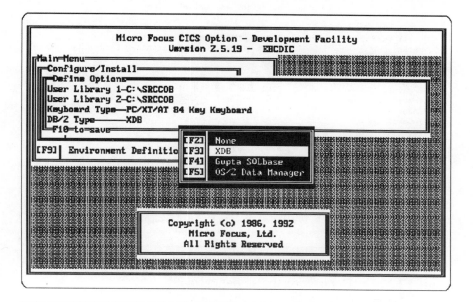

Figure 4.6.   Selecting an SQL preprocessor.

* [F4] *Gupta*
* [F5] *OS/2 Data Manager*

Once an SQL tool is selected, programmers should give some thought to how COBOL programs will be stored in directories. It is more common for COBOL/SQL source code to be stored in separate directories than non-SQL programs. Separate directories are not necessary for MCO to compile programs correctly.

CONFIGURE SCREEN

MCO provides a function to configure the basic presentation of screens, as shown in Figure 4.7.

* Changing default colors
* Selecting a monitor type
  Monochrome
  Color

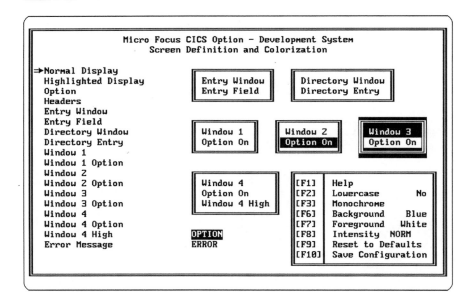

Figure 4.7.   Configuring the screen displays.

- Selecting upper- or lower-case text support
- Saving configuration

From the MCO main menu press [*F9*], and then press [*F4*] *Configure Screen*. Each window or message box is listed on the left side of the screen. The right side displays how each window or message box appears in MCO. A selection indicator located to the left of the window message labels positions to a new item using the up or down arrow keys.

Altering Color. Windows and message boxes can be presented in colors different from the MCO defaults by selecting [*F9*], from the MCO main menu pressing [*F9*], and then pressing [*F4*] *Configure Screen*.

Position the cursor to the window on the left side of the screen, and use the function keys in the list box to change colors:

- [*F6*] *Background*
- [*F7*] *Foreground*

When selecting a different color, press the appropriate function key until the color you want is displayed in the list box work area. Colors can be reset to MCO defaults at any time for windows and messages by pressing

- [*F9*] *Reset to Defaults*

When resetting the MCO defaults, all windows and message boxes are reset to the defaults.

Selecting Monitor Type. The screen development function allows selecting between a MONOCHROME or COLOR by pressing [*F3*]. This function key acts as a toggle, switching between the two selections.

Altering Intensity. The screen development function allows the intensity of text displays to be altered. From the MCO main menu press [*F9*], and then press [*F4*] *Configure Screen*.

Position the cursor to the window on the left side of the screen, and use the function key in the list box:

- [F8] *Intensity to select (NORM, HIGH)*

Upper or Lower Case. MCO defaults to upper-case sensitivity. If lower-case sensitivity is required, selecting case sensitivity is accomplished by pressing [F9] from the MCO main menu and then pressing [F4] *Configure Screen*.

Position the cursor to the window on the left side of the screen and use the function key in the list box:

- [F2] *Lower case*

Saving Configuration. Once the screen has been modified, the configuration must be saved by pressing

- [F10] *Save Configuration*

The configuration can be changed at any time. Once saved, press Escape twice to exit to the MCO main menu.

CICS RESOURCE FILES

MCO has to have the VSAM file definitions, transaction codes, program names, and so forth defined. See Figure 4.8.

MCO resources can be defined all at once or individually. Installing all tables is good for the first time when there is no chance of losing existing files. Installing one table is good practice for subsequent reinstallations of specific tables that have met an untimely demise.

MCO resource tables are defined by selecting the [F9] *Environment/Definition* from the MCO main menu. When defining the resource tables to CICS, two functions are provided:

- [F5] *Create All Control Files*
- [F6] *Create Individual Control Files*

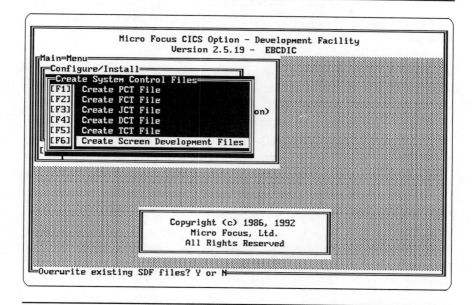

Figure 4.8.   Individual resource file definitions.

CICS RESOURCE TABLES

Loading tables will be covered in Chapter 5. MCO supports loading the following files:

- PCT   (Program Control Table)
- FCT   (File Control Table)
- JCT   (Journal Control Table)
- DCT   (Destination Control Table)
- TCT   (Terminal Control Table)
- SIT   (System Initialization Table)

In the list above, the first five resource tables can be imported from mainframe definitions migrated to the PC. The remaining tables are not organized in the same format on the PC and can not be imported.

Resource definition tables are stored as .DAT (data) and .IDX (index) files in the default directory C:\MFCICS\CICSRDT. File names are

- PCT   MCOPCT00.DAT and MCOPCT00.IDX
- FCT   MCOFCT00.DAT and MCOFCT00.IDX
- JCT   MCOJCT00.DAT and MCOJCT00.IDX
- DCT   MCODCT00.DAT and MCODCT00.IDX
- TCT   MCOTCT00.DAT and MCOTCT00.IDX
- SIT   stored as a control record on the FCT table

When upgrading from release 2.2x to release 2.5, the following resource datasets may need to be converted:

Release 2.2 x and prior Resource Files	Release 2.5 Resource Files
ISTSTPCT.DAT	MCOPCT00.DAT PCT
ISTSTPCT.IDX	MCOPCT00.IDX
ISTSTFCT.DAT	MCOFCT00.DAT FCT
ISTSTFCT.IDX	MCOFCT00.IDX
SCDFMSTR.DAT	MCOSDF00.DAT SDF
SCDFMSTR.IDX	MCOSDF00.IDX
SCDFSCRN.DAT	MCOSCR00.DAT
SCDFSCRN.IDX	MCOSCR00.IDX

To convert files, verify that a new directory has been created, even though it is not required. Converting previous release CICS tables might be necessary when a large application has already been defined on the PC.

Verify that the CICSCTL environment variable points to the correct directory, and from a command line type in CVT22RDT. When errors are detected reading the old files, the conversion process stops. If the conversion program finds no files on the

SCDFSCRN for a file on SCDFMSTR, the convert program writes out a dummy blank image to the MCOSCR00 file.

Directory Search Paths

As CICS Resource Definition Tables are being defined, MCO establishes the files in one of three directories, in the following order:

- CICSCTL path
  MCO creates the file in the first directory path found on this SET statement in the AUTOEXEC.BAT or CONFIG.SYS.
- CICSTEST path
  MCO creates the file in the first directory path found on this SET statement in the AUTOEXEC.BAT or CONFIG.SYS.
- Current Directory path
  If no SET statements define directories to create the RDT files to, MCO establishes them in the current directory.

Establish All Resource Files

MCO provides the capability of establishing all resource files at one time, which is very useful for the first-time installation. This function can also be used to reinstall the resource tables by wiping clean all information on existing tables within the defined directory path.

If the default directory path has been used, reinstalling all resource tables might be the last resort. MCO will prevent any accidental overlaying of a resource file by prompting for a confirmation to overlay an existing resource file (see Figure 4.9). Press [F5] *Create All Control Files*

Answering "Y" to the confirmation request purges all existing entries for the resource file being reloaded. There is no backup function within MCO to recover from any accidental deletions, so exercise care when selecting to use this function.

Establish Individual Resource Files

MCO provides the capability of establishing individual resource files, which is very useful after previously installing all resource

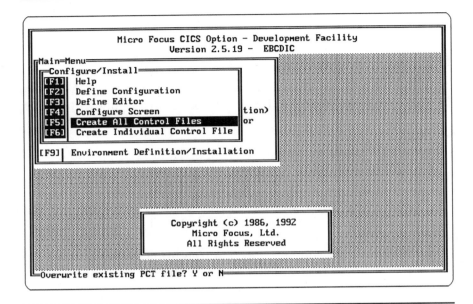

Figure 4.9. Installing all resource tables.

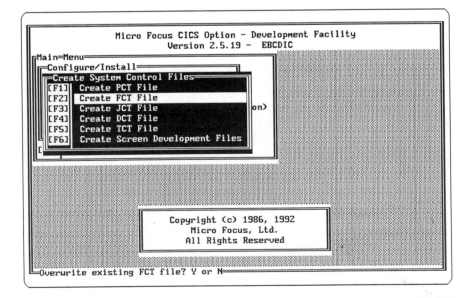

Figure 4.10. Using the individual install option.

tables. Once the resource files have been established, this function is best used to rebuild portions of the CICS resources. MCO still prevents any accidental overlaying of a resource file by prompting with a confirmation request, as shown in Figure 4.10, to overlay an existing resource file. From the MCO main menu press [*F9*], and then press [*F6*] *Create Individual Control Files*.

Answering "Y" to the confirmation purges all existing entries for the specific resource file being reloaded. Remember that there is no backup function within MCO to recover from any accidental deletions, so exercise care when using this function. Individual CICS resource files are not required for all programs to execute.

SUMMARY

The MCO product provides a limited capability of configuring the presentation of the menus and submenus. MCO does allow for changing the color display of windows (menus and submenus) and messages boxes. MCO provides an interface to other PC-based tools supporting either SQL processing or edit packages.

5

Loading MCO Resource Tables

After the CICS resource tables have been defined, programmers can load various tables to support an application. CICS resources defined in MCO prior to developing an application are the following:

- Transactions
- Data files
- Journals
- Transient data queues
- Terminal types
- System parameters

This chapter examines the process of loading CICS resources (see Figure 5.1):

- PCT
- FCT
- JCT
- DCT
- TCT
- SIT
- SQL preprocess options

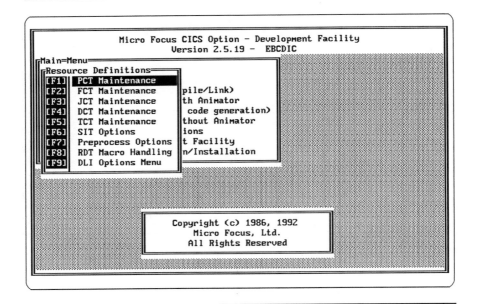

Figure 5.1.   Submenu for defining CICS resources.

CICS MULTIPLE REGIONS

MCO is a single-task processor, not capable of emulating the mainframe multi-tasking. MCO supports one terminal and cannot run more than one at a time.

Directory Search Paths

As CICS Resource Definition Tables are updated or used, MCO searches for the files in one of four directories, in the following order:

- CICSCTL path—MCO searches in the first directory path found on this SET statement in the AUTOEXEC.BAT or CONFIG.SYS.
- CICSTEST path—MCO searches in the first directory path found on this SET statement in the AUTOEXEC.BAT or CONFIG.SYS.

- CICS path—MCO searches in the first directory path found on this SET statement in the AUTOEXEC.BAT or CONFIG.SYS.
- Current Directory path—If no SET statements are found, MCO searches in the current directory.

PCT—PROGRAM CONTROL TABLE

Programs that run within the CICS emulator have to be mapped to a four-character transaction ID (see Figure 5.2). The only programs that need to be defined here are those accessed by a terminal user or by CICS command:

```
EXEC CICS RETURN
     TRANSID
END-EXEC.
```

No other programs should be defined here. On the mainframe, a Processing Program Table (PPT) would additionally define

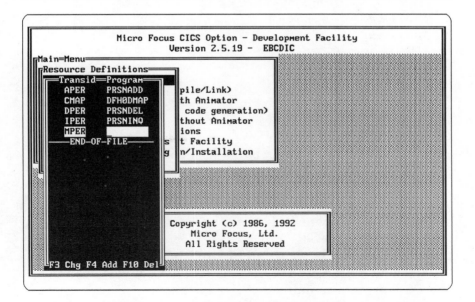

Figure 5.2. Adding an FCT transaction ID/program.

- All programs used in CICS commands
    LINK
    XCTL
- MAPSETs name
- Programs defined in the PCT

On the PC, no PPT table exists because the CICS emulation facility resolves programs dynamically. To modify the FCT table, press [F7] *CICS Resource Definitions* from the MCO main menu, and then press [F1] *PCT Maintenance*.

At emulation (execution) time, after a transaction has been invoked, CICS searches the PCT until a match on the transaction ID is found. Once the transaction ID is located, the executable program associated with it is searched for in the PATH/ directory defined in the CICSTEST variable. At that point the program begins execution and is positioned for debugging the program.

This submenu supports modifying PCT entries by selecting one of the following options:

- [F3] *Chg*
- [F4] *Add*
- [F8] *Load*
- [F10] *Del*

Add PCT Entries

Once the [F4] *Add* function key is selected, an empty input area opens up where the highlight bar is positioned. The first field typed in is the four-character transaction ID. Once typed in, press the Enter key to accept the value.

At that point the program name field opens an empty input area. Type in a value and press the Enter key. After pressing Enter, the message TRID ADDED is displayed in the lower portion of the screen, as shown in Figure 5.3.

Once a transaction ID/program name entry has been made, the PCT process remains in the add function. To exit the add function, press Escape.

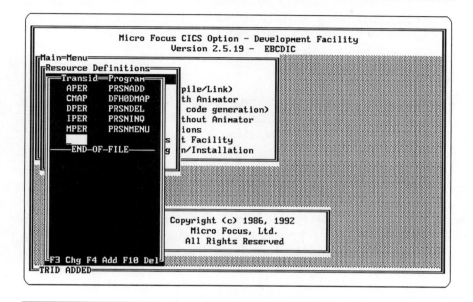

```
                Micro Focus CICS Option - Development Facility
                        Version 2.5.19 -  EBCDIC
  ┌Main=Menu
  ┌Resource Definitions
   ┌Transid═Program
    APER     PRSNADD     │pile/Link)
    CMAP     DFHODMAP    │th Animator
    DPER     PRSNDEL     │  code generation)
    IPER     PRSNINQ     │thout Animator
    MPER     PRSNMENU    │ions
                        s│t Facility
    ──END-OF-FILE──     g│n/Installation


                        ┌─────────────────────────
                        │ Copyright (c) 1986, 1992
                        │    Micro Focus, Ltd.
                        │   All Rights Reserved
  └F3 Chg F4 Add F10 Del
  └TRID ADDED
```

Figure 5.3.   Successfully added PCT entry.

Change PCT Entries

If the [*F3*] *Chg* function key is pressed, the program name field of the line that the highlight bar is positioned on can be modified. Once the program is typed over, press Enter. After pressing Enter, the message TRID UPDATED is displayed in the lower portion of the screen. Only the program name field can be changed. To facilitate changing the transaction ID, delete the entire entry and then add a new entry to the PCT file.

Once a program name entry has been modified, press Escape to save the updated information and return to the PCT submenu.

Delete PCT Entries

Deleting is done by pressing the [*F10*] *Del* function key for the transaction ID/program name on the highlighted line. The delete function displays a confirmation message "Delete this TRID? Y or N" in the lower portion of the screen. To confirm the delete, press "Y"; any other keystroke cancels the delete. Pressing Escape returns to the PCT submenu.

Load PCT Entries

Loading PCT entries from mainframe DFHPCT macros is done by selecting [*F8*] *Load*, which is not displayed on the PCT submenu. Prompt for load file after pressing [*F8*] as in Figure 5.4.

FILE SUPPORT

MCO does not provide any functions for file management. File definitions or editing should be done by other PC-based products. Micro Focus COBOL provides a file management function that meets most programmers' needs.

Once the PC file has been converted to an appropriate VSAM

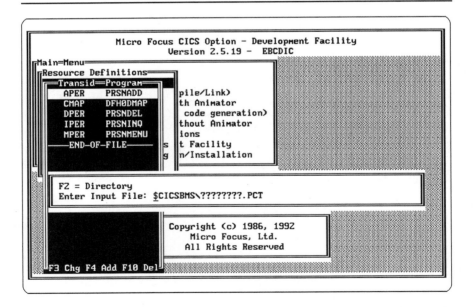

Figure 5.4.   Prompt for loading MCOs FCT file.

file structure, adding the VSAM file definition to the resource table allows programs to access the file. MCO supports VSAM files, Alternate Indexes, and Journal file formats.

Alternate Indexes

Alternate Indexes can be created for primary (ESDS or KSDS) files. The FCT entry for a primary file must be defined before the Alternate Index file can be defined.

Alternate Indexes are defined in a two-step process: create the FCT file entry and then generate the Alternate Index. These files will have to be defined manually in the [F7] *CICS Resource Definitions* function.

Create the FCT Entry. The primary file must be defined prior to running the generate Alternate Index step. Once the primary file is defined, add a new file definition to the FCT table (see Figure 5.5). Identify the file as an Alternate Index. In defining the file, do the following:

- Specify key length/location.
- Type in the primary file name in the primary file ID field.
- Press [F10] to update record and save the Alternate Index definition.

Generate the Alternate Index. Once the Alternate Index definition has been defined, position the highlight bar to the Alternate Index summary definition and press [F7] *Generate Alternate* (see Figure 5.6). This reads the primary file and generates an Alternate Index record for each record on the primary file.

Open and Close Files

Files can be defined on the FCT as opened each time the CICS emulation facility is invoked by answering "Y" to the open file question during the add or change process. Files can be left closed and manually opened prior to executing any transaction ID by using the CSMT transaction provided with the MCO product.

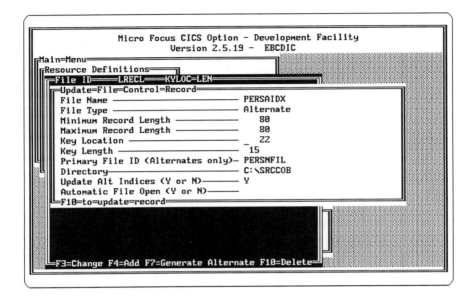

Figure 5.5.   Defining an Alternate Index file.

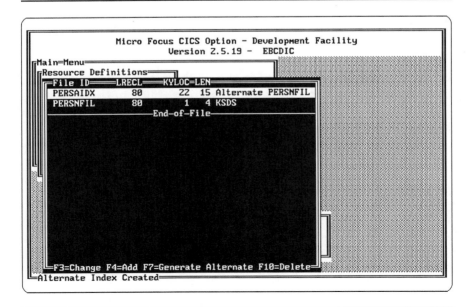

Figure 5.6.   Generating the Alternate Index file.

Refer to Appendix A for CICS transactions provided with MCO and their uses.

FCT—FILE CONTROL TABLE

The File Control Table (FCT) is used to allow transparent I/O access between CICS and data files. Data files (non-DB2 or IMS) accessed in MCO must be defined in the FCT.

Files must be defined, but they do not have to be defined before the first actual access of a file in the emulation facility. MCO adds definitions to the FCT table for new primary files opened during an emulation session.

All VSAM files that are accessed within the CICS emulator should be defined as an FCT entry (see Figure 5.7). To modify the FCT table, press [F7] *CICS Resource Definitions* from the MCO main menu, and then press [F2] *FCT Maintenance*.

This submenu supports modifying FCT entries by pressing a function key:

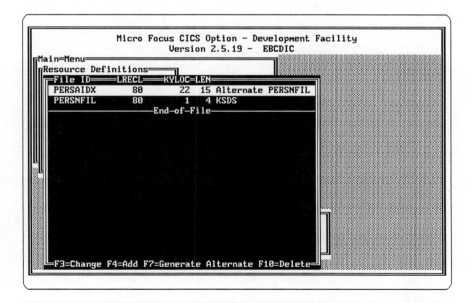

Figure 5.7.   FCT summary file information submenu.

- *[F3] Change*
- *[F4] Add*
- *[F7] Generate Alternate*
- *[F8] Load*
- *[F10] Delete*

In order to add or update an FCT entry, programmers must type in the file name. This identifies a new file for add or an existing file for change and delete processing.

Add FCT Entries. Once the *[F4] Add* function key is pressed, a detail FCT entry submenu displays entry fields to define a VSAM file. Figure 5.8 reflects the data values for an indexed sequential fixed-length file. When adding key locations, the location is relative to 1, not 0, as on the mainframe.

The following fields can be entered during the add process:

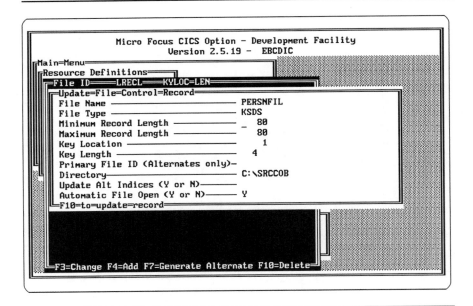

Figure 5.8. Sample display of KSDS definition.

- File type—Identifies the type of VSAM file (KSDS, ESDS, RRDS, Alternate Index) that the file is.
- Minimum and maximum record lengths—A number between 1 and 32,767 that identifies a record's length. Fixed-length files have the same values.
- Key location—The start position of the key.
- Key length—The length of the key field, a numeric value between 1 and 125.
- Primary file ID—Only allowed when defining an Alternate Index, gives the name of the primary file.
- Directory path—Directory in which the file will be stored; if not provided, the directory found on the CICSDAT variable is used.
- Update Alt index—When set to "Y," all Alternate Indexes are updated automatically.
- Automatic file open—When set to "Y," this file will be opened automatically each time the emulation process is invoked.

The file name field cannot be changed once the add FCT function is invoked. To change the file name, press Escape from the detail submenu and start the add over again.

Change FCT Entries. Once the *[F3] Change* function key is pressed, data for the file is displayed for modifying existing file information. The submenu displayed appears exactly as the add submenu.

The following fields can be modified during the change process:

- Minimum and maximum record lengths—A number between 1 and 32,767 bytes that identifies the record lengths. Fixed-length files have the same values.
- Key location—The start position of the key.
- Key length—The length of the key field, a numeric value between 1 and 125.
- Primary file ID—Only allowed when defining an Alternate Index, gives the name of the primary file.
- Directory path—Directory in which the file will be stored; if not provided, the directory found on the CICSDAT variable is used.
- Update Alt index—When set to "Y," all Alternate Indexes are updated automatically.

- Automatic file open—When set to "Y," this file will be opened automatically each time the emulation process is invoked.

The file name field cannot be changed. To accomplish changing a file name, delete the current FCT entry and add a new FCT entry.

The file type (KSDS, ESDS, RRDS, Alternate Index) cannot be modified. To do so, delete the existing entry and add a new entry to the FCT.

Delete FCT Entries. Prior to deleting an FCT entry, position the highlight bar to the file definition to be purged, then press [F10] Delete. No confirmation message is presented on the screen. Only the FCT entry is deleted. The physical file remains intact on the hard disk.

Load FCT Entries. MCO provides a function to load mainframe DFHFCT macros, [F8] Load, shown in Figure 5.9. The load function is not displayed on the FCT submenu, but it is available.

JCT—JOURNAL CONTROL TABLE

MCO provides a facility to store journal records, a special set of sequential records. Journals contain the necessary information to reconstruct events or change data. Journals are often used as audit trails, a file of additions or changes to a data file, and a log of transaction processing in the system. The JCT file contains all journal definitions that are used by the CICS emulator. Journal records are written via the EXEC CICS JOURNAL command. The JCT process (Figure 5.10) is invoked from the MCO main menu by pressing [F7] and then pressing [F3] JCT Maintenance.

Journal files are slightly different on the PC from those on the mainframe. The two differences are the following:

- Journaling is supported, but not the writing of system journal records.
- MCO writes out single-record blocks.

Once a CICS emulation session is started, MCO opens the journal file the first time it is referenced in the session and closes it at the end of a session.

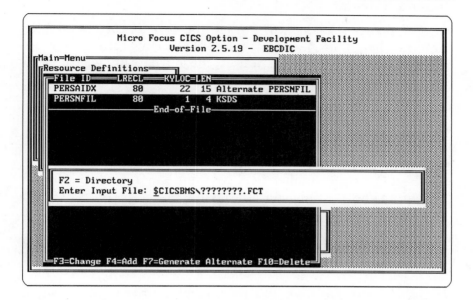

Figure 5.9.   Loading mainframe FCT macros.

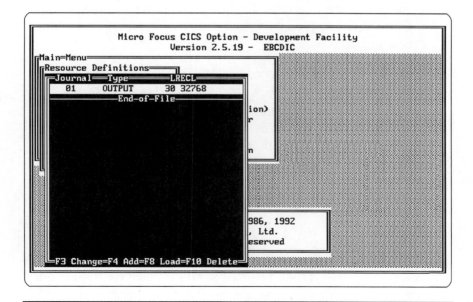

Figure 5.10.   Display of journal file summary.

Journal Format

MCO supports a version of the journal format that is simpler than that found on the mainframe. MCO writes records to a file one logical record at a time. Mainframe journals are written as a block of collected records. The actual format of the files is different on the PC as well:

- Records on the PC do not contain a four-byte prefix to define the block length.
- The PC file contains only one label record.
- The PC record number field contains the number 1. On the mainframe, it would contain the number of the record within the current block.

Two journal record types exist on the PC: the journal label record and the user journal record.

Journal Label Record. A journal label record contains a value that identifies the characteristics of a file in the system. It is made up of the system header segment and the label record segment.

- System header segment
     Defines the record length
     System ID
     Record number (set to 1)
- Label record segment
     The journal ID taken from the JFILEID
     The block number (set to 1)
     Volume date (00yyddd)
     Volume sequence number (set to 1)
     Relative TTRO (set to low values)
     Track balance (set to low values)
     Time written (hhmmsss)
     Run time (hhmmsss)
     Date written (00yyddd)

User Journal Record. The user journal record stored on the journal file contains three segments: the system prefix segment, the user prefix segment, and the user data segment.

- System prefix segment
    Contains the prefix length, always 20
    Task number
    Time stamp (hhmmsss)
    Transaction ID
    Terminal ID
- User prefix segment
    Prefix length
    User prefix data
- User data segment
    User data

Add JCT Entries. Once the *[F4] Add* function key is pressed, an input area opens up on the highlighted bar. Key in a two-digit number (journal ID), identifying the journal file, and press Enter.

After the journal ID is typed in, a detail JCT entry submenu is displayed (see Figure 5.11). When typing in a numeric value, press the space bar first to clear the field of the current value.

The following fields can be entered during the add process:

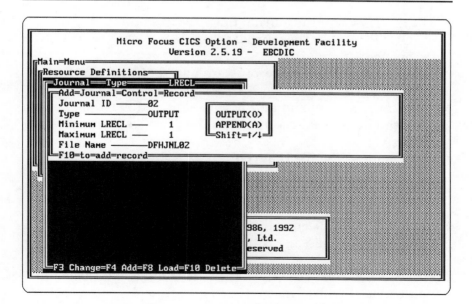

Figure 5.11.   Defining a journal file.

- Type—How will the journal file be written?
  OUTPUT(O)—The journal file is cleared each time a file is opened.
  APPEND(A)—New records are added at the end of an existing journal file.
- Minimum and maximum LRECL—Minimum and maximum length of a journal record. Fixed-length files have the same values.
- File name—The file that contains the journal.

The journal ID field cannot be changed once the add JCT function is invoked. To change the journal ID, press Escape from the detail submenu and start the add over again.

Change JCT Entries. Once the [F3] *Change* function key is pressed and a detail JCT entry submenu is displayed, existing FCT values can be modified. The journal ID field cannot be changed. To facilitate a change of the journal ID, delete the current JCT entry and add a new JCT entry.
The following fields can be modified during the change process:

- Type—How will the journal file be written to?
  OUTPUT(O)—The journal file is cleared each time a file is opened.
  APPEND(A)—New records are added at the end of an existing journal file.
- Minimum and maximum LRECL—Minimum and maximum length of a journal record. Fixed-length files have the same values.
- File name—The file that contains the journal.

Delete JCT Entries. Prior to deleting a JCT entry, first position the highlight bar to the journal definition to be purged. Next, press [F10] *Delete*, and the entry is deleted from the JCT. No confirmation message is presented on the screen.

Load JCT Entries. Pressing [F8] *Load* prompts for the name of a mainframe DFHJCT macro file to load into MCO, as shown in Figure 5.12.

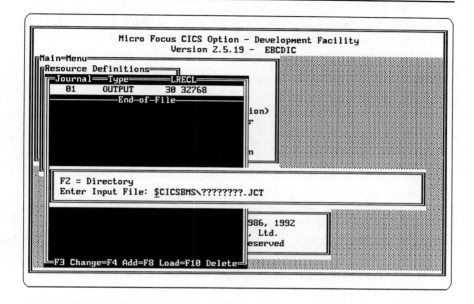

Figure 5.12.   Using a mainframe file to load JCT.

DCT—DESTINATION CONTROL TABLE

The DCT is provided to set up transient data queues for CICS transactions requiring the use of temporary queues. MCO only requires that a DCT entry be established for extra-partition destinations. Definitions for intra-partition destinations can be entered, but they do not impact the emulation environment.

Intra-queues are stored in TEMPSTRG, an indexed file, and can be used for both input and output. They are used primarily for destinations (terminal or output destination) within the CICS environment. Some uses for intra-partition datasets are the following:

- Message switching
- Broadcast messages
- Routing of output to multiple terminals
- Data queuing
- Data collection

Extra-partition queues are stored in a previously identified sequential file and can be defined as input or output. These files are accessible to programs within or outside of the CICS region. Uses for extra-partition data sets are the following:

- Logging data
- Statistics
- Transaction error messages
- Passing data for read destructive processing

Add DCT Entries. Once the *[F4] Add* function key is pressed, an input area opens up on the highlighted bar. Key in a destination ID and press Enter. The detail DCT entry submenu (see Figure 5.13) allows programmers to define queues as either intra-partition or extra-partition. When typing in a numeric value, press the space bar first to clear the current value from the field.

The following fields can be entered during the add process:

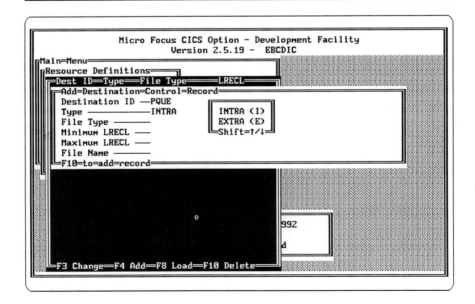

Figure 5.13. Define temporary destination queues.

- Type—Define the type of queue (this is the only required field if the queue selection is intra):
     Intra (I)—Used primarily for destinations (terminal or output destination) within the CICS environment.
     Extra (E)—Files accessible to programs within or outside of the CICS region.
- File type—Identify the manner in which the file will be used:
     Input—The queue is defined as an input file.
     Output—The queue is defined as an output file.
     Extend—Append new records at the end of the existing file.
- Minimum and maximum LRECL—Minimum and maximum length of a record. Fixed-length files have the same values.

The destination ID field cannot be changed once the add DCT function is invoked. To change the destination ID, press Escape from the detail submenu and start the add over again.

When defining an extra-partition queue, all of the fields are required (see Figure 5.14).

Change DCT Entries. Once the [F3] *Change* function key is pressed, a detail DCT entry submenu is displayed, and data values can be modified. The destination ID field cannot be changed. To change it, delete the current DCT entry and add a new DCT entry.

The following fields can be modified during the change process:

- File type—Identify the manner in which the file will be used:
     Input—The queue is defined as an input file.
     Output—The queue is defined as an output file.
     Extend—Append new records at the end of the existing file.
- Minimum and maximum LRECL—Minimum and maximum length of a record. Fixed-length files have the same values.

Delete DCT Entries. Prior to deleting a DCT entry, position the highlight bar to the destination definition to be purged. Next, press [F10] *Delete*, and the entry is deleted. No confirmation message is presented on the screen.

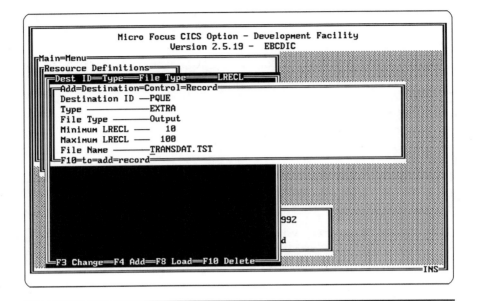

```
              Micro Focus CICS Option - Development Facility
                      Version 2.5.19 -  EBCDIC
┌Main=Menu
│┌Resource Definitions
││┌Dest ID═══Type═══File Type═══════LRECL
│││┌Add═Destination═Control═Record
││││ Destination ID ──PQUE
││││ Type ───────────EXTRA
││││ File Type ───────Output
││││ Minimum LRECL ──     10
││││ Maximum LRECL ──    100
││││ File Name ───────TRANSDAT.TST
│││└F10═to═add═record




                                                        992

                                                       d

│└F3 Change══F4 Add══F8 Load══F10 Delete                         INS
```

Figure 5.14. Define an extra-partition queue.

Load DCT Entries. Pressing [*F8*] *Load*, prompts for the name of a mainframe DFHDCT macro file to load into MCO, as shown in Figure 5.15.

TCT—TERMINAL CONTROL TABLE

MCO requires terminals defined to it that will be used in an emulation session. They are defined on the TCT file, as shown in Figure 5.16.

Add TCT Entries. Once the [*F4*] *Add* function key is pressed, an input area opens up on the highlighted bar. Key in a terminal ID and press Enter. The detail TCT entry submenu (see Figure 5.17) allows programmers to define terminals and printers to MCO. When typing in a numeric value, press the space bar first to clear the current value from the field.

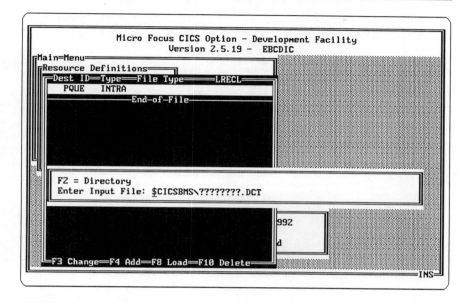

Figure 5.15. Loading DCT entries from mainframe.

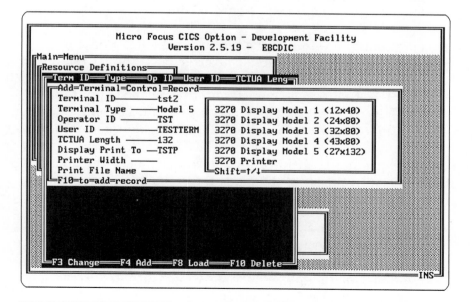

Figure 5.16. Define terminals to the TCT file.

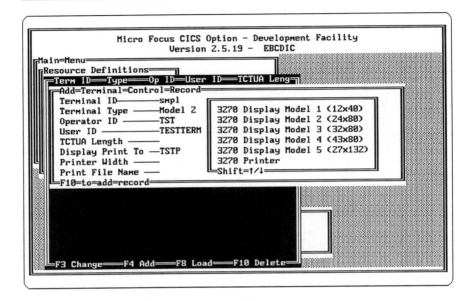

Figure 5.17.   Defining terminals for use in CICS.

The following fields can be entered during the add process:

- Terminal type—Define the terminal type (CRT or printer).
- Operator ID—Up to three-character operator ID related to this terminal.
- User ID—Up to eight-character user ID related to this terminal
- TCTUA—A numeric value between 0 and 255 defining the size (in bytes) of the Terminal Control Table User Area.

The terminal ID field cannot be changed once the add TCT function is invoked. To change the terminal ID, press Escape from the detail submenu and start the add over again.

Change TCT Entries. Once the [*F3*] *Change* function key is pressed, a detail TCT entry submenu is displayed. Existing TCT values can be modified. The terminal ID field cannot be changed. To change it, delete the current TCT entry and add a new TCT entry.

The following fields can be modified during the change process:

- Terminal type—Define the terminal type (CRT or printer).
- Operator ID—Up to three-character operator ID related to this terminal.
- User ID—Up to eight-character user ID related to this terminal.
- TCTUA—A numeric value between 0 and 255 defining the size (in bytes) of the Terminal Control Table User Area.

Delete TCT Entries. Prior to deleting a TCT entry, position the highlight bar to the terminal definition to be purged. Next, press [*F10*] *Delete* and the entry is deleted. No confirmation message is presented on the screen.

Load TCT Entries. Pressing [*F8*] *Load* prompts for the name of a mainframe DFHTCT macro file to load into MCO, as shown in Figure 5.18.

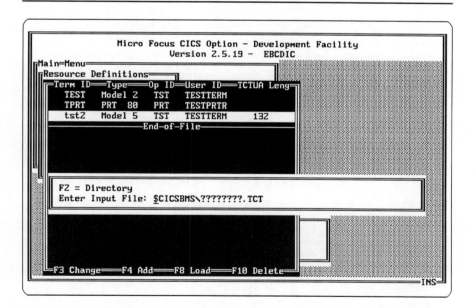

Figure 5.18.   Load TCT from mainframe files.

SIT—SYSTEM INITIALIZATION TABLE

This file contains various system parameters used by CICS applications and defined in MCO (see Figure 5.19). There is not a separate add, change, or delete function when updating the SIT file. When typing in a numeric value, press the space bar first to clear the current value from the field.

To modify values defined in the SIT table, just overtype the existing value. To delete an existing value, space it out.

The following fields can be updated on the SIT file:

- TWA (Transaction Work Area) size—A numeric value between 0 and 32,767 bytes that defines the size of the Transaction Work Area. The default size is 0.
- CWA (Common Work Area)—A numeric value between 0 and 32,767 bytes that defines the size of the Common Work Area. The default size is 0.
- TD/TS Max—The maximum size (in bytes between 0 and 32,767) of records that can be written to TSQ (temporary stor-

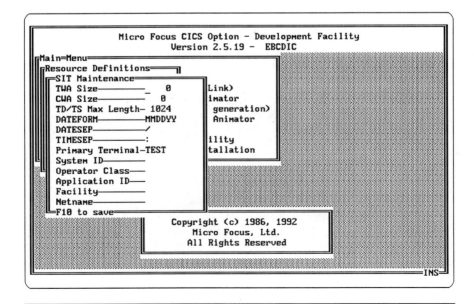

Figure 5.19. Setting CICS level definitions.

age queue) and for intra-partition TDQ (transient data queue). The size defined here also applies to the START and RETRIEVE data areas. The default is 1,024 bytes.

- DATE FORM—Identify the format to be used by date fields. The default is MMDDYY.
    MMDDYY
    DDMMYY
    YYMMDD
    YYDDMM
- DATESEP—Select the value to be used as a separator between the date, month, and year when used in the FORMATTIME command. The default is "/".
- TIMESEP—Select the value to be used as a separator between the hours and minutes when used in the FORMATTIME command. The default is ":".
- Primary terminal—Identifies the terminal ID to use in the CICS emulation session. The default value is "TEST."
- Operator class—Three-byte operator class field used in routing of data.
- Application ID—Eight-byte character string that defines the system owning the transaction.
- Facility—Value identifies the identifier of the facility that initiated the transaction.
- Netname—Eight-byte character string identifying the name of a logical unit in a VTAM network or PC network

CICS Command Address. MCO allows programs to access system information via two CICS storage areas:

- CWA (Common Work Area)—This CICS address area is used to pass information between application programs.
- TWA (Transaction Work Area)—Passes information between application programs, as long as they are in the same task.

PREPROCESS OPTIONS

The options toggled on in this function are used by the preprocess/check process to prepare programs for execution. MCO must have the following defined:

- What should be done when syntax errors occur?
- What mainframe COBOL dialect should be used?
- Should interfaces be made to other databases?

These directives can be set here as a default for all preprocess/ check processing, or they can be set from the Checker submenu each time a program is to be checked for syntax errors. Establish the environment here to cover preprocess/check needs for 80 percent of the programs.

The preprocess function provides programmers with the capability (see Figure 5.20) to define their PC CICS environment as nearly as possible to the mainframe environment.

Syntax Errors

When the preprocess/check function is invoked, this directive instructs the preprocess/check facility either to stop at all syntax errors or complete the check collecting all errors. To turn the

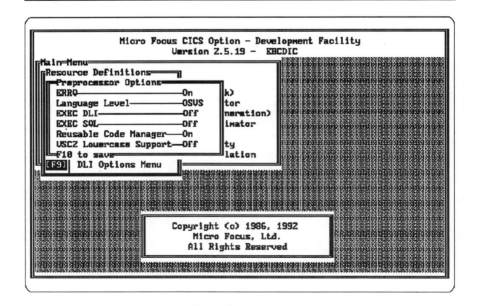

Figure 5.20. Selecting compile options.

pause on, position the cursor to the ERRQ option and press Enter until the option value is "on."

Language

MCO supports the following mainframe dialects:

* OSVS
* VSC2
* VSC2 release 1
* VSC2 release 2
* VSC2 release 3

To select a language, position the cursor on the language field and press Enter until the correct value is displayed.

Database Access

The Micro Focus Checker does not recognize commands such as the following:

* EXEC CICS
* EXEC DL/I
* EXEC SQL

MCO provides its own translator to convert EXEC CICS commands into COBOL recognizable code for the Checker. MCO also interfaces with IMSVS86 and XDB or Database Manager to convert EXEC DL/I and EXEC SQL commands, respectively.

MCO has to define the interfaces to DL/I or DB2 databases by toggling on the option from the Preprocessor Options submenu. Position the cursor to either field and press Enter until "on" appears in the option value.

The DL/I and SQL options will only display on the Preprocessor Options submenu if an IMSVS86 or a DB2 system is installed on the PC.

Reusable Code Manager

This option only appears if the reusable code preprocessor has been installed, supporting reusable code. Position the cursor to this field and press Enter to turn the option "on." Figure 5.21 reflects the preprocess options established and then saved by pressing [*F10*].

MACRO HANDLING

MCO provides a submenu for importing and exporting RDT entries (see Figures 5.22 and 5.23). This can be very useful for distributing definitions from one PC to another when programmers are not on a LAN.

MCO allows for RDT entries to be imported or exported to a PC file, file name.RDT. Individual RDT files or all RDT files can be selected for importing or exporting.

DL/I OPTIONS

To maintain DL/I databases, MCO interfaces with IMSVS86 if it is installed on the PC to perform IMS functions:

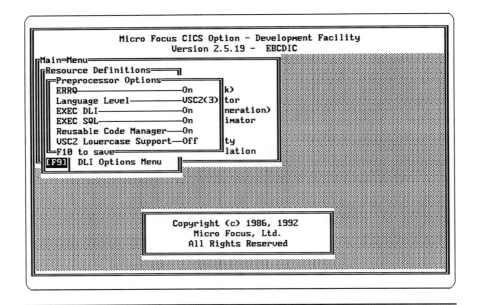

Figure 5.21. Preprocess/check directive setting.

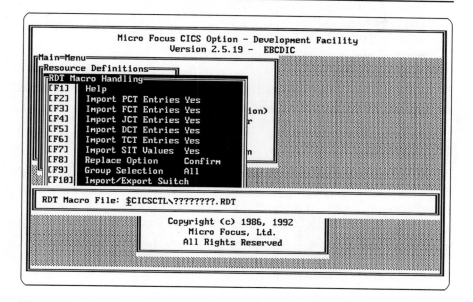

Figure 5.22.   Import selection of RDT files.

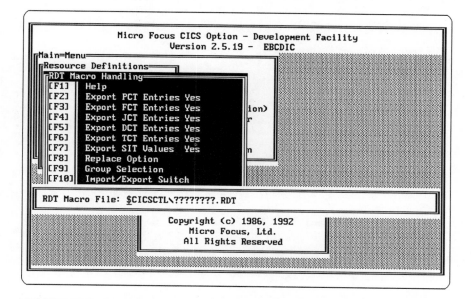

Figure 5.23.   Export RDT entries to other users.

- PSB generation
- DBD generation
- ZEROLOAD
- DL/I utilities

When interfacing with an IMS database, it is handy to have access to IMSVS86 on a CICS submenu.

SUMMARY

MCO provides a menu-driven process to load the Resource Definition Tables that CICS emulation requires to execute programs. The function is well laid out and Help is available on many screens even if [F1] is not displayed. Unless the particular program being tested supports many files, the loading of RDT files will generally go quickly.

6

Developing BMS Screens

To complete business functions, on-line applications require an interface between programs and terminals. The typical interface between the keyboard and the CPU is provided by screens. Via screens the customer responds to function selections and provides data input to process a request.

Screens are supported in CICS by BMS macros. If you are experienced in assembler language, BMS macros will be familiar. Macros are assembler statements that generate additional statements.

MCO supports the interface much as BMS macros do on the mainframe. MAPs provide a user friendly method of transmitting requests between the customer and CICS programs. "User friendly" is relative; compared to card processing, screen displays are user friendly.

MCO provides a facility to paint BMS MAPs and generate macros that can be transferred to the mainframe. This chapter will examine importing BMS macros, copying MAPs, and three methods for creating or editing BMS macros:

- Editing native macros
- Painting MAPs
- Field updating

As the paint facility is examined, screen development will be covered by the phases of MAPSET/MAP development:

- Define the MAPSET
- Define the MAP
- Paint the screen
- Modify fields on a MAP

BMS MAP COMPONENTS

When the development effort requires BMS macros for displaying data on terminals, programmers can start from scratch or use a template from existing macros. Copying existing code and making minor changes is often the preferred approach. In developing BMS files, the following three components are required:

- DFHMSD macros—Coded twice defining the beginning and end of a MAPSET.
- DFHMDI macros—Coded once for each MAP being defined.
- DFHMDF macros—Coded for each field (data or literal) being defined.

The basic components of macros are discussed in Appendix B of this book. The overview presented here should be sufficient to allow CICS programmers to code basic BMS macros.

CICS SCREEN DEVELOPMENT

MCO supports the building of macro files containing one or more MAPs per MAPSET. When developing MAPSETs, files are generated during the creation process. MCO provides a directory search facility for locating a MAPSET or a single MAP in a MAPSET.

BMS Files Generated

MCO stores BMS files in CICS in two resource files established within the Environment/Definition function:

- MCOSDF00—CICS screen master file, stored as a data file (.DAT) and an index file (.IDX). This file contains a definition of the BMS MAPs defined to CICS.

- MCOSCR00—File that contains an image of the screen stored as a data file (.DAT) and an index file (.IDX).

As programmers use functions within CICS to edit BMS MAPs, various PC files are created:

- filename.BMS—Contains the BMS macros for a MAPSET.
- filename.MST—The generated (assembled) MAPSET used by the emulator to handle SEND MAP and RECEIVE MAP commands.
- filename.EXT—Contains extracts from the MCOSDF00 screen definition master file. Extracted MAPSET definitions can be passed from PC to PC.

The screen development functions of MCO, shown in Figure 6.1, are executed from the MCO main menu by pressing [*F8*] *BMS Screen Development*.

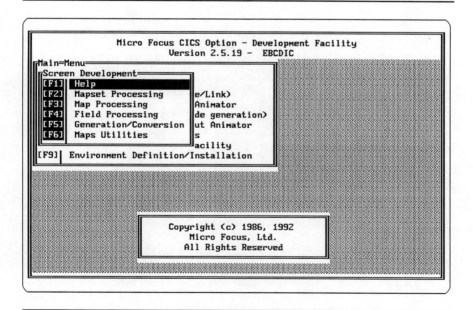

Figure 6.1.   Screen development submenu of MCO.

Searching for BMS Files

When editing macro files, the *F2=directory* feature provides an easy method of locating MAPSETs or specific MAPs within a MAPSET (see Figure 6.2). To select a MAP for editing, position the cursor to the specific MAPSET/MAP line and press Enter.

SCREEN DEVELOPMENT

Development of MAPSET/MAPs begins with the import function. If the development effort is for a new application, the import section will not be as critical. Screen development within MCO focuses on the following:

- Importing existing MAPSET/MAPs
- Editing MAPSET/MAPs
- Painting MAPSET/MAPs
- Field updating
- Copying MAPSET/MAPs

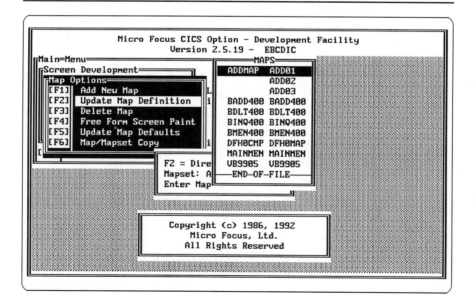

Figure 6.2.   MAPSET search containing many MAPs.

IMPORTING SCREENS

MCO supports importing macros from the mainframe. This is the first step when maintaining existing BMS source code. Once the code is imported into CICS, it can be loaded into the screen painter or an editor and modified per requirements. MCO provides programmers support for importing the following:

- BMS macros
- MFS macros
- Forms definitions

The import function shown in Figure 6.3 is accessed from the Screen Development submenu by pressing [*F5*] *Generation/Conversion*.

With import procedures, most emphasis is on importing BMS macros. The normal flow in developing or editing CICS applications will require BMS support. It is possible that programmers will import MFS macros and then generate BMS macros as part of converting from IMS to CICS. This book's focus is on CICS devel-

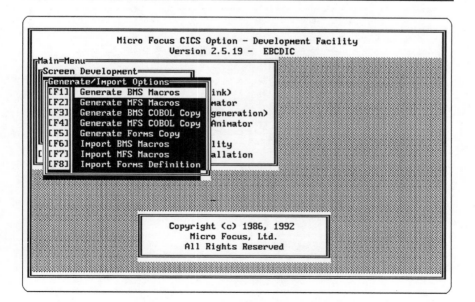

Figure 6.3. Import, copybook, and macro submenu.

opment and maintenance, not on IMS to CICS conversions. The process of importing Forms will only be touched on briefly.

Importing BMS Macros

Mainframe BMS macro files can be imported, and they will function on the PC using MCO. Importing assumes the input file is syntactically correct and simply loads the file in the CICS RDT file. As shown in Figure 6.4, a window box opens with question marks where programmers should identify the macro file name being imported, with a file extension of .BMS. From the Generate Import Options submenu, select the type of file being imported by pressing [F6] *Import BMS Macros.*

As CICS searches for the BMS macro files, MCO uses the specific directory path entered in the file name window. If no directory path is typed into the window, MCO searches the following directories in the order presented below:

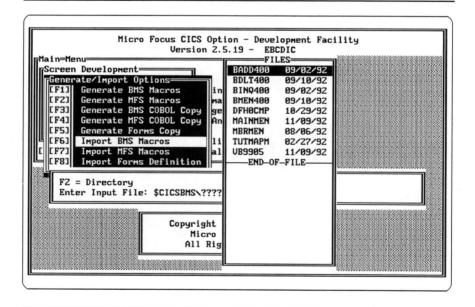

Figure 6.4.   Import BMS macro directory search.

- CICSBMS path
  MCO searches in the first directory path found on this SET statement in the AUTOEXEC.BAT or CONFIG.SYS.
- CICSSRC path
  MCO searches in the first directory path found on this SET statement in the AUTOEXEC.BAT or CONFIG.SYS.
- CICSTEST path
  MCO searches in the first directory path found on this SET statement in the AUTOEXEC.BAT or CONFIG.SYS.
- Current Directory path
  If no SET statements are found, MCO searches in the current directory.

After selecting the import of BMS macros, the submenu displayed provides function keys (Figure 6.5) to define how to handle the following:

- Comments
- Type of macros

Programmers must identify how to import the macro file by selecting one of the functions supported. All of the functions import a file; handling comments is the difference between them:

- [F1] *Macros are CICSVS86*—Identifies the macros as being generated by CICSVS86 or MCO; mainframe macros are easily imported with this selection.
- [F2] *Ignore Comments*—Instructs MCO to ignore anything in the comment area of the macros.
- [F3] *Comments are SDF1*—Identifies the comments in the format of SDF 1.
- [F4] *Comments are SDF2*—Identifies the comments in the format of SDF 2.

As the macros are being loaded into MCO, the MAPSET name is automatically added to the CICS MAPSET resource table. When loading a MAPSET, if MCO detects that the MAPSET already exists, a prompt is displayed to prevent an accidental overlay:

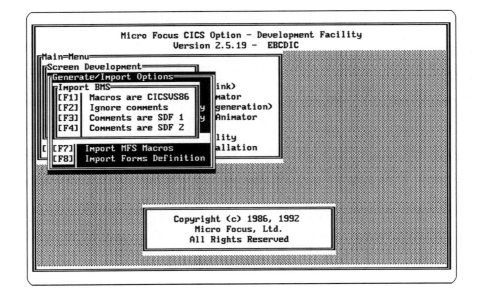

```
         Micro Focus CICS Option - Development Facility
                 Version 2.5.19 -  EBCDIC
┌Main=Menu
 ┌Screen Development
  ┌Generate/Import Options
   ┌Import BMS                      │ink>
   │ [F1]  Macros are CICSUS86      │mator
   │ [F2]  Ignore comments       │y │generation>
   │ [F3]  Comments are SDF 1     │y │Animator
   │ [F4]  Comments are SDF Z     │y │
   │                                │lity
 [ │ [F7]  Import MFS Macros        │allation
   │ [F8]  Import Forms Definition  │



              ┌──────────────────────────────┐
              │    Copyright (c) 1986, 1992   │
              │       Micro Focus, Ltd.       │
              │      All Rights Reserved      │
              └──────────────────────────────┘
```

Figure 6.5.   Define manner to import BMS code.

MAPSET already exists—Overwrite? Y or N? MAINMEN

If the file name is not readily available to you, use the directory
search, *F2=Directory*, to assist in locating the file, as shown in
Figure 6.4.

Importing MFS Macros

Mainframe MFS macro files can be imported. Like importing BMS
macro files, the MFS file is assumed to be syntactically correct.
Any MFS MFLD statements that do not match to a BMS DFLD
statement are not converted. From the Generate Import Options
submenu press [F7] *Import MFS Macros* to import MFS files. A
window box prompts for a file name.BMS, or the directory facility
is available to locate MFS macros.

As CICS searches for the MFS macro files, MCO uses the

specific directory path entered in the file name window. If no directory path is typed into the window, MCO searches the following directories in the order presented below:

- CICSMFS path—MCO searches in the first directory path found on this SET statement in the AUTOEXEC.BAT or CONFIG.SYS.
- CICSTEST path—MCO searches in the first directory path found on this SET statement in the AUTOEXEC.BAT or CONFIG.SYS.
- Current Directory path—If no SET statements are found, MCO searches in the current directory.

Importing Forms

MCO allows Forms to be imported for generating copybook files in the Micro Focus Forms-2 format. This format supports using the Micro Focus ADIS feature. Forms supported here are for PC-based applications running, not for migration to the mainframe.

Screens generated through Forms-2 incorporate the attribute byte as part of fields. The import function attempts to insert attributes into the format expected by CICS, but it may overlay portions of a field on the screen.

Any literal or data value found in line 1, column 1 is lost, and no field can be greater than 255 characters. From the Generate Import Options submenu press [F8] *Import Forms Definition* to import Forms.

As CICS searches for the Forms-2 files, MCO uses the specific directory path entered in the file name window. If no directory path is typed into the window, MCO searches the following directories in the order presented below:

- CICSFORM path
  MCO searches in the first directory path found on this SET statement in the AUTOEXEC.BAT or CONFIG.SYS.
- CICSTEST path
  MCO searches in the first directory path found on this SET statement in the AUTOEXEC.BAT or CONFIG.SYS.

- Current Directory path

     If no SET statements are found, MCO searches in the current directory.

BMS MACRO EDITING

After either importing the macro file or creating macros from scratch, the file can be edited by using the previously selected editor package. Appendix C documents an alternative BMS file edition. From the MCO main menu, select the [F2] *Edit* to invoke an edit package (Figure 6.6).

This example reflects using the Micro Focus COBOL Editor as the tool for editing BMS macro files. In editing macros directly, it is important for programmers to read Appendix B and find a CICS reference manual.

Once a file of macros is available, the MAPSET and MAP definitions can be edited in the MCO BMS Screen Development

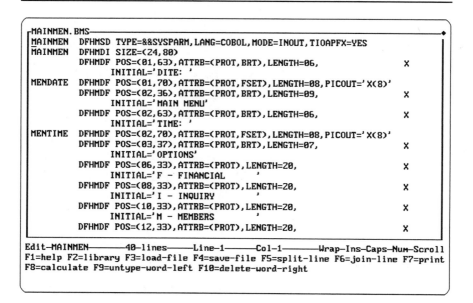

```
┌MAINMEN.BMS───────────────────────────────────────────────────────────────────◆
│MAINMEN  DFHMSD TYPE=&&SYSPARM,LANG=COBOL,MODE=INOUT,TIOAPFX=YES
│MAINMEN  DFHMDI SIZE=(24,80)
│         DFHMDF POS=(01,63),ATTRB=(PROT,BRT),LENGTH=06,                        X
│                INITIAL='DITE: '
│MENDATE  DFHMDF POS=(01,70),ATTRB=(PROT,FSET),LENGTH=08,PICOUT='X(8)'
│         DFHMDF POS=(02,36),ATTRB=(PROT,BRT),LENGTH=09,                        X
│                INITIAL='MAIN MENU'
│         DFHMDF POS=(02,63),ATTRB=(PROT,BRT),LENGTH=06,                        X
│                INITIAL='TIME: '
│MENTIME  DFHMDF POS=(02,70),ATTRB=(PROT,FSET),LENGTH=08,PICOUT='X(8)'
│         DFHMDF POS=(03,37),ATTRB=(PROT,BRT),LENGTH=07,                        X
│                INITIAL='OPTIONS'
│         DFHMDF POS=(06,33),ATTRB=(PROT),LENGTH=20,                            X
│                INITIAL='F - FINANCIAL      '
│         DFHMDF POS=(08,33),ATTRB=(PROT),LENGTH=20,                            X
│                INITIAL='I - INQUIRY        '
│         DFHMDF POS=(10,33),ATTRB=(PROT),LENGTH=20,                            X
│                INITIAL='M - MEMBERS        '
│         DFHMDF POS=(12,33),ATTRB=(PROT),LENGTH=20,                            X
│
Edit-MAINMEN───────40-lines──────Line-1────────Col-1────────Wrap-Ins-Caps-Num-Scroll
F1=help F2=library F3=load-file F4=save-file F5=split-line F6=join-line F7=print
F8=calculate F9=untype-word-left F10=delete-word-right
```

Figure 6.6.   Native macros loaded into editor.

function; even the data fields can be edited in MCO. A macro file can be loaded into the screen painter feature to perform all aspects of screen development with a minimum of BMS knowledge.

BMS MAPSET/MAP PROCESSING

The process of developing screens in BMS is broken into specific phases that correspond to specific macro statements found in BMS files. The three phases of development are the following:

- MAPSET development
- MAP development
- Field development

Each phase provides a set of functions that supports establishing, modifying, and deleting MAPSET/MAPs.

Once a MAPSET/MAP is completed, the remaining process is to generate BMS macros and COBOL copybooks and to assemble (generate a test definition). Generating copybooks is useful whether the file is created in an editor or by a painter and certainly, creation of an executable applies to any BMS file.

MAPSET CREATION

Enhancing BMS files is invoked from the MCO main menu by selecting *[F8] BMS Screen Development* and accessing the Screen Development submenu, as shown in Figure 6.4.

The submenu provides access to functions supporting all three phases of BMS file generation, as well as copybook and macro generation. MAPs cannot be defined unless a MAPSET is first defined. To invoke the MAPSET Options submenu, as shown in Figure 6.7, press *[F2] MAPSET Processing*.

The MAPSET Options submenu supports adding, changing, and deleting MAPSETS via function keys:

- *[F1] Add New MAPSET*
- *[F2] Update MAPSET Definition*
- *[F3] Delete MAPSET*
- *[F4] Update MAPSET Defaults*

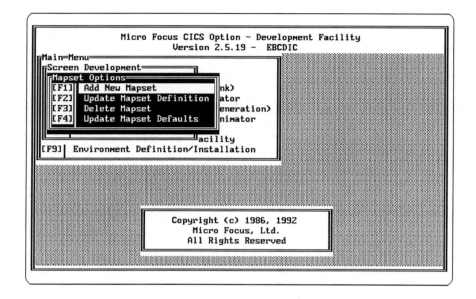

Figure 6.7.   MAPSET maintenance submenu.

Prior to working on MAPSET definitions, defaults should be established that mirror standards established for mainframe CICS applications.

Update MAPSET Defaults. To begin the process of developing MAPSETs, define the defaults as shown in Figure 6.8. Appendix B provides a more detailed definition of the various MAPSET options. The following are those frequently used in mainframe applications:

- TYPE=&SYSPARM
- LANG=COBOL
- MODE=INOUT
- TERM=3270-2
- TIOAPFX=YES
- STORAGE=AUTO

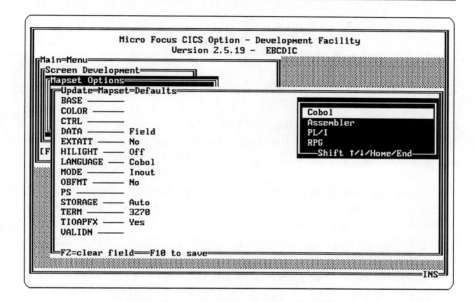

```
                 Micro Focus CICS Option - Development Facility
                         Version 2.5.19 -  EBCDIC
 Main Menu
   Screen Development
     Mapset Options
       Update Mapset Defaults
        BASE
        COLOR
        CTRL                          Cobol
        DATA         Field            Assembler
        EXTATT       No               PL/I
 [F     HILIGHT      Off              RPG
        LANGUAGE     Cobol              Shift ↑/↓/Home/End
        MODE         Inout
        OBFMT        No
        PS
        STORAGE      Auto
        TERM         3270
        TIOAPFX      Yes
        VALIDN

        F2=clear field   F10 to save
                                                              INS
```

Figure 6.8.   Set default options for MAPSETs.

Updating MAPSET defaults processing is entered by pressing [*F4*] *Update MAPSET Defaults.*

Add New MAPSET. Once the add process is selected, a window will open prompting programmers for a new MAPSET name. MCO does not support programmers creating a new MAPSET if the name already exists on the MCO resource files. If, during the installation of the RDT files, the programmer created several copies in different directories, the same MAPSET name could be used.

Once the Add MAPSET submenu is displayed, default values can be overridden by positioning the cursor to an option and typing in a new value, or using the [*F2*] *Clear Field* to clear out a field and typing in a value. When a window opens for selecting a parameter, use the Shift/arrow keys to select from the list and then press Enter. Creating a new MAPSET is accessed from the Screen Development submenu (see Figure 6.9) by pressing [*F1*] *Add New MAPSET.*

Once the MAPSET options have been typed in, the MAPSET needs to be saved before using Escape. To save the MAPSET, press [*F10*] *Save*. Once the MAPSET is saved, the MAP function can be invoked to create a MAP within the newly defined MAPSET.

Update MAPSET Definition. MAPSET options can be altered after the MAPSET has been saved. To update an existing MAPSET, invoke the Update MAPSET submenu. To update a MAPSET, MCO prompts for the name of an existing MAPSET file name, as shown in Figure 6.10, by pressing [*F2*] *Update MAPSET Definition*.

MCO requires that the MAPSET file name already exists and is defined on the MCO resource files. The Update MAPSET submenu allows the current values to be overridden by typing in a new value. Prior to changing a value, use the [*F2*] *Clear Field* to clear out the current value.

As the cursor is positioned to an option, a window opens allowing the selection of values from a list. To select items in a window, use the Shift/arrow keys to position to the specific parameter and press Enter. Once the MAPSET options have been modified, save the MAPSET before escaping from the screen by pressing [*F10*] *Save*.

Delete MAPSET. As part of cleaning the CICS resource tables, occasionally MAPSETs must be deleted. The delete MAPSET function does not delete any files associated with the MAPSET, just the resource file definition is deleted:

- file name.BMS
- file name.CPY
- file name.MST

To delete a MAPSET, type in the name at the prompt, as shown in Figure 6.11, by pressing [*F3*] *Delete MAPSET*. MCO prompts for a confirmation of the delete with the following message: Delete this Mapset? Y or N?

As MAPSETs are deleted from the resource files, the MAPSETs are unavailable for further activity within the BMS Screen Development function. Since the MAPSET files (.BMS, .CPY, and .MST) are

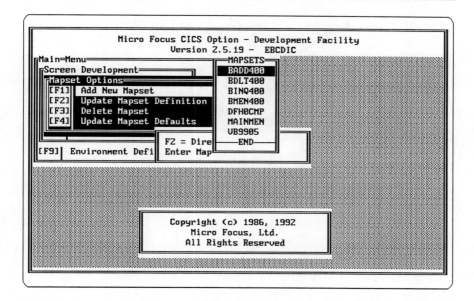

Figure 6.9.   Adding a new MAPSET to CICS.

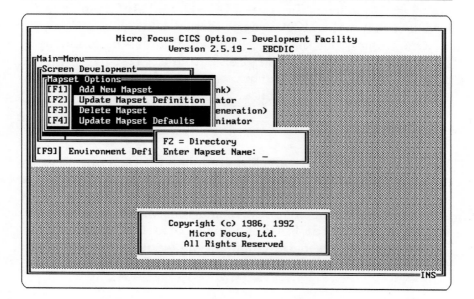

Figure 6.10.   Updating MAPSET option values.

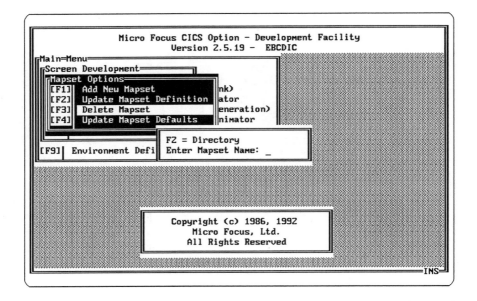

Figure 6.11. Deleting MAPSET definitions in CICS.

not physically deleted, the actual MAPSET and MAPs can be easily loaded back into the MCO resource files.

One thing about the delete function that can be confusing is that even after deleting a MAPSET from the resource files, the executable .MST file can still be displayed using the CMAP transaction in the emulation facility.

MAP CREATION

BMS file processing is invoked from the MCO main menu by selecting [*F8*] *BMS Screen Development*, as shown in Figure 6.12. The MAP Options submenu provides access to functions supporting development of MAP macros. MAPs cannot be defined unless a MAPSET is first defined. To invoke MAP functions from the BMS Screen Development submenu, press [*F3*] *MAP Processing*.

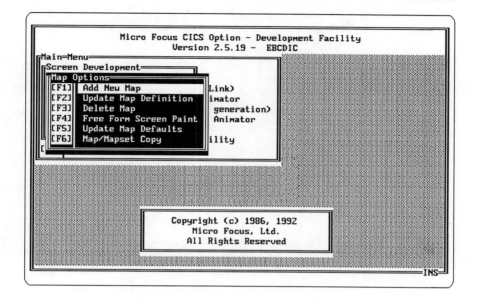

Figure 6.12.   CICS MAP submenu options.

The MAP menu supports adding, changing, and deleting MAPS by function key selections:

- *[F1] Add New MAP*
- *[F2] Update MAP Definition*
- *[F3] Delete MAP*
- *[F4] Free Form Screen Paint*
- *[F5] Update MAP Defaults*
- *[F6] Map / Mapset Copy*

Similar to working with MAPSETs, programmers should establish defaults that mirror standards for mainframe CICS applications.

Update MAP Defaults. The Update MAP Defaults submenu is displayed in Figure 6.13 and is accessed from the MAP Options submenu by pressing *[F5] Update MAP Defaults*.

Appendix B provides a more detailed definition of the various

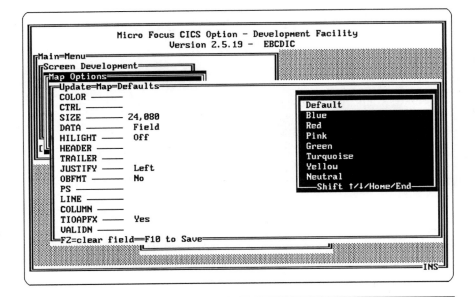

Figure 6.13. Establishing MAP default options.

MAP options. The following is the most frequently used in main-frame applications:

- SIZE=(24,80)

Add New MAP. Once a MAPSET has been defined, one or more MAPs can be created for it. The MAP Options layout is the same screen used by the Update MAP Default function; to create new MAPs press [*F1*] *Add New MAP*.

In order to establish a new MAP, an existing MAPSET name must first be typed in (see Figure 6.14). MCO then prompts via a second window for a MAP file name. As part of creating new MAPs, MCO verifies that the name typed in the window does not already exist. Like the MAPSET function, if CICS resource files have been installed in different directories, the same MAP name can be used more than once.

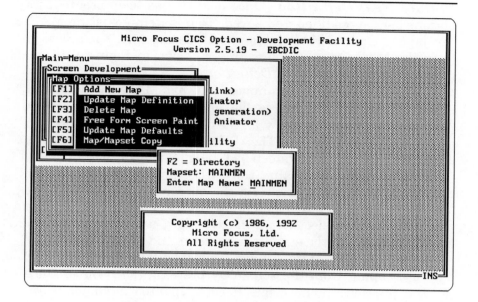

Figure 6.14.   Adding a new MAP to existing MAPSET.

Default values can be replaced with custom values, although it might be better to use only the default values for consistency among MAPs.

To erase a current value, use the space bar or press [*F2*] *Clear Field*. When a window box opens, listing values for an option, use the Shift/arrow keys to select from the list and then press Enter.

Once the MAP options are typed in, the MAP needs to be saved before using Escape. To save a MAP press [*F10*] *Save*. Pressing Escape without saving the MAP exits the function with no MAP created.

Once [*F10*] is pressed to save the MAP, the message "Record Updated" is displayed in the lower portion of the screen. Escape should be pressed to exit from the MAP function. After pressing Escape, MCO closes the MAP window and opens up the Free Form Screen Painter. The screen painter is discussed later in this chapter.

Update MAP Definition. Once a MAP has been created, its options can be modified and saved. To update an existing MAP, invoke the Update MAP submenu. Updating MAPs is accessed from the MAP Options submenu, as shown in Figure 6.15, by pressing [*F2*] *Update MAP Definition*.

To update a MAP, programmers type in a MAPSET name that exists on the CICS resource file and press Enter. MCO then prompts, via a second window, for the name of a MAP that is defined on the MCO resource files. The Update MAP submenu allows the current values to be overridden by typing in a new value.

Prior to changing a value, the [*F2*] *Clear Field* can be used to clear out the current value. As the cursor is positioned to the options, a window box opens allowing the selection of a value from the list. To select items in a window, use the Shift/arrow keys to position to the specific parameter and press Enter.

Once the MAP options have been modified, save the MAP before escaping from the screen by pressing [*F10*] *Save*. Once [*F10*] is pressed, the message "Record Updated" is displayed in

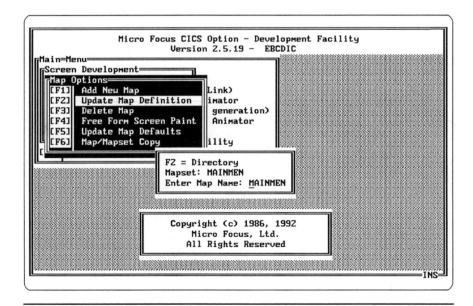

Figure 6.15.   Update MAP options to new values.

the lower portion of the screen. Escape should then be pressed to exit from the MAP function.

Unlike the Add New MAP function, the Update MAP function does not access the screen painter for modifying the screen. To modify the actual screen image, do one of the following:

- Edit the macros
- Invoke the screen painter—([F4] Free Form Screen Paint from the Map Options submenu)
- Invoke field updates

Delete MAP. CICS retains MAP definitions on resource files until they are deleted. Like the MAPSET delete, physical files are not deleted:

- file name.BMS
- file name.CPY
- file name.MST

To delete a MAP, type in the MAPSET name and press Enter. MCO opens a second window prompt for the specific MAP name to be deleted (Figure 6.16) by pressing [*F3*] *Delete MAP*.

When deleting MAPs, MCO prompts for a confirmation of the delete with the following message: Delete this MAP? Y or N? As MAPs are deleted from the resource files, they are unavailable for further activity within the BMS Screen Development function. Since MAP files (.BMS, .CPY, and .MST) are not physically deleted, the actual MAP can be easily loaded back into MCO resource files.

As in the delete MAPSET function, deleting MAPs only deletes from the resource files. The executable .MST file can still be displayed using the CMAP transaction in the emulation facility.

FREE-FORM SCREEN PAINTING

MCO provides a function to draw screens with a paint facility that allows the following:

- Literal placement on the screen
- Data entry field definitions

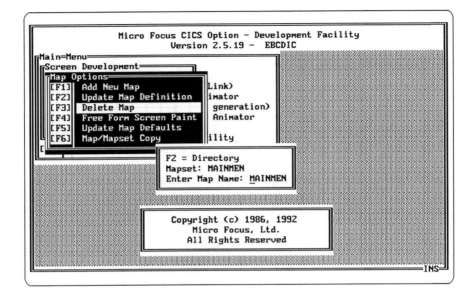

Figure 6.16.   Deleting a MAP from a MAPSET.

The paint facility provides programmers with a tool for defining a screen's layout. Using a painter allows screens to be developed with minimal knowledge of BMS macros. Using the paint facility is a three-step process:

1. Invoke the paint facility.
2. Paint (draw) the screen.
3. Exit the painter.

Invoking the Paint Facility

The Free Form Screen Painter function can be invoked in two different manners: from the Add New MAP function, and directly from the MAP Options submenu. Whichever way the painter is accessed, the functions supported are the same. To invoke the screen painter (Figure 6.17) from the MCO main menu, press [*F8*] *BMS Screen Development.*

Once the Screen Development submenu is displayed, program-

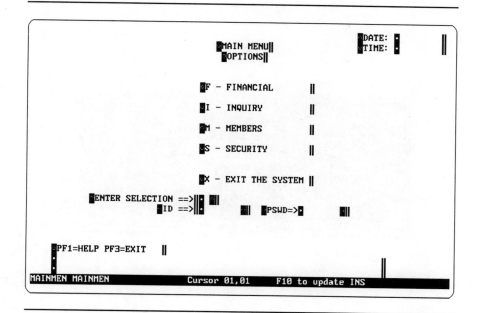

Figure 6.17.   Sample painted screen image.

mers can choose the Free Form Screen Painter directly or first establish MAPSET/MAP definitions. The painter can only be entered directly if loading an existing macro file.

The painter facility is function key driven. Pressing [*F1*] will provide the Help screen display of function key uses (Figure 6.18).

Indirect Access to the Painter. The Free Form Screen Painter is accessed when defining a MAPSET and MAP as part of the screen development function. The steps noted here were covered in detail in a previous section of this chapter.

- From the Screen Development submenu:
- Invoke the MAPSET function   [*F2*] *MAPSET Processing*
- Establish a MAPSET   [*F1*] *Add New MAPSET*
     Identify MAPSET options to use
     Save the MAPSET   [*F10*] *Save*
     Exit the MAPSET process   *Escape*
- Invoke the MAP function   [*F3*] *MAP Processing*

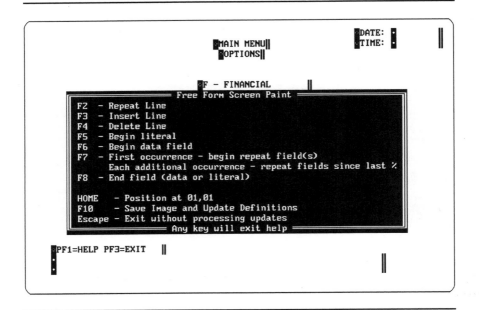

Figure 6.18.   Screen Painter function key HELP.

- Establish a MAP   [F1] *Add New MAP*
    Identify MAPSET the new MAP belongs to and press Enter
    Identify MAP options the MAP will use
    Save the MAP   [F10] *Save*
    Exit the MAP process   *Escape*
- Free-Form Screen Painter automatically entered

To update an existing MAP, the screen painter is used. The Update MAP Definition function does not support editing a MAP or access to the painter.

Direct Access to the Painter. MCO requires that an existing MAPSET/MAP be defined to access the screen painter. Once a screen image is built, programmers have to generate BMS macros from the Generate Import Options submenu. The steps outlined below are used to access the painter facility directly:

- From the Screen Development submenu:
- Invoke the screen painter   *[F4] Free Form Screen Paint*
    Identify MAPSET name   *Enter*
    Identify MAP name   *Enter*
- Establish a screen image   (painter functions)
    Save the screen image   *[F10] Save*
    Exit the painter   *Escape*
- Select data field   *Enter*
    Modify data field
    Save the modified field   *[F10] Save*
    Exit the field updates   *Escape*

To update an existing MAP, the Free Form Screen Painter is used because the Update MAP Definition function does not support or allow access to the painter.

Painting a Screen

Once the Free Form Screen Painter facility is invoked, a blank screen is displayed if adding a new MAP, or the image reflects the current screen, as shown in Figure 6.19.

Free Form Screen Painter function keys:

- *[F2] Repeat Line*—Copies the line that the cursor is currently on, subsequent lines shift down one line.
- *[F3] Insert Line*—A blank line is inserted prior to the current line the cursor is on.
- *[F4] Delete Line*—Deletes the line the cursor is on.
- *[F5] Start of Literal*—Sets an attribute byte for the start of a literal. Can be used to mark the end of a field by starting a new field.
- *[F6] Start of Data Field*—Sets an attribute byte for the start of a data field. Can be used to mark the end of a field by starting a new field.
- *[F7] Occurs Mark*—Use in place of [F6] to mark a data field that occurs multiple times. Can be used to mark the end of a field by starting a new field.
- *[F8] End of Field*—Marks the end of a data or literal field.

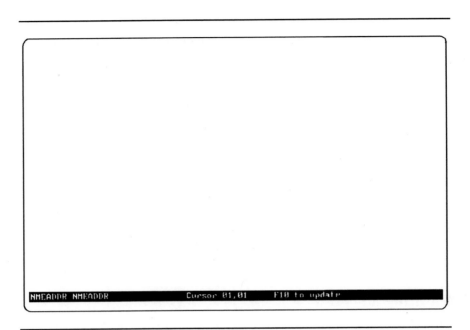

NMEADDR NMEADDR   Cursor 01,01   F10 to update

Figure 6.19.   Initial Free-Form Painter screen.

- *[F10] Save Image*—Saves the image to resource files.
- *Escape*—Exit without saving.

While the painter screen is displayed, the cursor position is always present in the lower portion of the screen. Use the arrow keys to move the cursor around on the screen. Using the Home key always returns the cursor to line 1, column 1. Painting the MAP sample shown in Figure 6.17 was started by identifying literal definitions:

- Position cursor to start point of a literal.
  [F5] is pressed to set the attribute byte for a literal.
- Type in the literal.
  [F8] is pressed to mark the end of a literal. *[F5]*, *[F6]*, or *[F7]* could also be used.

Define a single data field definition by doing the following:

- Position cursor to start point of data field.

  [*F6*] is pressed to set the attribute byte for a data field.
- Use the space bar or the right arrow key to mark the data field size.

  [*F8*] is pressed to mark the end of a literal. [*F5*], [*F6*], or [*F7*] could also be used.

To save the MAP, press [*F10*], and the MAPSET/MAP is defined to CICS. A macro file or copybook file is not generated as part of the screen painting process. After pressing Escape to exit the painter facility, the Update Field Options submenu is displayed (Figure 6.20). The data field names have a particular significance in the naming convention:

- FLD1733

  FLD—Identifies this as a data field.

  17—Identifies the line the field is on.

  33—Identifies the column the field starts in.

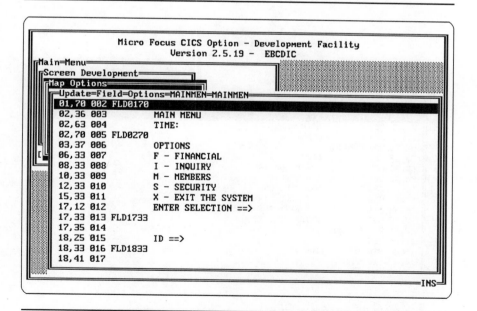

Figure 6.20.   Screen painter-generated field name.

At this point programmers would not want to bring these data field names into a COBOL program. It would be too difficult to figure out which fields were which. For example, which would be more meaningful in a COBOL program—FLD1733 or MENSEL?

Converting field names to more meaningful ones is accomplished by positioning to a field and pressing Enter, displaying the Update Field Options submenu (see Figure 6.21).

Fields are updated one at a time by overtyping the currently displayed values. The submenu provides the following keys for programmer use:

- *PgUp*—For scrolling up to the previous field.
- *PgDn*—For scrolling down to the next field.
- *[F9] Clear Field*—Clear out the value of the option that the cursor is located on.
- *[F2] View*—Displays the painter screen reflecting any changes made to the fields.

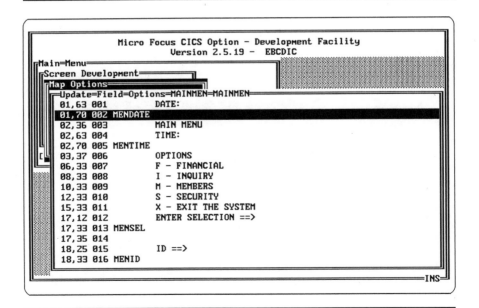

Figure 6.21.   Modified field names changed.

- [*F10*] *Save*—Saves the changes made to the current field.
- *Escape*—To exit the Update Field Options submenu.

As fields are modified, MCO does not permit the use of scrolling from one field to the next without saving or exiting from the current changes. Any attempt to exit prompts with the message:

`Exit without saving? Y or N?`

If a more complicated screen is needed with multiply occurring data fields (Figure 6.22), MCO supports repeating groups:

- Position cursor to start point of data field.
  [*F7*] is pressed to set the attribute byte for a repeated data field size.
  Use the space bar or the right arrow key to mark the data field size.
  [*F8*] is pressed to mark the end of a literal or data field.

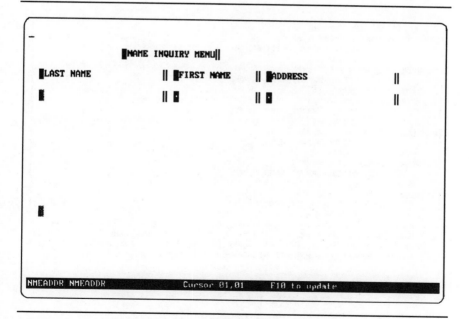

Figure 6.22. Defining "occurs" data fields.

- Position the cursor on the line to repeat group through.
- [F7] is pressed a second time to mark the end of the repeated group.

In a repeated group, all other markers ([F5], [F6], or [F7]) are overlayed within the group. The overlay can cause syntax problems when the starting attribute that is overlayed is within the repeated group and the ending marker is outside the repeating group.

MCO supports BMS macros similar to mainframe CICS in that no occurs code exists in the macro file (Figure 6.23). Fields in an occurs definition are defined as individual fields.

When the copybook is generated by MCO, the repeating group field groups are defined as a table with an occurs clause (Figure 6.24). If your mainframe environment does not support a painter with similar capabilities, the generated copybook is an excellent reason to use the painter and transfer code to the mainframe.

```
-NMEADDR.BMS-
 * FLD0703-GRP<03>.FLD0703
 FLD0703   DFHMDF POS=(07,03),                               X
                  ATTRB=(UNPROT,NORM,FSET),                  X
                  LENGTH=023
 FLD0729   DFHMDF POS=(07,29),                               X
                  ATTRB=(UNPROT,NORM,FSET),                  X
                  LENGTH=015
 FLD0747   DFHMDF POS=(07,47),                               X
                  ATTRB=(UNPROT,NORM,FSET),                  X
                  LENGTH=024
 FLD0803   DFHMDF POS=(08,03),                               X
                  ATTRB=(UNPROT,NORM,FSET),                  X
                  LENGTH=023
 FLD0829   DFHMDF POS=(08,29),                               X
                  ATTRB=(UNPROT,NORM,FSET),                  X
                  LENGTH=015
 FLD0847   DFHMDF POS=(08,47),                               X
                  ATTRB=(UNPROT,NORM,FSET),                  X
                  LENGTH=024
 _
 Edit-NMEADDR--------52-lines------Line-41-----Col-1--------Wrap-Ins-Caps-Num-Scroll
 F1=help F2=library F3=load-file F4=save-file F5=split-line F6=join-line F7=print
 F8=calculate F9=untype-word-left F10=delete-word-right
```

Figure 6.23.   Macro file with a repeated group.

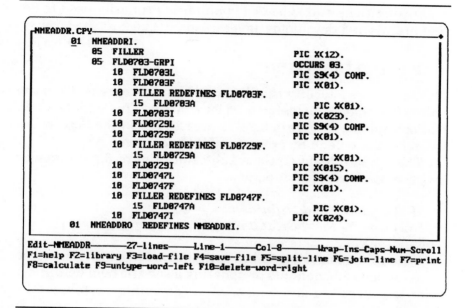

```
┌NMEADDR.CPY─────────────────────────────────────────────────────────────●
│    01  NMEADDRI.
│        05  FILLER                           PIC X(12).
│        05  FLD0703-GRPI                     OCCURS 03.
│            10  FLD0703L                      PIC S9(4) COMP.
│            10  FLD0703F                      PIC X(01).
│            10  FILLER REDEFINES FLD0703F.
│                15  FLD0703A                      PIC X(01).
│            10  FLD0703I                      PIC X(023).
│            10  FLD0729L                      PIC S9(4) COMP.
│            10  FLD0729F                      PIC X(01).
│            10  FILLER REDEFINES FLD0729F.
│                15  FLD0729A                      PIC X(01).
│            10  FLD0729I                      PIC X(015).
│            10  FLD0747L                      PIC S9(4) COMP.
│            10  FLD0747F                      PIC X(01).
│            10  FILLER REDEFINES FLD0747F.
│                15  FLD0747A                      PIC X(01).
│            10  FLD0747I                      PIC X(024).
│    01  NMEADDRO  REDEFINES NMEADDRI.
├──────────────────────────────────────────────────────────────────────────
│Edit─NMEADDR────────27─lines────────Line─1────────Col─8──────────Wrap─Ins─Caps─Num─Scroll
│F1=help F2=library F3=load-file F4=save-file F5=split-line F6=join-line F7=print
│F8=calculate F9=untype-word-left F10=delete-word-right
```

Figure 6.24.   MCO copybook with repeated group.

Exiting the Screen Painter

Exiting the screen painter can be done in these two different ways:

- Exit with saving
- Exit without saving

Once a screen image is finished, it should be saved by pressing [*F10*] *Update*. At the point that an image is saved, MCO validates the MAP and exits to the Update Field Options window. If errors are detected during the save process, CICS displays messages and the line/column of the error. To return to the painter to correct any errors, press Enter.

Once in the screen painter, pressing Escape without pressing [*F10*] causes the screen image to be deleted. If the painter had been entered through the Add New MAP function, the MAPSET/

MAP definitions still exist. The painter is primarily used to define literals and data fields on a screen.

MAP FIELD UPDATING

MCO provides a facility that is automatically accessed from the painter to update fields created in a MAP. The Update Field Options submenu (Figure 6.24) is accessed from the Screen Development submenu by pressing [*F4*] *Field Processing*.

The Update Field Options submenu (Figure 6.25) provides programmers with two functions:

- [*F1*] *Update Field Definitions*
- [*F2*] *Update Field Defaults*

When a field is being updated, the submenu used is the same as when updating defaults or updating a specific field definition. Prior to generating any screens with the painter, establish the

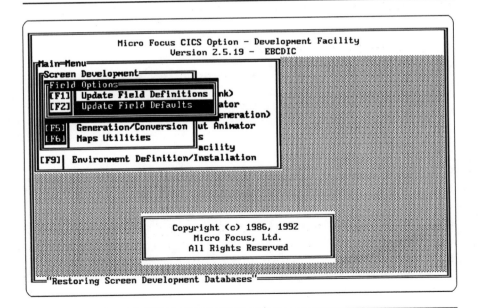

Figure 6.25.   Field Options editing submenu.

field default options that the majority of the data fields use. The screen painter utilizes defaults from MAPSET, MAP, and Fields that have been previously defined.

The only limitation to be aware of is that the Update Field Definitions function is not capable of changing a fields position (line/column). Use the painter to accomplish this. As done previously for MAPSET and MAP processing, the first step presented here is to establish default values.

Update Field Defaults

Prior to developing any MAPs via the screen painter, define the defaults to use (see Figure 6.26). Appendix B provides a more detailed definition of the various field options. The following are those frequently used in mainframe applications:

- LENGTH= number
- NAME=label

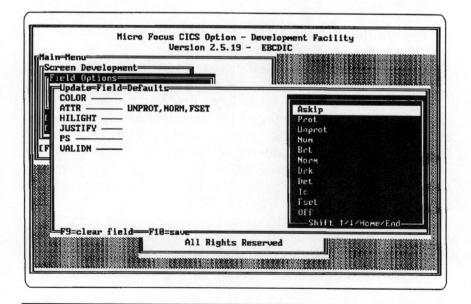

Figure 6.26. Updating field default options.

- ATTR=????
- INITIAL=???
- PICIN=?????
- PICOUT=?????

Updating data field defaults is entered from the Update Field Options submenu by pressing [F2] *Update Field Defaults*.

Update Field Definitions

Updating data fields is done after the MAPSET/MAP is created either with a native editor or through the screen painter. To modify a screen image to "add" a new field, use the painter or editor first. For existing fields, invoke Update Field Definitions. Invoking the Update Field Options submenu for data fields is a little more involved than accessing the defaults screen: press [F1] *Update Field Definitions*.

Fields are updated by identifying the MAPSET and MAP that will be edited in the Update Field functions, as shown in Figure 6.27:

- Type in the MAPSET name and press Enter.
- Type in the MAP name and press Enter.
- Select a field to update and press Enter.

Using the up or down arrow keys, programmers can position to the field option to be changed. On the right side of a screen, list boxes open as an option is moved onto. When only one item is listed in the box, programmers should type in a valid value.

Fields are updated one at a time by overtyping the currently displayed values (Figure 6.28). The following keys are for programmer use:

- *PgUp*—For scrolling up to the previous field.
- *PgDn*—For scrolling down to the next field.
- [F9] *Clear Field*—Clear out the value of the option that the cursor is located on.
- [F2] *View*—Displays the painter screen reflecting any changes made to the fields.

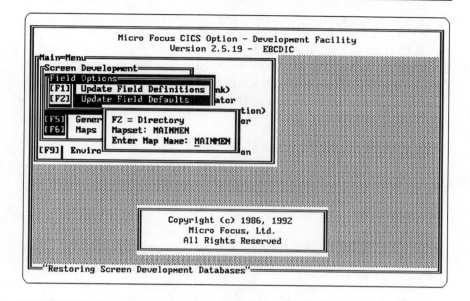

Figure 6.27.   Updating MAPSET field options.

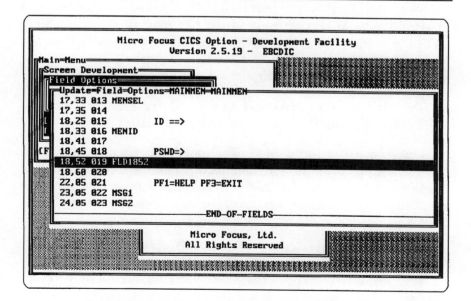

Figure 6.28.   Selecting a field to modify options.

- *[F10] Save*—Saves the changes made to the current field.
- *Escape*—To exit off of the Update Field Options submenu.

When lists are presented, the Shift/arrow keys are used to select from the list. Then press Enter. As fields are modified, MCO does not permit scrolling from one field to the next without saving or exiting from the current changes. Any attempt will prompt the message:

Exit without saving? Y or N?

Once the field options have been typed in, the MAPSET/MAP needs to be saved before using Escape. To save the MAPSET/ MAP, press *[F10] Save*.

MAPSET/MAP COPYING

Programmers should find the copy facility useful for copying and making minor changes to the copied file. The focus of this chapter is MAP/MAPSET development, the last function on the MAP.

Options submenu is the MAP/MAPSET Copy function (Figure 6.29). The copy facility is invoked by selecting from the MAP Options submenu. Press *[F5] MAP/MAPSET Copy*.

The copy facility supports two ways to copy files: copy a MAPSET and MAP to a new MAPSET/MAP file or use native DOS copy commands. The MCO copy facility requires that the input MAPSET and MAP be typed in (Figure 6.30). Once the selection is made to copy, do the following:

- Type in the input MAPSET name and press Enter.
- Type in the input MAP name and press Enter.

Once both the input MAPSET and MAP names have been typed in, MCO prompts for the output file names (Figure 6.31). When copying files within MCOs BMS Screen Development function, only one MAP can be copied at a time. Assuming that a MAPSET/MAP file already exists, do the following:

- Input MAPSET/MAP (NMEADDR/NMEADDR)

Programmers can copy the file to satisfy a couple of different needs:

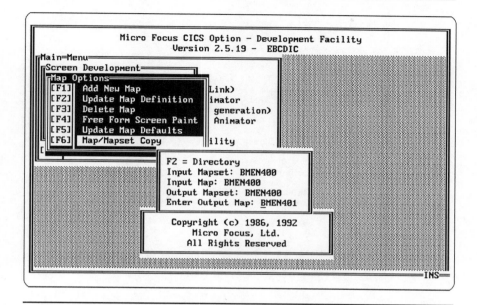

Figure 6.29.   Copying MAPSETs and MAPs.

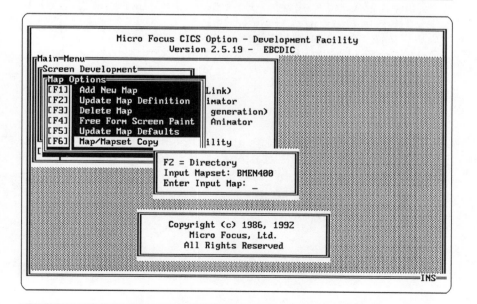

Figure 6.30.   Copy after MAPSET/MAP inputs keyed.

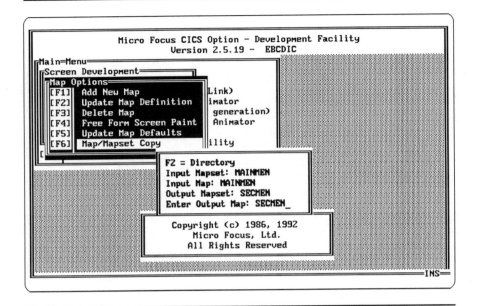

```
            Micro Focus CICS Option - Development Facility
                    Version 2.5.19 -  EBCDIC
┌Main=Menu═══════════════════════════════════════════
│┌Screen Development═══════════════════════╗
││┌Map Options═══════════════════╗
│││ [F1]  Add New Map              │Link>
│││ [F2]  Update Map Definition    │imator
│││ [F3]  Delete Map               │   generation>
│││ [F4]  Free Form Screen Paint   │ Animator
│││ [F5]  Update Map Defaults      │
│││ [F6]  Map/Mapset Copy          │ility
│[                                 ▼
│       ▼ ┌───────────────────────────┐
│         │ F2 = Directory             │
│         │ Input Mapset: MAINMEN      │
│         │ Input Map: MAINMEN         │
│         │ Output Mapset: SECMEN      │
│         │ Enter Output Map: SECMEN_  │
│         ├───────────────────────────┤
│         │ Copyright (c) 1986, 1992   │
│         │      Micro Focus, Ltd.     │
│         │    All Rights Reserved     │
│         └───────────────────────────┘
                                                    ═INS═
```

Figure 6.31.　Copying after output files named.

- Copy a MAP to a new MAP name within the same MAPSET.
   Update Output MAPSET/MAP
   (NMEADDR/NMEADDR and NMEPHON)
- Copy a MAPSET/MAP to a new MAPSET/MAP file.
   New Output MAPSET/MAP (NMEFILE/NMEFILE)

SUMMARY

MCO provides programmers with the tools to define MAPSETs, MAPS, and data field definitions. BMS macro files can be imported from the mainframe and loaded into either a selected edit package or into the screen painter. Macro files that are compatible with the mainframe and the functions can be generated in MCO, providing an easy-to-use set of tools.

7

BMS Macros, Copybooks, and Executables

The previous chapter covered the various features available to create and alter BMS files. At the conclusion of the chapter, the MAPSET/MAP created only existed on CICS Resource Definition Tables. To complete the MAPSET/MAP process, at least three files need to be generated.

This chapter covers the Generation/Conversion function relating to generating macro and copybook files:

- file name.BMS
- file name.CPY

and the MAP Utilities function for generating an executable file:

- file name.MST

The .BMS file contains the macro definitions of the screen image with the generated macros. BMS source code can be transferred to the mainframe. MCO provides programmers with the capability to generate either BMS or MFS macros. The .CPY file contains a definition of MAP(s) in COBOL format for use in working-storage. The .MST file is the equivalent of a mainframe-assembled executable file of the MAPSET/MAP.

Once a screen is developed, programmers can verify its appearance according to specifications without having a COBOL program ready for execution. The CMAP transaction provided with MCO uses the executable .MST file to display the screen on the terminal.

ACCESS TO GENERATING AND IMPORTING FUNCTIONS

Generating and Importing functions can be accessed from three different areas within the MCO. From the MCO main menu select [F8] *BMS Screen Development*, and select either [F5] *Generation/Import* or [F6] *MAP Utility* from an OS-command line.

Command Line Generation and Importing

When invoking a function from a command line, all commands are preceded by the following:

```
[XM switches] used for DOS based processing only
```

XM is used to invoke MCO and load the function into extended memory for processing. Switches can be provided to direct XM how to load the function.

Following the [XM switches] is the reference to MCO, keyed as either

```
MFCICS in a DOS environment
            or
PMFCICS in an OS/2 environment
```

Command Line Generation of a Test Definition. The command syntax for "assembling" a Test definition from the command line is

```
[XM switches] MFCICS mapgen mapset
```

• Mapset: the MAPSET file to generate the test definition for.

Command Line Importing BMS Macros. The command syntax for importing macros from the command line is

```
[XM switches] MFCICS bmsin dataset
```

- Dataset: the name of the dataset containing the BMS macros to import.

Command Line Generation of BMS Macros. The command syntax for generating a macro file from the command line is

```
[XM switches] MFCICS bmsgen mapset
```

- Mapset: the name of the MAPSET file name to be generated.

Command Line Generation of BMS Copybook. The command syntax for generating a copybook file from the command line is

```
[XM switches] MFCICS bmscopy mapset
```

- Mapset: the name of the MAPSET file name to generate the copybook from.

Command Line Importing MFS Macros. The command syntax for importing macros from the command line is

```
[XM switches] MFCICS mfsin dataset
```

- Dataset: the name of the dataset containing the MFS macros to import.

Command Line Generation of MFS Macros. The command syntax for generating a macro file from the command line is

```
[XM switches] MFCICS mfsgen mapset map
```

- Mapset: the name of the MAPSET file containing the MAP to be generated.
- Map: the name of the MAP to generate MFS macros from.

Command Line Generation of MFS Copybook. The command syntax for generating a copybook file from the command line is

```
[XM switches] MFCICS mfscopy mapset map
```

- Mapset: the name of the MAPSET file containing the MAP to be generated.
- Map: the name of the MAP to generate copybook file from.

MCO Menu Generation/Import

MCO provides an interactive function supporting generating and importing BMS files. The remaining sections of this chapter will examine the Generation and Import process in detail.

MACRO GENERATION

Within MCO, BMS macros are not required. The primary purpose of generating macros is to export MAPSET/MAPs to either another PC or the mainframe. MCO provides an extract utility that can also be used to transfer screens between PCs without a macro file available. I personally prefer to transfer a source file that can be edited, and the utility output of the extract is not editable.

BMS Macro Generation

Having macro files available comes in handy for quick edits that programmers often discover are needed when testing. In place of native editing of macro files, MCO provides a painter. The painter is not complicated, but if all they need to do is change a data field size to make it one byte larger, programmers often like to just make the change.

Whenever a change is made to the macro file, the file will have to be reimported into the CICS resource files. The point being that few keystrokes are saved using either the painter or native editing to edit screens. Generating BMS macros is part of the BMS Screen Development function [F8] from the MCO main menu (Figure 7.1). The Generate/Import Options submenu (Figure 7.2) is selected by pressing [F5] *Generation/Conversion* from the Screen Development submenu.

MAPSET/MAP macros are created in MCO from the Generate/Import Options submenu. MCO prompts for the MAPSET name, shown in Figure 7.3. After pressing Enter, MCO searches the

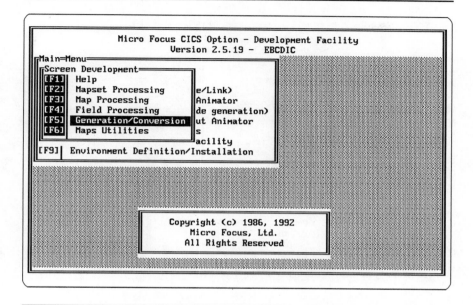

Figure 7.1.   MCO's screen development functions.

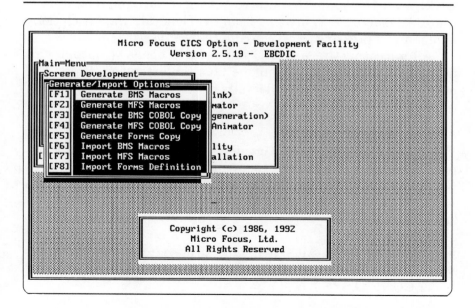

Figure 7.2.   Submenu for generating and importing.

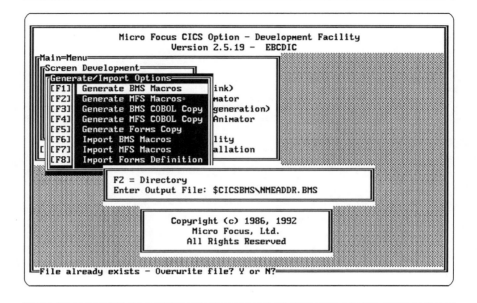

Figure 7.3. Generate macro file for this MAPSET.

CICS resource files for the entered MAPSET file name. Creation of the BMS macro file is invoked from the Generate/Import Options submenu by pressing [F1] *Generate BMS Macros.*

After locating the MAPSET name, MCO opens an output window box containing the file name plus the extension .BMS. The output directory\file name defaults to

```
$CICSBMS\MAPSET.BMS
```

Using the $CICSBMS, MCO creates the macro file in the directory established as part of the SET commands in either AUTOEXEC.BAT (DOS) or CONFIG.SYS (OS/2). If no directory path is typed into the window, MCO searches the following directories in the order presented below:

- CICSBMS path—MCO generates to or searches the first directory path found on this SET statement in the AUTOEXEC.BAT or CONFIG.SYS.

- CICSSRC path—MCO searches in the first directory path found on this SET statement in the AUTOEXEC.BAT or CONFIG.SYS.
- CICSTEST path—MCO searches in the first directory path found on this SET statement in the AUTOEXEC.BAT or CONFIG.SYS.
- Current Directory path—If no SET statements are found, MCO searches in the current directory.

After verifying the output file name, press Enter to generate the macro file. MCO displays one of two messages depending on whether or not the macro file already exists:

- Macro file does not exist.
  Generating BMS Macros
- Macro file already exists (see Figure 7.3).

When working with macros directly in an editor, programmers often like to have several options on a single line to display as many lines as possible in the editor, as shown in Figure 7.4.

When generating macros from an existing macro file, each option is moved to a separate line, as shown in Figure 7.5. MCO prompts if a file exists, preventing any accidental overlaying of macros.

MFS Macro Generation

MCO supports the generation of MFS MFLD statements by converting BMS DFLD statements. MFS macro files are created from CICS-generated BMS macro files. Generating MFS macros is part of the BMS Screen Development function [F8] from the MCO main menu.

Generating MFS macros is accessed from the Screen Development submenu by pressing [F5] *Generation/Conversion*, as shown in Figure 7.1, and then from the Generate/Import Options submenu, shown in Figure 7.2. Press [F2] *Generate MFS Macros*.

The procedure for generating MFS macro files is identical to that of generating BMS macros. MCO prompts for the MAPSET name. Type in the name, press Enter, and MCO searches the

```
┌─MAINMEN. BMS──────────────────────────────────────────────────────────────◆
│ MAINMEN   DFHMSD TYPE=&&SYSPARM,LANG=COBOL,MODE=INOUT,TIOAPFX=YES
│ MAINMEN   DFHMDI SIZE=(24,80)
│           DFHMDF POS=(01,63),ATTRB=(PROT,BRT),LENGTH=06,           X
│             INITIAL='DITE: '
│ MENDATE   DFHMDF POS=(01,70),ATTRB=(PROT,FSET),LENGTH=08,PICOUT='X(8)'
│           DFHMDF POS=(02,36),ATTRB=(PROT,BRT),LENGTH=09,           X
│             INITIAL='MAIN MENU'
│           DFHMDF POS=(02,63),ATTRB=(PROT,BRT),LENGTH=06,           X
│             INITIAL='TIME: '
│ MENTIME   DFHMDF POS=(02,70),ATTRB=(PROT,FSET),LENGTH=08,PICOUT='X(8)'
│           DFHMDF POS=(03,37),ATTRB=(PROT,BRT),LENGTH=07,           X
│             INITIAL='OPTIONS'
│           DFHMDF POS=(06,33),ATTRB=(PROT),LENGTH=20,               X
│             INITIAL='F - FINANCIAL       '
│           DFHMDF POS=(08,33),ATTRB=(PROT),LENGTH=20,               X
│             INITIAL='I - INQUIRY         '
│           DFHMDF POS=(10,33),ATTRB=(PROT),LENGTH=20,               X
│             INITIAL='M - MEMBERS         '
│           DFHMDF POS=(12,33),ATTRB=(PROT),LENGTH=20,               X
│
├────────────────────────────────────────────────────────────────────────────
│ Edit—MAINMEN────40-lines────Line-1────Col-1────Wrap—Ins—Caps—Num—Scroll
│ F1=help F2=library F3=load-file F4=save-file F5=split-line F6=join-line F7=print
│ F8=calculate F9=untype-word-left F10=delete-word-right
```

Figure 7.4. Multiple options per statement.

```
┌─MAINMEN. BMS──────────────────────────────────────────────────────────────◆
│ MAINMEN   DFHMSD TYPE=&&SYSPARM,                                  X
│             LANG=COBOL,                                           X
│             MODE=INOUT,                                           X
│             TIOAPFX=YES
│ MAINMEN_  DFHMDI SIZE=(24,80)
│           DFHMDF POS=(01,63),                                     X
│             ATTRB=(PROT,BRT),                                     X
│             LENGTH=006,                                           X
│             INITIAL='DITE: '
│ MENDATE   DFHMDF POS=(01,70),                                     X
│             ATTRB=(PROT,FSET),                                    X
│             LENGTH=008,                                           X
│             PICOUT='X(8)'
│           DFHMDF POS=(02,36),                                     X
│             ATTRB=(PROT,BRT),                                     X
│             LENGTH=009,                                           X
│             INITIAL='MAIN MENU'
│           DFHMDF POS=(02,63),                                     X
│             ATTRB=(PROT,BRT),                                     X
├────────────────────────────────────────────────────────────────────────────
│ Edit—MAINMNZ────91-lines────Line-5────Col-8────Wrap—Ins—Caps—Num—Scroll
│ F1=help F2=library F3=load-file F4=save-file F5=split-line F6=join-line F7=print
│ F8=calculate F9=untype-word-left F10=delete-word-right
```

Figure 7.5. One option per line macro sample.

resource files for the MAPSET file name. After the MAPSET file is located, an output window opens with the input file name plus the extension .MFS, as shown in Figure 7.6. The output directory/file name defaults to

```
$CICSTEST\MAP.MFS
```

Using the $CICSTEST, MCO creates the macro file in the directory established as part of the SET commands found in AUTOEXEC.BAT (DOS) or CONFIG.SYS (OS/2). If no directory path is typed into the window, MCO searches the following directories in the order below:

- CICSMFS—MCO searches in the first directory path found on this SET statement in the AUTOEXEC.BAT or CONFIG.SYS.
- CICSTEST—MCO searches in the first directory path found on this SET statement in the AUTOEXEC.BAT or CONFIG.SYS.

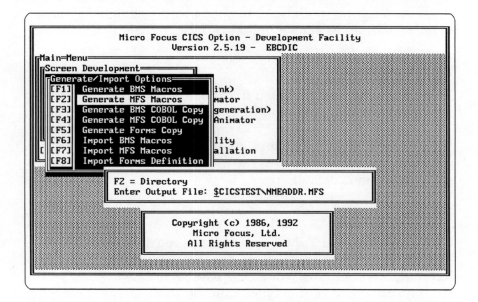

Figure 7.6.   Output file prompt for MFS dataset.

- Current Directory—If no SET statements are found, MCO searches in the current directory.

Once the output file name is verified, pressing Enter generates the macro file. Once the macro file is generated, the MFS code can be genned in IMSVS86 to create an executable screen image. MCO displays one of two messages when generating the macro file:

- Macro file does not exist message.
  Generating MFS Macros
- Macro file already exists message (see Figure 7.6).

COBOL COPYBOOK GENERATION

After a screen has been developed and verified, programmers can construct the COBOL program. To complete the program, a copybook file defining the screen image is needed.

Generating a COBOL copybook file is part of the BMS Screen Development function [*F8*] from the MCO main menu. Invoke the Generate/Import Options submenu by pressing [*F5*] *Generation/Conversion*, as shown in Figure 7.1.

BMS Copybook

BMS copybooks are generated from the Generate/Import Options submenu (Figure 7.7). Press [*F3*] *Generate BMS COBOL Copybook*.

To generate a copybook, MCO prompts for the MAPSET name. Type in the name, press Enter, and an output window box opens with the input file name plus the extension .CPY. The output directory/file name defaults to

```
$CICSCPY\MAPSET.CPY
```

Using the $CICSCPY, MCO creates the copybook file in the directory established as part of the SET commands in either AUTOEXEC.BAT (DOS) or CONFIG.SYS (OS/2).

If no directory path is typed into the window, MCO searches the following directories in the order presented below:

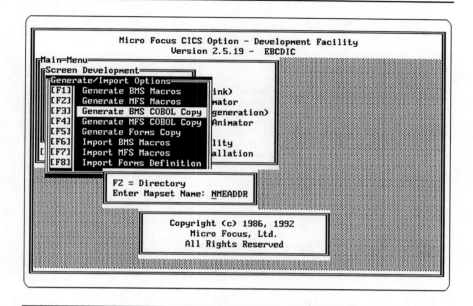

Figure 7.7.   Generating a COBOL copybook file.

- CICSMFS path
  MCO searches in the first directory path found on this SET
  statement in the AUTOEXEC.BAT or CONFIG.SYS.
- CICSTEST path
  MCO searches in the first directory path found on this SET
  statement in the AUTOEXEC.BAT or CONFIG.SYS.
- Current Directory path
  If no SET statements are found, MCO searches in the current directory.

Once the copybook generation process is invoked, MCO displays two messages, depending on the results:

- Copybook file does not exist.
  Generating BMS Copybook
- Copybook file already exists (see Figure 7.8).

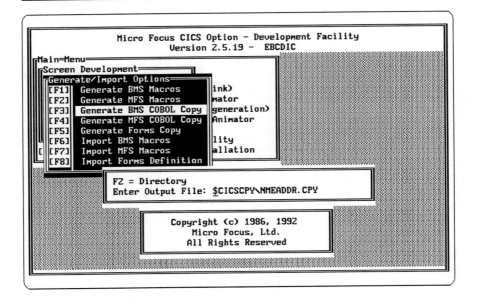

Figure 7.8.   Identifying an output copybook file.

Copybook files can be created to contain either the eight-character DFHMDF macro name or a COBOL-generated name (see Figure 7.9). The COBOL-generated name is created in the Free-Form Screen Painter or from the Field Processing function.

MFS Copybook

When generating a copybook file, MCO generates each field name as an eight-character macro name from the DFHMDF macro name. When the BMS screen is defined, the programmer can select to use COBOL names (see Figure 7.9). Defining COBOL names can be accomplished within the Free-Form Screen Painter or from the Field Processing function.

MFS copybook files are generated from CICS-generated BMS macro files, or from importing MFS macros and then generating BMS macros from the MFS file. To generate a MFS COBOL copybook from the Generate/Import Options submenu, press [*F4*] *Generate MFS COBOL Copybook.*

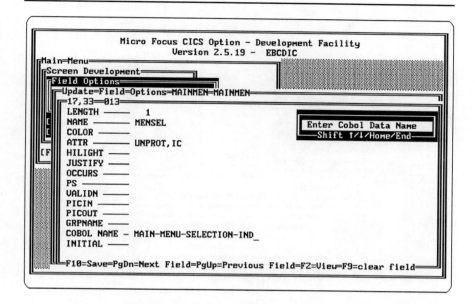

Figure 7.9.   Copybook with macro and COBOL names.

When generating a copybook, MCO prompts for the MAPSET name. After typing it in, press Enter. The next prompt is for the MAP name. As with the MAPSET, press ENTER.

Once the MAPSET and MAP names are entered, an output window opens with the MAP name plus the extension .CPY, as shown in Figure 7.10. The output directory/file name defaults to

```
$CICSCPY\MAP.CPY
```

Using the $CICSCPY, MCO creates the copybook file in the directory established as part of the SET commands in either AUTOEXEC.BAT (DOS) or CONFIG.SYS (OS/2).

Once the copybook generation process is invoked, MCO displays two messages, depending on the results:

- Copybook file does not exist.
    Generating MFS Copybook
- Copybook file already exists (see Figure 7.10).

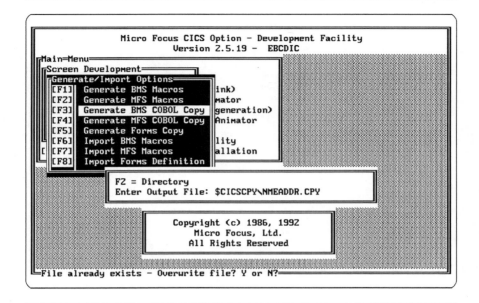

Figure 7.10. Defining the output MFS copybook.

EXECUTABLE GENERATION

The previous chapter explained how to create MAPSETs and MAPs, and the preceding sections of this chapter covered generating macro and copybook files. The final function to deal with is generating a test definition, the equivalent of a mainframe assemble.

The Generate Test Definition function is not found on the Generate/Import Options submenu where you might expect it. (It would certainly save several keystrokes if it were there!) Creating an executable is part of the BMS Screen Development functions located off of the MCO main menu. Selecting from the Screen Development submenu, the Utilities submenu [*F6*] *MAP Utility* (Figure 7.11), select the Generate Test Definition function by pressing [*F5*] *Generate Test Definition*.

From the Utilities submenu, programmers are prompted by MCO for the MAPSET name. After pressing Enter, the MAPSET

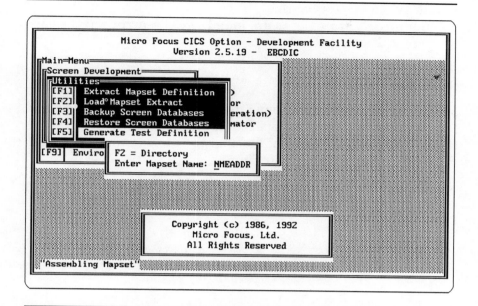

Figure 7.11.   Assembling a MAPSET/MAP file.

is assembled and a message is displayed in the lower portion of the screen.

As part of the assemble, MCO generates a file name.MST dataset as the executable MAPSET/MAP. The .MST dataset can be executed in the emulation process to view the screen image for meeting the customer's requirements.

As CICS updates or searches for the BMS Test Definition files, MCO uses the specific directory path. If no directory path is provided, MCO searches the following directories in the order presented below:

- CICSMAPS path
  MCO searches in the first directory path found on this SET statement in the AUTOEXEC.BAT or CONFIG.SYS.
- CICSTEST path
  MCO searches in the first directory path found on this SET statement in the AUTOEXEC.BAT or CONFIG.SYS.

- Current Directory path
  If no SET statements are found, MCO searches in the current directory.

SUMMARY

MCO provides functions to generate BMS macro files and copybook files to support an application. Executable files are created within the BMS screen Development function and can be transferred from PC to PC, but not to the mainframe.

8

BMS Utilities

The two previous chapters covered the various features available to create and alter BMS files, generation of BMS files (macro and copybook), and generation of an executable file. MCO provides various utilities to assist programmers in managing BMS resources.

This chapter covers the Map Utility functions, the last MAP function we will examine. It is used to do the following:

- Extract MAPSET definitions
- Load MAPSET definitions
- Backup and restore the screen databases

The following files are created or used during the execution of these utilities:

- file name.EXT
- MCOSDF00.BAK
- MCOSCR00.BAK

ACCESS TO UTILITY FUNCTIONS

Utility functions can be accessed from two different areas within MCO. From the MCO main menu, select [F8] *BMS Screen Devel-*

opment. Select *[F6] MAP Utility*, or invoke from an OS-command line. The Generate Test Definition Utility function was covered in the previous chapter.

Command Line Use

When invoking a function from a command line, all commands are preceded by

```
[XM switches] used for DOS based processing only
```

XM is used to invoke MCO and load the function into extended memory for processing. Switches can be provided to direct XM how to load the function.

Following the [XM switches] is the reference to MCO, keyed as either

```
MFCICS in a DOS environment
```

or

```
PMFCICS in an OS/2 environment
```

Command Line Access. The command syntax for using utilities from the command line is

```
[XM switches] MFCICS extract mapset
```

• Mapset: the name of the MAPSET file to load the definition into.

Command Line Extract Access. The command syntax for using the extract utility from the command line is

```
[XM switches] MFCICS extract mapset
```

• Mapset: the name of the MAPSET file to extract the definition from.

Command Line Load Access. The command syntax for using the load utility from the command line is

```
[XM switches] MFCICS load mapset
```

- Mapset: the name of the MAPSET file to load the definition into.

MCO Menu Utilities

MCO provides an interactive set of menus supporting utilities functions. The remaining sections of this chapter will examine the MAP utility process in detail.

MAPSET UTILITIES

MCO supports five utilities (Figure 8.1) to manage MAPSET definitions and databases. The utility functions are located within the [F8] *BMS Screen Development* function by pressing [F6] *MAP Utility*.

The following utilities are provided as part of the MCO CICS application development tool:

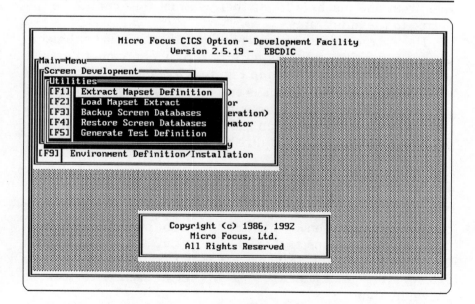

Figure 8.1.   Utilities submenu.

- Extract MAPSET Definitions
- Load MAPSET Extract
- Backup Screen Databases
- Restore Screen Databases
- Generate Test Definition—Executable MAP, covered in the previous chapter

Extract Mapset Definitions

The Extract MAPSET Definitions function is the only method provided by MCO to copy all information in a MAPSET to another file. MAPSET definitions can contain one or more MAP definitions in a single file. Using the MAP/MAPSET Copy function only allows the selection of a single MAP within a MAPSET.

The native DOS copy command can be used to accomplish the same thing when copying an entire BMS macro file, but the resulting file needs to be imported into CICS on the other machine.

The extract function is used to copy a file when no macro file exists. Using the extract process allows programmers to transfer files from one machine to another. Extract files cannot be imported to the mainframe.

The extract utility is invoked from the Utilities submenu. The extract utility prompts for a MAPSET file name to extract information from, as shown in Figure 8.2.

Once the input file name is entered, pressing Enter appends to the end of the file name the extension .EXT (Figure 8.3). Pressing Enter after the extension is displayed causes the extract file to be created in the current directory.

Load Mapset Extract

The Load MAPSET function is the only method provided by MCO to copy all information in a MAPSET from one machine to another. The load process expects the file to be in the format of an extract file. The extract utility is invoked from the Utilities submenu. The extract utility prompts for a MAPSET file name .EXT to load, as shown in Figure 8.4.

Pressing Enter after typing in the file name causes the current directory to be searched for the file name .EXT. Once the file is located, MCO examines the CICS resource files to determine

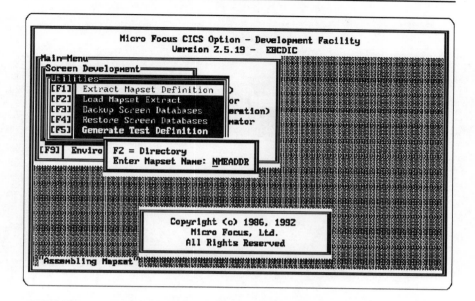

Figure 8.2.   Prompt for MAPSET name to extract.

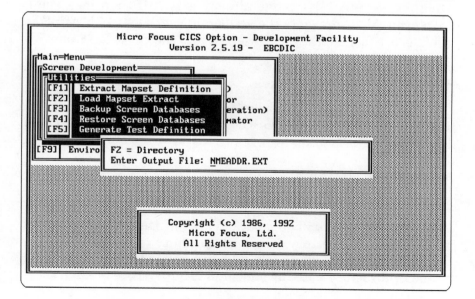

Figure 8.3.   MCO assigns the file name extension.

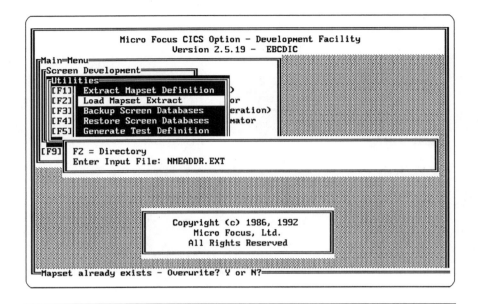

```
        Micro Focus CICS Option - Development Facility
                  Version 2.5.19 -  EBCDIC
┌Main=Menu═══════════════════════════════════════════
 ┌Screen Development════════════════════╗
  ┌Utilities═══════════════════════════╗
   [F1]  Extract Mapset Definition      ╟──┐
   [F2]  Load Mapset Extract            ║  or
   [F3]  Backup Screen Databases        ║  eration)
   [F4]  Restore Screen Databases       ║  mator
   [F5]  Generate Test Definition       ║
 ┌──────────────────────────────────────────────────┐
  [F9]    F2 = Directory
          Enter Input File: NMEADDR.EXT
 └──────────────────────────────────────────────────┘

            ┌──────────────────────────────────┐
            │    Copyright (c) 1986, 1992      │
            │        Micro Focus, Ltd.         │
            │        All Rights Reserved       │
            └──────────────────────────────────┘

└Mapset already exists - Overwrite? Y or N?═══════════
```

Figure 8.4.   Loading an extract file into MCO.

whether the MAPSET name already exists. If so, a message is displayed. MCO prevents the accidental overlaying of MAPSETs. As files are loaded, they are inserted into the CICS RDT files.

Backup Screen Databases

The Backup Screen Databases function is provided to back up the screen databases (MCOSDF00.DAT and MCOSCR00.DAT). The files are backed up to

- MCOSDF00.BAK
- MCOSCR00.BAK

As the screen files are being backed up, the .BAK files are created in the current directory. The backup utility is invoked from the Utilities submenu. The backup utility does not prompt for a file name or directory path, as shown in Figure 8.5.

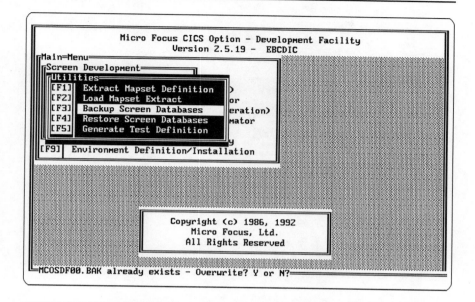

Figure 8.5.   Screen Development database backup.

If the backup file name already exists, a message is displayed. MCO prevents the accidental overlaying of previously created backup files.

Restore Screen Databases

The Restore Screen Databases function is provided to recover the screen development files (MCOSDF00.DAT and MCOSCR00.DAT) in the current directory. The files are recovered from

- MCOSDF00.BAK
- MCOSCR00.BAK

and the following files are rebuilt:

- MCOSDF00.IDX
- MCOSCR00.IDX

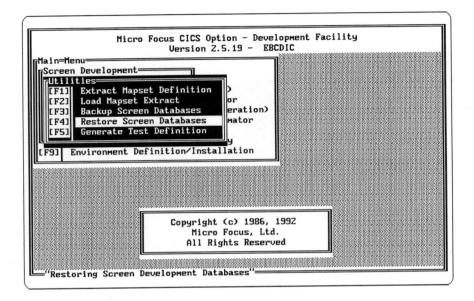

Figure 8.6.   Restore the screen development files.

The restore utility is invoked from the utilities submenu and does not prompt for a file name or directory path, as shown in Figure 8.6.

If the backup file name already exists, a message is displayed. MCO prevents the accidental overlaying of previously created backup files.

SUMMARY

The utility functions are useful in maintaining a backup and recovery of the CICS Screen Development database. The extract/load functions allow for full MAPSET files to be copied. MCO provides useful utilities for programmers to maintain the CICS application development environment.

9

Editing and Checking CICS COBOL Programs

Once the BMS code is complete and copybook files have been generated, programmers can begin the development of the CICS COBOL programs. When developing source code in MCO, there are no surprises, primarily because there is no editor.

This chapter examines various topics concerning editing and checking CICS COBOL programs on the PC. As noted in previous chapters, MCO interfaces with the edit package selected in the Environment/Definition function, because of the interactive interface with Micro Focus COBOL. A brief examination of the editor is presented in this chapter.

In covering the checking of COBOL programs, the interface discussed here is to Micro Focus COBOL. Checking options and preprocess options are covered in this chapter.

EDITING CICS PROGRAMS

Prior to beginning any edit process within MCO, programmers accessed [F9] *Environment Definitions* and selected the edit package to use. The list of edit packages MCO interfaces with, shown in Figure 9.1, is selected from the Configuration/Install submenu ([F9] *Environment/Definition*) from the main menu by pressing [F3] *Define Editor.*

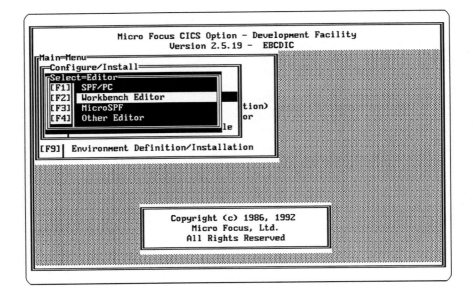

Figure 9.1. Establishing the default edit tool.

At the time the edit function is invoked, MCO interfaces to the previously selected edit package:

- *[F1] SPF/PC*
- *[F2] Workbench Editor*
- *[F3] Micro SPF*
- *[F4] Other*

If a different editor package is required, the *[F4] Other* function key is pressed, and the executable file name for the edit software is selected.

THE MICRO FOCUS COBOL EDITOR

Micro Focus COBOL's (the Workbench) edit package is well worth considering as the edit tool because it interactively interfaces with the Checker and Animator functions invoked from

MCO. The manner in which these functions relate to each other can speed up the debugging process. Because of this, I am including a brief examination of the Micro Focus COBOL edit menus. Detailed information can be found in the book *Micro Focus CO-BOL Workbench for the Application Developer*.

General Edit Characteristics

Menus are presented to programmers in a hierarchical manner. The workbench provides significant information to programmers via the HELP and HYHELP functions.

Micro Focus supports wide records allowing records with up to 250 characters and large files of up to 999,999 records to be brought into the Editor. An information line appears on each screen, providing a current status of the editor's settings. Escape from any menu will return to the previous level (one up). The editor provides these three menus:

- Edit main menu (see Figure 9.2)
- Edit Alt menu
- Edit Ctrl menu

Edit Main Menu. Micro Focus COBOL's edit package can be invoked from the MCO CICS main menu by pressing [F2] *Edit*. The Edit main menu's function is primarily for (1) processing lines of COBOL code, (2) character processing, and (3) invoking the COBOL processor for checking and animating programs. The Edit main menu provides access to two additional submenus, the Alt and Ctrl menus.

Edit Alt Menu. From the Edit main menu an alternate menu is accessed by pressing and holding down the Alt key (see Figure 9.3). Pressing Shift/F1 continuously displays the Alt menu. The Alt menu supports these functions:

- Loads and saves files
- Compiles library
- Deletes words
- Splits and joins lines of code

```
┌BILLPYMT.CBL──────────────────────────────────────────────────────────◆
│007000     ADD 1 TO BILL-COUNT.
│007300
│007300     IF BILL-TYPE IS EQUAL TO 'B'
│007300     THEN
│007300         CALL BILLRPT USING WRK-BILL-RECORD
│007400     ELSE
│007300         CALL BILLLATE USING WRK-BILL-RECORD.
│007400
│007600     GO TO 0300-MAIN-PROCESSING.
│007400
│007700 0300-EXIT.
│007800     EXIT.
│008200*
│008200*   CLOSE FILE AND GENERATE FINAL DISPLAY LINE
│008200*
│008200 0900-CLOSE-ROUTINE.
│008300     MOVE BILL-COUNT TO TOT-LINE-BILLS.
│008400     DISPLAY TOTAL-LINE.
│008500     CLOSE BILLINPT BILLTYPE.
│
```

```
Edit─BILLPYMT───────96─lines───────Line─85────Col─27────────Wrap─Ins─Caps─Num─Scroll
F1=help F2=COBOL F3=insert-line F4=delete-line F5=repeat-line F6=restore-line
F7=retype-char F8=restore-char F9=word-left F10=word-right       Alt Ctrl Escape
```

Figure 9.2.   Micro Focus COBOL main edit menu.

```
┌BILLPYMT.CBL──────────────────────────────────────────────────────────◆
│007300     IF BILL-TYPE IS EQUAL TO 'B'
│007300     THEN
│007300   _   CALL BILLRPT USING WRK-BILL-RECORD
│007400     ELSE
│007300         CALL BILLLATE USING WRK-BILL-RECORD.
│007400
│007600     GO TO 0300-MAIN-PROCESSING.
│007400
│007700 0300-EXIT.
│007800     EXIT.
│008200*
│008200*   CLOSE FILE AND GENERATE FINAL DISPLAY LINE
│008200*
│008200 0900-CLOSE-ROUTINE.
│008300     MOVE BILL-COUNT TO TOT-LINE-BILLS.
│008400     DISPLAY TOTAL-LINE.
│008500     CLOSE BILLINPT BILLTYPE.
│007700 0900-EXIT.
│007800     EXIT.
│
```

```
Edit─BILLPYMT───────116─lines──────Line─93────Col─13────────Wrap─Ins─Caps─Num─Scroll
F1=help F2=library F3=load-file F4=save-file F5=split-line F6=join-line F7=print
F8=calculate F9=untype-word-left F10=delete-word-right               Escape
```

Figure 9.3.   Micro Focus COBOL Alt edit menu.

Edit Ctrl Menu. The Ctrl menu (Figure 9.4) can be accessed from the Edit main menu by pressing and holding down the Ctrl key. Pressing Shift/F2 continuously displays the Ctrl menu. The Ctrl menu performs some more advanced functions:

- Finds and replaces text strings
- Processes blocks of text
- Does window processing
- Clears memory

CHECKING CICS PROGRAMS

One area that mainframe programmers can relate to is the time spent submitting jobs to be compiled and waiting through what seems like an endless queue of jobs. With minimal testing initiators capability available on the mainframe, programmers lose valuable time waiting for jobs to execute.

```
┌BILLPYMT.CBL─────────────────────────────────────────────────◆
007700 0100-EXIT.
007800      EXIT.
006700 0300-MAIN-PROCESSING.
006800      READ BILLINPT INTO WRK-BILL-RECORD
006900           AT END GO TO 0300-EXIT.
007300
007000      ADD 1 TO BILL-COUNT.
007300
007300      IF PARM-VALUE IS EQUAL TO 'B'
007300      THEN
007300         CALL BILLRPT USING WRK-BILL-RECORD
007400      ELSE
007300         CALL BILLLATE USING WRK-BILL-RECORD.
007400
007600      GO TO 0300-MAIN-PROCESSING.
007400
007700 0300-EXIT.
007800      EXIT.
008200*

Edit─BILLPYMT───────118-lines───Line-100───Col-46───────Wrap-Ins-Caps-Num-Scroll
F1=help F2=find F3=block F4=clear F5=margins F6=draw/forms F7=tags F8=word-wrap
F9=window F10=scroll ←/→ (move in window) Home/End (of text) Pgup/Pgdn
```

Figure 9.4.   Micro Focus COBOL Ctrl edit menu.

Migrating to the PC is not going to eliminate the repetitive nature of syntax checking or debugging a program, but it will shorten the time between submission and execution of jobs. In fact, since there is no queue, MCO provides programmers with the opportunity to produce more in the same amount of time.

In MCO JCL is not used. Compiles begin as soon as the program name is typed in and Enter is pressed. It is not unheard of for MCO users to increase their productivity well over 50 percent using the interactive MCO features.

The MCO compile process is controlled by directives similar to the mainframe compiler options. Most companies allow programmers to control the compile process by the directives they select. Directive selection is one area in which standardization used by a project team is a good idea.

MCO offers a menu-driven compile process with function keys providing toggling support for selection of directives. The MCO menu system distinguishes between the syntax Check and Compile functions. Whether mainframe or PC, programs must be free of syntax errors. MCO provides an effective interface to the CICS translator and then to the Micro Focus Check function. CICS commands must be translated to COBOL-recognizable code before the Check function can begin.

The interactive connection between the Check and Edit functions provides programmers with a tremendous advantage over mainframe syntax debugging. As MCO checks a program, several files are processed as inputs and more are generated as outputs (see Figure 9.5).

The compiler (checking) takes in source code (program and copy files) if no syntax errors are detected, as shown in Figure 9.6. An intermediate file (.INT) and reference file (.IDY) are created with the same file name as the program. The .INT and .IDY files are both used in the animation of programs, as well as input into the Compile function. Compiling strips the file of code used to animate and "optimizes" to a .GNT or .OBJ file.

When syntax errors are encountered, MCO automatically invokes the Micro Focus COBOL Editor if it is the default edit package. As shown in Figure 9.7, the edit main menu is displayed with the cursor positioned to the first syntax error in the file.

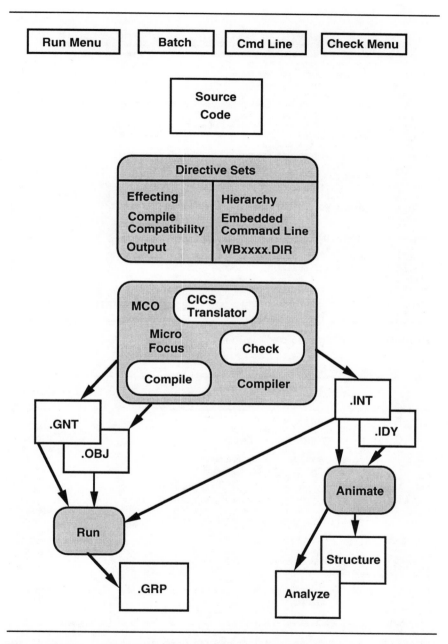

Figure 9.5.   MCO/Micro Focus compiler interface.

```
413*    TERMINATE THE PROGRAM IF OPTION 'X' HAS BEEN SELECTED.     *
414* * * * * * * * * * * * * * * * * * * * * * * * * * * * * * * * *
415     MOVE 'PROCESSING COMPLETE - GOODBYE' TO MESSAGE-AREA.
416     MOVE +29 TO MESSAGE-LENGTH.
417 0990-SEND-MESSAGE.
418* * * * * * * * * * * * * * * * * * * * * * * * * * * * * * * * *
419*    CLEAR THE SCREEN AND SEND A MESSAGE TO THE TERMINAL BEFORE  *
420*    TERMINATING THE PROGRAM.                                    *
421* * * * * * * * * * * * * * * * * * * * * * * * * * * * * * * * *
422     EXEC CICS SEND
423        FROM(MESSAGE-AREA)
424        LENGTH(MESSAGE-LENGTH)
425        ERASE
426     END-EXEC.
427     EXEC CICS RETURN END-EXEC.
428* * * * * * * * * * * * * * * * * * * * * * * * * * * * * * * * *
429*    INCLUDE A GOBACK STATEMENT TO AVOID A COMPILER WARNING.     *
430* * * * * * * * * * * * * * * * * * * * * * * * * * * * * * * * *
431     GOBACK.
* Micro Focus COBOL Version 3.0.22   L2.4 revision 001
*
* Total Messages:      0
* Data:       1940    Code:       2922
* Checking terminated
***
```

Figure 9.6. Sample check with no syntax errors.

```
┌MAINMEN.CBL─────────────────────────────────────────────────◆
│           MOVE LOW-VALUES TO MAINMENO
│           MOVE 'Y' TO WS-COMM-SCRN-IND                     000138
│           GO TO 0100-SEND-MAIN-MENU                        000139
│       ELSE                                                 000140
│           MOVE DFHCOMMAREA TO WS-COMMAREA                  000140
│           MOVE 'N' TO WS-COMM-SCRN-IND.                    000141
│                                                            000142
│   * * * * * * * * * * * * * * * * * * * * * * * * * * * *  000143
│   *   PERFORM ROUTINE TO READ MAP FROM TERMINAL         *  000144
│   * * * * * * * * * * * * * * * * * * * * * * * * * * * *  000145
│       PERFORM 0300-RECEIVE-MAP THRU 0300-EXIT.            000146
│                                                            000232
│       EXEC CICS RECEIVE                                    000228
│           MAP('MAINMEN')                                   000229
│           INTO(MAINMENI)                                   000230
│       END-EXEC.                                            000231
│                                                            000147
│   * * * * * * * * * * * * * * * * * * * * * * * * * * * *  000148
│   *   PERFORM MAIN LOGIC ROUTINE                        *  000149
└
Edit-MAINMEN───────302-lines───Line-79───Col-42───Wrap-Ins-Caps-Num-Scroll
F1=help F2=library F3=load-file F4=save-file F5=split-line F6=join-line F7=print
F8=calculate F9=untype-word-left F10=delete-word-right
 *  12-S Operand MAINMENO is not declared
```

Figure 9.7. Check with syntax errors detected.

Syntax Errors in the Source Code. When checking CICS programs, three general types of syntax errors occur:

- CICS errors—CICS preprocessor-generated syntax errors.
- COBOL errors—Syntax errors identified by the Micro Focus Checker.
- SQL, DL/I, RCM errors—Syntax errors detected prior to the check taking place.

MCO completes the syntax check no matter how many errors are detected. CICS generates four types of errors:

- Unsupported or invalid functions
  If CICS detects any unsupported or invalid functions, they are replaced with a NO OP (no operation). The following prompt occurs:
  - S   —terminate the preprocessor.
  - N   —Insert a NO OP and the code is ignored.
  - A   —Forces an ABEND at run time, but the program is preprocessed and checked.
  - Z   —Zooms through the preprocess without stopping at other errors. Any other errors default to NO OP.
- Unsupported or invalid options
  If CICS detects any unsupported or invalid options, they are ignored, and the following prompt occurs:
  - S   —Terminate the preprocessor.
  - N   —Insert a NO OP and the code will be ignored.
  - I   —Ignores the option, but the rest of the EXEC CICS command is preprocessed.
  - Z   —Zooms through the preprocess without stopping at other errors. Other errors default to ignore.
- COPY file errors
  COPY file errors are identified if CICS (1) cannot find the file, (2) cannot open the file, or (3) the copy file name is not in mainframe format.
  - Y   —The program continues checking and pauses at each syntax error.
  - N   —The program ends checking and is positioned in the editor.

Z —Zooms through the preprocess without stopping at other errors.

- COBOL errors

    Y —The program continues checking and pauses at each syntax error.

    N —The program ends checking and is positioned in the editor.

    Z —Zooms through the preprocess without stopping at other errors.

SETTING UP THE CHECK PREPROCESS OPTIONS

Prior to initiating a check, the preprocess resources that are to be used during the compile process have to be defined. A detailed examination is found in the chapter on *Loading CICS Resource Tables*. MCO preprocess resources are defined from two different submenus: the Define Configuration submenu, accessed by pressing [*F9*] *Environment/Definition Installation*, and then selecting [*F2*] *Define Configuration* (see Figure 9.8).

The remaining preprocess directive options are set from the Preprocess Options submenu (Figure 9.9) which is accessed from the main menu by selecting [*F7*] *CICS Resource Definitions* and then selecting [*F7*] *Preprocess Options*.

ACCESS TO PROGRAM CHECKING

Program checking functions can be accessed from two different areas within MCO: (1) from the MCO main menu, press [*F3*] *Check (Preprocess/Compile/Link)*, or (2) from an OS-command line.

Command Line Checking

Programs can be checked from a command line. The following functions are accessed from command lines:

- Preprocess/check
- Compile—see chapter on *Compiling and Running CICS CO-BOL Programs*
- Emulation—see chapter on *Animating CICS COBOL Programs*

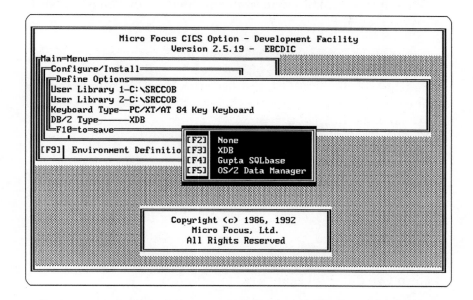

Figure 9.8.   Selecting the SQL preprocessor.

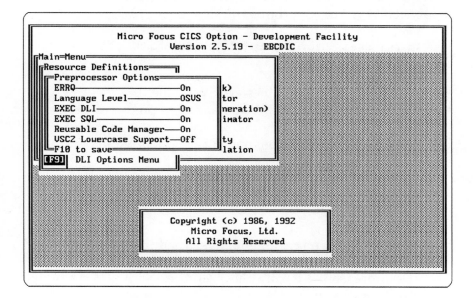

Figure 9.9.   Setting default check directives.

When invoking a function from a command line, all commands are preceded by

```
[XM switches] used for DOS based processing only
```

XM is used to invoke MCO and load the function into extended memory for processing. Switches can be provided to direct XM how to load the function.

Following the [XM switches] is the reference to MCO, keyed as either

```
MFCICS in a DOS environment
            or
PMFCICS in an OS/2 environment
```

Preprocess/check. The preprocess/check functions can be invoked in two different manners:

- CICS-option preprocess/check
- Invoke the preprocessor from the check function

The command syntax for executing the CICS-option preprocess/check typed in on a command line is

```
[XM switches] MFCICS CHECK file name [mco-options]
[checker directives]
```

- File name—Identifies the source code file.
- MCO-options—Identify the language and preprocessor options used.
     Language—Select from one of the supported dialects:
     OS/VS
     VSC2
     VSC2(1)
     VSC2(2)
     VSC2(3)
     If more than one language is typed in on the command line, only the last is used.
     Preprocessor—Identify the preprocessor functions to use in the check process.

> DLI   IMSVS86 EXEC DLI
> DB2   EXEC SQL
> RCM   Reusable Code Manager

The command syntax for executing the preprocesor from the checker is to type on a command line

```
CHECK file name [checker directives]
preprocess($cics\cicsprep) mco-options [preprocess]....
```

- File name—Identifies the source code file. The source code is searched for in the current directory. MCO does not search the directory found on the SET environment ($CICSSRC) statement in the CONFIG.SYS (OS/2) or AUTOEXEC.BAT (DOS) files unless coded in the check window box:
  MCO-options—Identifies a seven-character string of flags:
  mco-options:=lang case errq debug dli sql rcm
  Lang—Select from one of the supported dialects:
  O   OS/VS
  V   VSC2
  1   VSC2(1)
  2   VSC2(2)
  3   VSC2(3)
  Case—Identify text case sensitivity:
  U   OS/VS or VS COBOL II upper case only
  L   VS COBOL II allows use of lower case
  Errq—Identify how the checker should handle syntax errors:
  Q   instructs the checker to pause at each error
  Z   collects errors but does not stop on each error
  Debug—Identify the debugging mode to use:
  N   does not generate the debug output
  C   generates COBOL source output
  D   debugs trace listing output
  B   generates the debug trace and COBOL source
  Dli—Identify if DL/I code will be supported:
  N   does not support EXEC DLI
  Y   supports EXEC DLI using the IMSVS preprocess directive
  Sql—Identify if SQL code will be supported:
  N   does not support EXEC SQL

Y   supports EXEC SQL using the OS/2 Database Manager

G   supports EXEC SQL using the GUPTA

X   supports EXEC SQL using the XDB

Rcm—Identify if the Reusable Code Manager will be supported:

N   does not support RCM

Y   supports RCM with explicit directives on the command

X   supports RCM with the CICS-option calling the RCM preprocessor

MCO MENU CHECKING

MCO provides a syntax checking function on the main menu. The remaining sections of this chapter will examine the check process in detail.

The MCO Check Menu

The MCO Check Menu (Figure 9.10) offers programmers the ability to check a program by supplying the program name and selecting directives to use. The Check function is invoked by pressing [F3] *Check with Animation*. The check submenu passes directive values to the compiler based on function key settings. With the exception of the [F2] and [F4] keys, all other function keys toggle directives or directive sets to ON or OFF.

- [F2] *Directory*—Used to search directories for a file.
- [F3] *ERRQ*—Used to control the pause option in the Micro Focus check function.
- [F4] *Language Level*—Used to toggle the language dialect.
- [F5] *EXEC SQL*—Toggle setting to invoke an SQL precompiler.
- [F6] *EXEC DLI*—Toggle setting to invoke DL/I processor.
- [F7] *Batch Check*—Identifies the program being checked as program with no CICS commands embedded in the code.
- [F8] *RCM*—Invokes the Reusable Code Manager.
- [F9] *Debug Trace Options*—Select the debug mode to use.
  COBOL Source Output—Generates a COBOL file with all

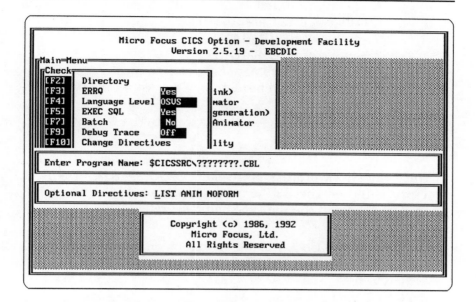

Figure 9.10.   MCO program syntax check submenu.

EXEC CICS and copy files fully expanded to file name .MCC. The .MCC file can be run through the checker to generate executable code. The directive batch must be toggled on to check the expanded code.

DEBUG Trace—File contains a list of all records passed from the CICS option preprocessor to the checker and all other preprocessors. The generated file is file name .MCD and contains the following information:

where the code passed to the checker came from
the RESP-MAIN value passed to the checker
the RESP-MORE value passed to the checker
the source code passed to the checker

A sample DEBUG Trace file might look like:

111222333>>44444444444(80 characters)xx where:

111 = source of code
    SRC source file
    CPY copy files

      MCO CICS Option
      OTH some other preprocessor
      222 = value of RESP-MAIN
      333 = value of RESP-MORE
      >> = identifies the start of the source record
      444 = up to eighty characters of source record passed to
      the checker
- [F10] *Change Directives*—Allows access to the window box to input or alter directives.

Once the check process is invoked, MCO searches the first directory found on the SET environment variable in a specific order, depending on the file type being searched for:

- COBOL Source Code—If no file extension is provided, MCO searches for file name .CBL, then file name .COB.
      $CICSSRC
      $CICSTEST
      current directory
- Copy/Include (COPY, -INC, ++INCLUDE) files—If no file extension is provided, MCO searches for file name .CPY, then file name .CBL. MCO displays a warning message if the name is not mainframe compatible.
      current directory
      $CICSCPY
      $CICSSRC
      $COBCPY

MCO generates the intermediate and reference files to specific directories:

- .INT and .IDY files
      $CICSTEST
      current directory

The check submenu provides three default directives that can be overridden by selecting [F10] *Directives* prior to initiating the syntax check:

- NOLIST—Does not display source code to the screen during a check.
- ANIM—Generates the .IDY file for animation.
- NOFORM—Prevents form feed characters from being inserted into the source code file.

MCO requires certain directives to be in use and forces these directives into the checking of CICS programs (they cannot be overridden):

- DEFAULT BYTE"00"—Initializes working storage fields with no values to low values.
- VSC2 or OSVS—Identifies the COBOL dialect to use for:
  COMP
  NOTRUNC—Required for binary address processing.
  ALTER—Required to handle ABEND error processing.
  CICS—Required to support the use of BLL cell processing. Only used for OSVS programs.
  MF—Provides support for Micro Focus extensions to COBOL.

The directive REMOVE should never be used when checking CICS programs. It allows reserved words to be removed from the reserved list.

Check Directives

Directives are similar to mainframe compile options and control the actions of the compiler. Figure 9.5 shows the COBOL.DIR file and indicates that other PC files containing directives are available with a .DIR extension in MCO:

- WBOSVS.DIR
- WBVSC21.DIR
- WBVSC22.DIR
- WBVSC23.DIR

The directive files loaded after the install can be left alone, but the directive WARNING(3) should be changed to a value (2) that emulates the mainframe better. The COBOL.DIR file is not required for a program to check, but it gives programmers flexibility when using directives. The following are some of the more common directives used by mainframe programmers (defaults are underlined):

- [*NO*] ALTER—Enables the use of ALTER statements in a program.
- [*NO*] ANALYZE—Enables the Analyze feature during Animation.
- [*NO*] ANIM—Compiles a program to be run in the Animator.
- [*NO*] ASMLIST—Causes production of an assembler listing.
- ASSIGN (dynamic | external)—Specifies default method of file assignment.
- CHARSET(*ASCII* | EBCDIC)—Specifies the character set for input and output data.
- [*NO*] CSI—Produces a .CSI analysis file for use in COBOL Source Information.
- DIRECTIVES (file name)—Enables loading of a directive set from the specified file name.
- [*NO*] EDITOR, EDITOR (MF)—Instructs the compiler to send error messages to a file in a format compatible with the Micro Focus Editor.
- [*NO*] LIBRARIAN—Enables use of -INC in program source code.
- [*NO*] LIST, LIST (destination), LIST()—Controls production and destination of a compile listing.
  (con:)   —The console
  (prn:)   —Printer
  ()   —File with the same file name as the program and .LST extension.
  NOLIST   —Produce no listing
- [*NO*] NESTCALL—Enables checking a nested call program.
- OMF (code type)—Controls type of object code produced (gnt) or (obj).
- [*NO*] PANVALET—Enables use of ++INCLUDE in program source code.
- [*NO*] PREPROCESS—Instructs the compiler to take the source program from a preprocessor instead of a source file.

- [_NO_] REF—Used for comparing check and assembler listings.
- [_NO_] SQL—Enables recognition of EXEC SQL and passes them to an SQL precompiler.
- [_NO_] STRUCT—Enables the Structure Chart feature during Animation.
- [_NO_] WARNING, WARNING (integer)—Specifies the lowest severity level of errors that are to be reported.
    (3)—All error messages, U, S, E, W or I
    (2)—U, S, E, W only
    (1)—U, S, E only
    NOWARNING—U, S only
- [_NO_] XREF—Causes production of a Cross Reference listing.

SUMMARY

Editing CICS programs is accomplished by interfacing with other edit packages. Because of the interactive relationship with the Micro Focus COBOL Editor, Checker, and Animator, I recommend it as the default edit package.

Checking is one area that provides the opportunity to make the syntax checking more efficient than on the mainframe. In combination with the immediate nature of checking a program on the PC and the interactive connection to the Micro Focus COBOL Editor, productivity should increase.

10

Animating CICS COBOL Programs

MCO does not provide an animation tool, but it interfaces with Micro Focus COBOL (the Workbench). The interface to the Animator begins when a transaction is keyed into the CICS region. The Animator has quite an impressive set of features, offering the ability to closely debug all aspects of a CICS COBOL program and deliver higher-quality, error-free code. This chapter examines topics related to the debugging or animating function of the workbench: (1) invoking the CICS region, and (2) using the Animator.

The Animator provides programmers with functions to display lines of source code while debugging and provides control over the speed of execution.

GENERAL ANIMATOR CHARACTERISTICS

The Animator provides the capability for three types of animation:

- Basic animation—A program or application on one PC can be animated as the active session.
- Cooperative animation—When testing in a LAN environment, programmers can start animating a program on a PC different from the one they are working on. To invoke cooperative animation from a DOS or OS/2 command line, type in

```
ANIMUSER USER-MACHINE 'netname'
```

- Cross-session animation—Programmers can animate a program on one PC in two different sessions, (available on OS/2). Only one cross-session animation can take place on one machine.

When using cooperative animation or cross-session animation, the Animator is limited to 4 breakpoints (methods of stopping program execution) versus 100 in basic animation. Prior to invoking the Animator, the source code must be checked. The Animator function utilizes files displayed in Figure 10.1 and listed here:

- .ANL—Analyzer file for printing
- .CBL—COBOL source code file
- .CPY—COBOL copybook or include file
- .CSI—COBOL source information file
- .IDY—Check-generated reference file
- .INT—Check-generated intermediate file (executable)
- .LBR—Run-time system
- .PRT—Structure chart print file

Along with the function key-driven features, the workbench provides many letter-driven features, some of which contain submenus. Some of the letter-driven functions are for setting breakpoints, viewing and changing data values, and resetting the execution point in a program's logic.

ACCESS TO PROGRAM EMULATION WITH ANIMATION

Emulating a program using the Animator can be accessed from two different areas: from the MCO main menu by pressing [*F4*] *Emulation Facility with Animator*, or from an OS-command line.

Command Line Emulation

Programs can be animated from a command line. When invoking a function from a command line, all commands are preceded by

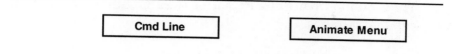

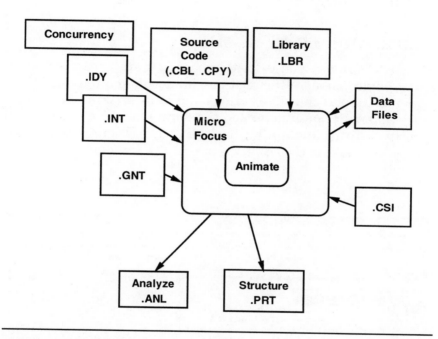

Figure 10.1. Animator inputs and outputs.

```
[XM switches] used for DOS based processing only
```

XM is used to invoke MCO and load the function into extended memory for processing. Switches can be provided to direct XM on how to load the function.

Following the [XM switches] is the reference to MCO, keyed as either

```
MFCICS in a DOS environment
            or
PMFCICS in an OS/2 environment
```

The command syntax for executing the animator function from the command line is

```
[XM switches] MFCICS animate [transid]
```

- Transid—The transaction ID to be started as soon as the emulator is initialized.

MCO Emulation Using the Menus

The MCO CICS region is for the most part similar to the mainframe environment, although there is one major difference. MCO does not support multiple regions and multi-tasking. MCO provides an emulation function on the main menu. The Emulation Facility with Animation function, shown in Figure 10.2, is accessed by pressing [F4] *Emulation with Animation.*

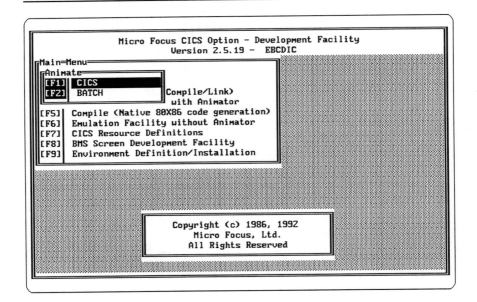

Figure 10.2. Selecting the CICS test emulator.

Once the emulation facility is invoked, programmers can select to emulate a CICS on-line program or a batch program:

- *[F1] CICS*
- *[F2] Batch*

For the purposes of this book, the MCO CICS on-line environment (*F1 CICS*—see Figure 10.3) will be the focus. The batch section of this chapter covers the access to emulating a batch program from within MCO. In either test environment, the Animator functions are the same.

After the emulation screen is presented, a transaction ID is typed in and Enter (Ctrl + Enter) is pressed to begin the execution (animation) of the program. As shown in Figure 10.4, the transaction ID can be typed in with or without clearing the screen. To clear the screen and then type in a transaction ID, press Ctrl + Home.

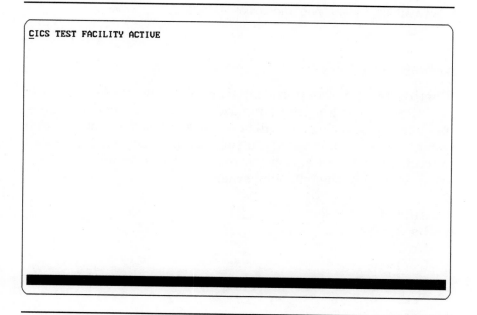

Figure 10.3.   Emulation access screen.

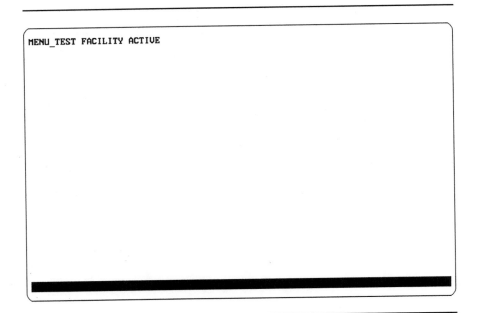

`MENU_TEST FACILITY ACTIVE`

Figure 10.4.   Identifying transaction ID to run.

Animator Presentation

Whether the emulation is started from an MCO screen or from an OS-command line, the animation process provides the same functions, so covering one will be sufficient. The Animator is well worth a close examination, but there is too much here to use all functions during an animation session. The Animator features are discussed in the following order:

- Animation modes
- Backtrack
- Breakpoints
- Queries
- Find and Locate
- Text
- Reset

ANIMATION MAIN MENU

Once the program begins animating, the cursor is positioned to the first executable line in the procedure division (Figure 10.5). The information line reflects function and file name, a reminder of which function and file the programmer is using.

ANIMATION MODES

Before looking at the features of the Animator, the actual mode of animation should be discussed. The mode of animation determines the speed, whether displays are automatically produced, and whether the code will be visible on the screen:

- Step
- Wch (Watch: Step with monitors)
- Go

```
 198*    SET THE ERROR HANDLING CONDITIONS.                     * 00012800
 199* * * * * * * * * * * * * * * * * * * * * * * * * * * * * * * 00012900
 200     EXEC CICS HANDLE CONDITION                               00013000
 201         ERROR(0900-ERROR-DETECTED)                           00013100
 202     END-EXEC.                                                00013200
 203* * * * * * * * * * * * * * * * * * * * * * * * * * * * * * * 00013300
 204* DETERMINE WHETHER TO SEND OR RECEIVE A MAP.              * 00013400
 205* * * * * * * * * * * * * * * * * * * * * * * * * * * * * * * 00013500
 206     IF  EIBCALEN EQUAL TO ZEROES                             00013600
 207     THEN                                                     00013700
 208         MOVE LOW-VALUES TO MAINMENO
 209         MOVE 'Y' TO WS-COMM-SCRN-IND                         00013800
 210         GO TO 0100-SEND-MAIN-MENU                            00013900
 211     ELSE                                                     00014000
 212         MOVE DFHCOMMAREA TO WS-COMMAREA                      00014010
 213         MOVE 'N' TO WS-COMM-SCRN-IND.                        00014100
 214                                                              00014200
 215* * * * * * * * * * * * * * * * * * * * * * * * * * * * * * * 00014300
 216* PERFORM ROUTINE TO READ MAP FROM TERMINAL               * 00014400
 217* * * * * * * * * * * * * * * * * * * * * * * * * * * * * * * 00014500
 218     PERFORM 0300-RECEIVE-MAP THRU 0300-EXIT.                 00014600
Animate-MAINMEN────────────────────Level=01-Speed=5-Ins-Caps-Num-Scroll
F1=help F2=view F3=align F4=exchange F5=where F6=lookup   F9/F10=word-</> Escape
Animate Step Wch Go Zoom nx-If Prfm Brk Rst Env Qury Find Locate txt Do Alt Ctrl
```

Figure 10.5.   MCO-invoked Animator main menu.

- Animate (Go: with monitors)
- Perform, Step
- Perform, Exit
- Zoom

Once positioned to the Animator main menu, pressing one of the highlighted characters (e.g., A for Animate) begins the execution of the program.

Step. Step is invoked by pressing the S when on the Animator main menu. As the S is pressed, only the current statement is executed and the cursor is positioned to the next sequential instruction in the program.

The speed of the Step feature can be increased by holding down the S. This will execute and move to the next line fairly quickly. Don't forget that PCs have a keyboard buffer area, and holding down the S will fill the buffer area with S commands. This can inadvertently cause the execution beyond a point in the file where the programmer wanted to stop execution to examine the code more closely.

This feature is useful for very slow and methodical execution of code and should always be considered one feature to use when narrowing in on a problem or for the initial test of complex code.

The advantage of this feature is in the slow speed of the execution, allowing for very close examination of a program. But the very aspect that provides the advantage (slowness) is also a disadvantage. Using Step as the sole debugging aid would negatively impact the timeliness of the testing phase.

Wch. Wch (watch) is invoked by pressing the W when on the Animator main menu. As the W is pressed, only the current statement is executed and the cursor is positioned to the next sequential instruction in the program.

The difference between Step and Wch is the display of temporary boxes showing the data field value before and after the code is executed. The speed of the Wch feature can be increased by holding down the W. This will execute and move to the next line fairly quickly. As with step, holding down the W will fill the buffer area with W commands. This can inadvertently cause the execution beyond a point in the file where the programmer wanted to stop and examine the code more closely.

This feature is also useful for very slow and methodical execution of code when data values need to be viewed. It should always be considered one feature to use in problem resolution or initial testing of complex code. The advantage of this feature is in the slowing of the execution to allow for very close examination of a program and displaying of data field values.

Go. Go executes lines of code sequentially, according to the logical flow of the program. As the code is executed, it is displayed on the screen. Go is like an automatic Step feature. The default speed for Go is 5; the current speed is always displayed on the information line.

The speed with which the animator can execute within Go varies from 0 to 9 or Z for Zoom. Zero (0) is quite slow, even on a 486 machine. Step or Wch might be a better choice. Speed 9 is fast, but not as fast as Zoom, and just try to watch the code! The optimum range is anywhere between 4 and 7; higher or lower is personal preference.

The speed can be changed at any time by pressing one of the numbers on the keyboard. For example, to change from the default of 5, press 6. The speed can be set to other than the default prior to pressing the G to invoke the Go function, or once animation is in progress. When the speed is changed, several lines of code will continue at the previous speed until the buffer is cleared out. When it is necessary to stop the automatic execution from within Go, press Escape.

This function is useful for execution of the code and should always be considered one feature to use while debugging a program. The advantage of this feature is in the automatic execution of code at controllable speeds. Sometimes the automatic execution can go right past the point where the programmer wanted to observe the process. Using Go followed by Step or Wch can be a very effective way to test programs.

Animate. Animate executes lines of code sequentially according to the logical flow of the program, just as Go did. As the code is executed, it is displayed on the screen along with before and after images of data field values. Animate is like an automatic Wch feature. The default speed for Animate is 5.

The current speed is always displayed on the information line. The animator can execute speeds within animate from 0 to 9 or Z for Zoom. Zero (0) is quite slow, even on a 486 machine. Step or Wch might be a better choice. Speed 9 is fast (not as fast as Zoom), but again, the code is barely visible. Set the range where it is comfortable for you. It will vary by programmer and machine.

The speed can be changed at any time by pressing one of the numbers on the keyboard. For example, to change from the default of 5, press 4. The speed can be set to other than the default prior to pressing the A to invoke the Animate function. When the speed is changed, several lines of code will continue at the previous speed until the buffer is cleared out. When it is necessary to stop the automatic execution, press Escape.

Animate is useful for careful execution of the code and can be considered a feature to use when debugging a program. The advantage of this feature is in the automatic execution of code at controllable speeds and the display of data values. Sometimes the automatic execution can go right past the point where the programmer wanted to observe the process. When this occurs, the programmer can restart prior to the failing code.

Zoom. Zoom executes lines of code sequentially, according to the logical flow of the program. As the code is executed, it is not displayed on the screen. Zoom is extremely fast; if the code being tested will display a user screen, the screen will be displayed. When it is necessary to stop the automatic execution from within Zoom, press Ctrl + Break simultaneously to stop execution.

This function is often used by programmers without giving any of the other animation features a workout. Use the other features first, and when the code is error free, then think of using Zoom.

Perform. Perform provides two methods for Zooming through lines of code. The first method is to Perform, Step, which allows the program to be flashed through a performed routine or a subprogram. The second method is to Perform, Exit, which will Zoom through the remaining lines of code of a performed routine.

No matter which is selected (Step or Exit), the execution stops and the cursor is positioned to the next instruction after the "perform or call." The Perform submenu provides some functions that are similar to those found on the Animator main menu:

- *F2=View*
- *F3=Align*
- *F4=Exchange*
- *F5=Where*
- *F6=Look-up*
- *F9/F10=Word*

These functions will be defined later in this chapter. One handy aspect of the Animator is that each submenu provides these functions for programmer use. The placement of the animator features was well thought out. From the Animator main menu press P, highlighted in the Prfm, to invoke the perform submenu (see Figure 10.6). Press P for Pfrm, and then select one of the following:

- Step—When the current statement is a perform or call, press S and Zoom through the routine or subprogram. No lines of code will be displayed on the screen, but the code will be executed. Unlike Zoom mode, Ctrl+Break does not interrupt the execution of the code.
- Exit—When the current statement is within a performed routine, press E and Zoom through the remaining code. No lines of code will be displayed on the screen, but the code will be executed. If the cursor is not within the range of a perform, an error message will display. Pressing Ctrl+Break will not stop the execution of the code.

Combining Animator Modes

The modes of debugging can be varied by each programmer. It is more a matter of which functions they are most comfortable with. The following is at least one successful approach to using one or more of the animation features. To begin the initial debugging, it is always recommended to do the following:

```
 218     PERFORM 0300-RECEIVE-MAP THRU 0300-EXIT.                00014600
 219                                                             00023200
 220     EXEC CICS RECEIVE                                       00022800
 221         MAP('MAINMEN')                                      00022900
 222         INTO(MAINMENI)                                      00023000
 223     END-EXEC.                                               00023100
 224                                                             00014700
 225* * * * * * * * * * * * * * * * * * * * * * * * * * * * * *  00014800
 226*   PERFORM MAIN LOGIC ROUTINE                            *  00014900
 227* * * * * * * * * * * * * * * * * * * * * * * * * * * * * *  00015000
 228     PERFORM 0500-EDIT-SCREEN THRU 0500-EXIT.               00015100
 229                                                             00015200
 230 0100-SEND-MAIN-MENU.                                       00015300
 231* * * * * * * * * * * * * * * * * * * * * * * * * * * * * *  00015400
 232*   GET THE CURRENT DATE AND TIME THROUGH CICS.           *  00015500
 233* * * * * * * * * * * * * * * * * * * * * * * * * * * * * *  00015600
 234     EXEC CICS ASKTIME                                      00015700
 235         ABSTIME(ABSOLUTE-TIME)                             00015800
 236     END-EXEC.                                              00015900
 237* * * * * * * * * * * * * * * * * * * * * * * * * * * * * *  00016000
 238*   FORMAT THE DATE AND TIME FOR DISPLAY IN THE MAP.      *  00016100
Perform-level———————————————————Level=01-Speed=5-Ins-Caps-Num-Scroll
F1=help F2=view F3=align F4=exchange F5=where F6=look-up  F9/F10=word-</> Escape
Step Exit
```

Figure 10.6. Perform submenu features.

- Establish breakpoints
- Display key fields
- Select the mode of animation

Start by using Go set to a speed of 4 or 5, just fast enough not to require continuous pressing of S or W. Go is a great place to start because the displays are suppressed except for those set on in the query process. If the displays are not a bother or are useful, then use Animate instead.

While closely watching the flow of the program logic and displays of selected fields, programmers can interrupt the execution as necessary. Pressing Escape forces a keyboard interrupt. At this point additional fields can be queried and/or altered. In fact, even the program flow can be altered.

Many of these items will become clear after the remaining sections of this chapter. Once the execution is interrupted, try

Wch to execute a line at a time with displays. The displays should not be bothersome now since the execution is probably going at a snail's pace. If the displays are still a problem, use the Step feature. Either of these two features is exceptional for close-quarter debugging ("I think the problem is here, but I'm not really certain"). Combining the capabilities of the Animator features is a very effective testing strategy.

General Animator Features

The Animator function provides several basic features that are conveniently placed on several submenus. These features are shown on the Animator main menu in Figure 10.7. The following are the menus and submenus that support these common functions:

- Animator main menu
- Backtrack

```
 198*    SET THE ERROR HANDLING CONDITIONS.                         * 00012800
 199* * * * * * * * * * * * * * * * * * * * * * * * * * * * * * * * 00012900
 200      EXEC CICS HANDLE CONDITION                                  00013000
 201          ERROR(0900-ERROR-DETECTED)                              00013100
 202      END-EXEC.                                                   00013200
 203* * * * * * * * * * * * * * * * * * * * * * * * * * * * * * * * 00013300
 204*    DETERMINE WHETHER TO SEND OR RECEIVE A MAP.                 * 00013400
 205* * * * * * * * * * * * * * * * * * * * * * * * * * * * * * * * 00013500
 206      IF  EIBCALEN EQUAL TO ZEROES                                00013600
 207      THEN                                                        00013700
 208          MOVE LOW-VALUES TO MAINMENO
 209          MOVE 'Y' TO WS-COMM-SCRN-IND
 210          GO TO 0100-SEND-MAIN-MENU                               00013800
 211      ELSE                                                        00013900
 212          MOVE DFHCOMMAREA TO WS-COMMAREA                         00014000
 213          MOVE 'N' TO WS-COMM-SCRN-IND.                           00014010
 214                                                                  00014100
 215* * * * * * * * * * * * * * * * * * * * * * * * * * * * * * * * 00014200
 216*    PERFORM ROUTINE TO READ MAP FROM TERMINAL                   * 00014300
 217* * * * * * * * * * * * * * * * * * * * * * * * * * * * * * * * 00014400
 218      PERFORM 0300-RECEIVE-MAP THRU 0300-EXIT.                    00014500
                                                                      00014600
Animate-MAINMEN────────────────────Level=01-Speed=5-Ins-Caps-Num-Scroll
F1=help F2=view F3=align F4=exchange F5=where F6=lookup   F9/F10=word-</> Escape
Animate Step Wch Go Zoom nx-If Prfm Brk Rst Env Qury Find Locate txt Do Alt Ctrl
```

Figure 10.7.   Animator main menu common features.

- Break
- Environment
- Locate
- Threshold-Level
- Query
- Reset
- Text
- Until

Common Animator Features

- *F2=view*—Allows the display of user-generated screens while animating. As code in the program is executed, the screen will change to reflect the newly entered characters. To return to only looking at the code, press any key.
- *F3=Align*—Causes the statement at the current cursor position to be positioned to the third line from the top of the screen.
- *F4=Exchange*—When the animation session has been split into two windows, *F4* switches between the two windows.
- *F5=Where*—Causes the cursor to be placed on the current executing line and then moves the line to the third line from the top of the screen.
- *F6=Lookup*—Causes a submenu to be displayed, providing two features:
  F2=Clear—Provided to clear out the line number buffer input area.
  Enter—Text line to display: type in the line number to locate and then press Enter.
- *F9/F10=Word*—A nice method of scrolling on a line of text without having to use the arrow keys. *F9=Word* moves the cursor to the next word to its left. *F10=Word* moves the cursor to the next word to its right.

Backtrack. Typically, during a debugging session, breakpoints are set and fields displayed and then the program is animated. Why then address backtrack at this time?

Backtrack is a feature well worth using for logic problems and perhaps best suited for the first few animation sessions. During the initial testing, it is quite possible (with new code) to accidentally go down the wrong path. With backtrack on (Figure 10.8), the session can be recorded and looked at, just as a videotape can be rewound and replayed. This is a super feature for figuring out how the program ended up in 0100-READ-ROUTINE when it should have been in 0110-GET-NEXT-RCD routine. Backtrack is a function located on the Environment submenu of the Animator. Press *E* for *Environment*, and then press *B* for *Backtrack*.

Besides the Animator common features, backtrack allows three features:

- Set—Turns on the recorder. The recorder can be turned on at the beginning of execution or at any time during execution.
- Unset—Stops collecting and recording lines executed for this session.

```
318*    MAP HAS BEEN RECEIVED AND A KEY OTHER THAN PF3 WAS PRESSED. * 00023700
319*    NOW DETERMINE WHICH SELECTION WAS MADE.                      * 00023800
320* * * * * * * * * * * * * * * * * * * * * * * * * * * * * * * * * 00023900
321*                                                                   00024100
322     IF  MENSELI = 'F'                                              00024000
323* * * * * * * * * * * * * * * * * * * * * * * * * * * * * * * * * * 00024100
324*    THE ADD SELECTION WAS MADE - TRANSFER CONTROL TO THE        * 00024200
325*    FINANCIAL PROCESS                                           * 00024300
326* * * * * * * * * * * * * * * * * * * * * * * * * * * * * * * * * 00024400
327         THEN                                                       
328             EXEC CICS XCTL                                        00024500
329                 PROGRAM('FINMEN')                                 00024600
330             END-EXEC.                                             00024700
331*                                                                   00024100
332     IF  MENSELI = 'I'                                             00024000
333* * * * * * * * * * * * * * * * * * * * * * * * * * * * * * * * * * 00024100
334*    THE ADD SELECTION WAS MADE - TRANSFER CONTROL TO THE        * 00024200
335*    INQUIRY PROCESS                                             * 00024300
336* * * * * * * * * * * * * * * * * * * * * * * * * * * * * * * * * 00024400
337         THEN                                                       
338             EXEC CICS XCTL                                        00024500
Backtrack = set─────────────────────────Level=01-Speed=5-Ins-Caps-Num-Scroll
F1=help F2=view F3=align F4=exchange F5=where F6=look-up  F9/F10=word-</> Escape
Set Unset Examine
```

Figure 10.8. Environment submenu.

- Examine—Allows the reviewing of previously recorded execution. The up and down arrows are used to scroll through the backtrack recording.

Breakpoint Characteristics. Prior to starting the animation process by the previously defined methods, it is always a good idea to establish breaks. Breaks are very useful when debugging a program. They allow a method of stopping the automatic execution for a more detailed examination of data fields or altering the logic path. Breaks are especially helpful when animating with Zoom. Breaks come in conditional and unconditional forms. No matter which type of break, they should be established prior to starting the animation execution.

Unconditional breaks are set at specific lines, and when execution gets to that line, it stops. Conditional breaks will stop the execution when some condition occurs, but the condition must be true for this to happen. A maximum of 100 breaks can be established in a session. Conditional and unconditional breaks cannot be set on the same line. To switch between breaks, the programmer would first have to clear the existing break and then establish another type of break. Starting with release 2.5, breaks can be saved from one animation session to another, unless the program is rechecked.

Breaks are probably one of the most useful features provided within the Animator. Without them, animation is somewhat like running a batch job from top to bottom. Effective debugging of a program is best accomplished with well-placed breaks and queries.

Breaks can be set from several areas within the Animator function. On the Animator main menu are found next-If, Break, and Env, all features that are breaks or support breaks.

Unconditional Breaks

Unconditional breaks are set from the Break submenu. They should be set prior to executing the program, but may be set after execution has started. The Break submenu is invoked from the Animator main menu (see Figure 10.9).

The Break submenu provides for establishing and removing

```
 218       PERFORM 0300-RECEIVE-MAP THRU 0300-EXIT.                          00014600
 219                                                                         00023200
 220       EXEC CICS RECEIVE                                                 00022800
 221            MAP('MAINMEN')                                               00022900
 222            INTO(MAINMEN)                                                00023000
 223       END-EXEC.                                                         00023100
 224                                                                         00014700
 225* * * * * * * * * * * * * * * * * * * * * * * * * * * * * * * * * *   * 00014800
 226*   PERFORM MAIN LOGIC ROUTINE                                        * 00014900
 227* * * * * * * * * * * * * * * * * * * * * * * * * * * * * * * * * *   * 00015000
 228       PERFORM 0500-EDIT-SCREEN THRU 0500-EXIT.                          00015100
 229                                                                         00015200
 230 0100-SEND-MAIN-MENU.                                                    00015300
 231* * * * * * * * * * * * * * * * * * * * * * * * * * * * * * * * * *   * 00015400
 232*   GET THE CURRENT DATE AND TIME THROUGH CICS.                       * 00015500
 233* * * * * * * * * * * * * * * * * * * * * * * * * * * * * * * * * *   * 00015600
 234       EXEC CICS ASKTIME                                                 00015700
 235            ABSTIME(ABSOLUTE-TIME)                                       00015800
 236       END-EXEC.                                                         00015900
 237* * * * * * * * * * * * * * * * * * * * * * * * * * * * * * * * * *   * 00016000
 238*   FORMAT THE DATE AND TIME FOR DISPLAY IN THE MAP.                  * 00016100
Break-points—On-count=unset————————————Level=01—Speed=5—Ins—Caps—Num—Scroll
F1=help F2=view F3=align F4=exchange F5=where F6=look-up  F9/F10=word-</> Escape
Set Unset Cancel-all Examine If Do On-count Zoom
```

Figure 10.9.   Animation submenu to set breaks.

breaks within an animator session. This submenu allows both conditional and unconditional break setting.

- Set—Establishes an unconditional break on the statement that the cursor is currently positioned to. The program will stop execution when the line of code is about to execute.
- Unset—Removes a break at the line that the cursor is positioned to.
- Cancel-all—Removes all breaks in a program.
- Examine—Each time that the E of Examine is pressed, the cursor will be positioned to the next line of code that has a break set and the type of break is displayed (Figure 10.10).
- Do—Allows programmers to code a temporary COBOL statement that will be executed just before the statement that contains the break (see Figure 10.11). When in Go or Zoom, the Do executes and then execution continues without stop-

```
320* * * * * * * * * * * * * * * * * * * * * * * * * * * * * * *   00023900
321*                                                               00024100
322    IF  MENSELI = 'F'                                           00024000
323* * * * * * * * * * * * * * * * * * * * * * * * * * * * * * *   00024100
324*   THE ADD SELECTION WAS MADE - TRANSFER CONTROL TO THE     * 00024200
325*   FINANCIAL PROCESS                                        * 00024300
326* * * * * * * * * * * * * * * * * * * * * * * * * * * * * * *   00024400
327        THEN                                                    
328            EXEC CICS XCTL                                      00024500
329                PROGRAM('FINMEN')                               00024600
330            END-EXEC.                                           00024700
331*                                                               00024100
332    IF  MENSELI = 'I'                                           00024000
333* * * * * * * * * * * * * * * * * * * * * * * * * * * * * * *   00024100
334*   THE ADD SELECTION WAS MADE - TRANSFER CONTROL TO THE     * 00024200
335*   INQUIRY PROCESS                                          * 00024300
336* * * * * * * * * * * * * * * * * * * * * * * * * * * * * * *   00024400
337        THEN                                                    
338            EXEC CICS XCTL                                      00024500
339                PROGRAM('INQMEN')                               00024600
340            END-EXEC.                                           00024700
Break-points—On-count=unset———————————Level=01-Speed=5-Ins-Caps-Num-Scroll
F1=help F2=view F3=align F4=exchange F5=where F6=look-up  F9/F10=word-</> Escape
Set Unset Cancel-all Examine If Do On-count Zoom
Break-point condition:        MENSELI = 'F'
```

Figure 10.10.   Examining established breaks.

```
320* * * * * * * * * * * * * * * * * * * * * * * * * * * * * * *   00023900
321*                                                               00024100
322    IF  MENSELI = 'F'                                           00024000
323* * * * * * * * * * * * * * * * * * * * * * * * * * * * * * *   00024100
324*   THE ADD SELECTION WAS MADE - TRANSFER CONTROL TO THE     * 00024200
325*   FINANCIAL PROCESS                                        * 00024300
326* * * * * * * * * * * * * * * * * * * * * * * * * * * * * * *   00024400
327        THEN                                                    
328            EXEC CICS XCTL                                      00024500
329                PROGRAM('FINMEN')                               00024600
330            END-EXEC.                                           00024700
331*                                                               00024100
332        ┌Enter—COBOL—statement—to—be—executed————              00024000
333* * *│ IF MENSELI EQUAL 'U' MOVE 'I' TO MENSELI_    │    * * * * 00024100
334*    T│                                             │         * 00024200
335*    I└─────────────────────────────────────────────┘         * 00024300
336* * * * * * * * * * * * * * * * * * * * * * * * * * * * * * *   00024400
337        THEN                                                    
338            EXEC CICS XCTL                                      00024500
339                PROGRAM('INQMEN')                               00024600
340            END-EXEC.                                           00024700
Do—————————————————————————————Level=01-Speed=5-Ins-Caps-Num-Scroll
F1=help F2=clear                                                   Escape
```

Figure 10.11.   Do break: Type in COBOL statement.

ping on the line where the break was established. If in Step mode, the Do statement is executed prior to executing the line where the break was established.

Conditional Breaks

Conditional breaks can be set from the Break submenu. They only execute when some predetermined condition is true. The following conditional breaks are found on the Break submenu:

- If—Allows programmers to key in a COBOL If test. The If, however, is not coded (see Figure 10.12). When the condition becomes true, the program stops execution on the line where the break was established.
- Zoom—Sets a breakpoint at the current line and Zooms through the code until reaching this statement.
- On-count—Allows programmers to type in a number between 2 and 255 inclusive and then using Set or the Do condition to

```
318*    MAP HAS BEEN RECEIVED AND A KEY OTHER THAN PF3 WAS PRESSED. * 00023700
319*    NOW DETERMINE WHICH SELECTION WAS MADE.                     * 00023800
320* * * * * * * * * * * * * * * * * * * * * * * * * * * * * * * * * 00023900
321*                                                                  00024100
322       ┌─Enter-condition:──────────────────────────────┐          00024000
323* * *  │MENSELI = 'F'_                                  │  * * * *  00024100
324*    T │                                                │       *  00024200
325*    F └────────────────────────────────────────────────┘       *  00024300
326* * * * * * * * * * * * * * * * * * * * * * * * * * * * * * * * * 00024400
327         THEN                                                      
328             EXEC CICS XCTL                                        00024500
329                 PROGRAM('FINMEN')                                 00024600
330             END-EXEC.                                             00024700
331*                                                                  00024100
332     IF  MENSELI = 'I'                                             00024000
333* * * * * * * * * * * * * * * * * * * * * * * * * * * * * * * * * 00024100
334*    THE ADD SELECTION WAS MADE - TRANSFER CONTROL TO THE       * 00024200
335*    INQUIRY PROCESS                                            * 00024300
336* * * * * * * * * * * * * * * * * * * * * * * * * * * * * * * * * 00024400
337         THEN                                                      
338             EXEC CICS XCTL                                        00024500
Break-points—On-count=unset───────────Level=01-Speed=5-Ins-Caps-Num-Scroll
F1=help F2=clear                                                   Escape
```

Figure 10.12.   Setting a conditional If break.

establish the break as shown in Figure 10.13. Once the program begins execution, the execution will stop on the designated line and every nth time that the line is executed.

Breaks can be combined as needed to assist in debugging a program. From the Break submenu set an On-count break (set to 3) and then select Do to set the break on a line of code. Once the Do is selected, type in a valid COBOL statement. The Do statement will then be executed after every third time the statement is executed.

Environment Breaks. The Env feature shown in Figure 10.14 allows several different breaks and is accessed from the Animator main menu by pressing *E* for Env.

Program-Break. Program-Break establishes a break at the entry point of the designated program as shown in Figure 10.15. All

```
320* * * * * * * * * * * * * * * * * * * * * * * * * * * * * * *  00023900
321*                                                              00024100
322    IF  MENSELI = 'F'                                          00024000
323* * * * * * * * * * * * * * * * * * * * * * * * * * * * * * *  00024100
324*   THE ADD SELECTION WAS MADE - TRANSFER CONTROL TO THE    *  00024200
325*   FINANCIAL PROCESS                                       *  00024300
326* * * * * * * * * * * * * * * * * * * * * * * * * * * * * * *  00024400
327        THEN                                                   00024500
328              EXEC CICS XCTL                                   00024500
329                  PROGRAM('FINMEN')                            00024600
330              END-EXEC.                                        00024700
331*                                                              00024100
332       ┌Enter─On─count┐'                                       00024000
333* * *  │ 003          │  * * * * * * * * * * * * * * * * * * *  00024100
334*   T  └──────────────┘    WAS MADE - TRANSFER CONTROL TO THE *  00024200
335*   INQUIRY PROCESS                                         *  00024300
336* * * * * * * * * * * * * * * * * * * * * * * * * * * * * * *  00024400
337        THEN                                                   00024500
338              EXEC CICS XCTL                                   00024500
339                  PROGRAM('INQMEN')                            00024600
340              END-EXEC.                                        00024700
Break-points─On-count=unset─────────────Level=01-Speed=5-Ins-Caps-Num─Scroll
F1=help F2=clear                                                   Escape
```

Figure 10.13. On-count: Type in countervalue.

```
320* * * * * * * * * * * * * * * * * * * * * * * * * * * * * * * 00023900
321*                                                               00024100
322      IF  MENSELI = 'F'                                         00024000
323* * * * * * * * * * * * * * * * * * * * * * * * * * * * * * * * 00024100
324*  THE ADD SELECTION WAS MADE - TRANSFER CONTROL TO THE      * 00024200
325*  FINANCIAL PROCESS                                         * 00024300
326* * * * * * * * * * * * * * * * * * * * * * * * * * * * * * * * 00024400
327         THEN                                                   00024100
328             EXEC CICS XCTL                                     00024500
329                 PROGRAM('FINMEN')                              00024600
330             END-EXEC.                                          00024700
331*                                                               00024100
332      IF  MENSELI = 'I'                                         00024000
333* * * * * * * * * * * * * * * * * * * * * * * * * * * * * * * * 00024100
334*  THE ADD SELECTION WAS MADE - TRANSFER CONTROL TO THE      * 00024200
335*  INQUIRY PROCESS                                           * 00024300
336* * * * * * * * * * * * * * * * * * * * * * * * * * * * * * * * 00024400
337         THEN                                                   00024100
338             EXEC CICS XCTL                                     00024500
339                 PROGRAM('INQMEN')                              00024600
340             END-EXEC.                                          00024700
Environment────────────────────────────Level=01-Speed=5-Ins-Caps-Num-Scroll
F1=help F2=view F3=align F4=exchange F5=where F6=look-up  F9/F10=word-</> Escape
Program-break Threshold-level Until Backtrack Flash(step/zoom) Mon-slide(on/off)
```

Figure 10.14.   Setting environment type breaks.

```
318*  MAP HAS BEEN RECEIVED AND A KEY OTHER THAN PF3 WAS PRESSED. * 00023700
319*  NOW DETERMINE WHICH SELECTION WAS MADE.                    * 00023800
320* * *┌Enter-name-of-program──────────────────────────┐* * * * 00023900
321*     │MAINMEN                                         │         00024100
322      │                                                │         00024000
323* * *└────────────────────────────────────────────────┘* * * * 00024100
324*  THE ADD SELECTION WAS MADE - TRANSFER CONTROL TO THE      * 00024200
325*  FINANCIAL PROCESS                                         * 00024300
326* * * * * * * * * * * * * * * * * * * * * * * * * * * * * * * * 00024400
327         THEN                                                   00024100
328             EXEC CICS XCTL                                     00024500
329                 PROGRAM('FINMEN')                              00024600
330             END-EXEC.                                          00024700
331*                                                               00024100
332      IF  MENSELI = 'I'                                         00024000
333* * * * * * * * * * * * * * * * * * * * * * * * * * * * * * * * 00024100
334*  THE ADD SELECTION WAS MADE - TRANSFER CONTROL TO THE      * 00024200
335*  INQUIRY PROCESS                                           * 00024300
336* * * * * * * * * * * * * * * * * * * * * * * * * * * * * * * * 00024400
337         THEN                                                   00024100
338             EXEC CICS XCTL                                     00024500
Program-break = set─────────────────────Level=01-Speed=5-Ins-Caps-Num-Scroll
F1=help F2=clear                                                        Escape
```

Figure 10.15.   Program-Break with program entered.

other programs can be Zoomed through. Only one active Program-Break is supported during an animation session. The following features are available on the Program-Break submenu:

- This—Establishes a Break on the program that is currently being executed.
- Select—Opens a window, allowing the programmer to type in the name of a program to stop execution at.
- Cancel—Removes the Program-Break that is currently set.

Program-Breaks are supported for subprograms accessed by CALL, not by XCTL and LINK CICS commands.

Threshold-Level. Defines a level within a program that all code (including subprograms) below the set level will be Zoomed through (Figure 10.16). The Threshold-Level remains set until removed by the programmer. It is set from the Environment submenu by pressing *T* of *Threshold-Level.*

```
396*    TERMINATE THE PROGRAM IF AN ERROR IS ENCOUNTERED.           * 00028500
397* * * * * * * * * * * * * * * * * * * * * * * * * * * * * * * * * * * 00028600
398      IF  EIBAID = DFHCLEAR                                         00028700
399         THEN MOVE INVALID-SELECTION-MESSAGE TO MSG10              00028800
400              GO TO 0100-SEND-MAIN-MENU.                           00028900
401      MOVE 'ENCOUNTERED AN ERROR' TO MESSAGE-AREA.                00029000
402      MOVE +20 TO MESSAGE-LENGTH.                                 00029100
403      GO TO 0990-SEND-MESSAGE.                                    00029200
404                                                                  00029300
405  0910-INVALID-SECURITY.
406      MOVE SPACES TO MSG10.
407      MOVE INVALID-SECURITY-MSG TO MSG10.
408      MOVE DFHBMFSE TO MENIDA.
409      GO TO 0100-SEND-MAIN-MENU.
410
411  0980-END-PROGRAM.                                               00029400
412* * * * * * * * * * * * * * * * * * * * * * * * * * * * * * * * * * * 00029500
413*    TERMINATE THE PROGRAM IF OPTION 'X' HAS BEEN SELECTED.       * 00029600
414* * * * * * * * * * * * * * * * * * * * * * * * * * * * * * * * * * * 00029700
415      MOVE 'PROCESSING COMPLETE - GOODBYE' TO MESSAGE-AREA.       00029800
416      MOVE +29 TO MESSAGE-LENGTH.                                 00029900
Threshold-level = 02─────────────────────Level=02-Speed=5-Ins-Caps-Num-Scroll
F1=help F2=view F3=align F4=exchange F5=where F6=look-up  F9/F10=word-</> Escape
Set Unset
```

Figure 10.16. Threshold-Level break setting.

Threshold-Level has these two features:

* Set—Set by positioning to the "perform or call" and pressing S. Once set, the Threshold-Level will appear on the information line.
* Unset—Removes the established Threshold-Level.

Until. Until establishes a condition test, displayed in Figure 10.17, that is tested prior to the execution of every line of code in the program. When the condition is true, the execution of the program stops. The *COBOL* statement must be a valid syntactically coded statement.

Only one Until break can be set in a program. Until provides these three features:

* Set—Establish a break similar to that of a conditional break by entering a statement in the window and pressing Enter.

```
396*    TERMINATE THE PROGRAM IF AN ERROR IS ENCOUNTERED.        * 00028500
397* * * * * * * * * * * * * * * * * * * * * * * * * * * * * * * 00028600
398        ┌Enter-condition:──────────────────────────────┐       00028700
399        │MENSELI = 'I'_                                 │       00028800
400        │                                               │       00028900
401        └───────────────────────────────────────────────┘       00029000
402        MOVE +20 TO MESSAGE-LENGTH.                            00029100
403        GO TO 0990-SEND-MESSAGE.                               00029200
404                                                               00029300
405 0910-INVALID-SECURITY.
406        MOVE SPACES TO MSG10.
407        MOVE INVALID-SECURITY-MSG TO MSG10.
408        MOVE DFHBMFSE TO MENIDA.
409        GO TO 0100-SEND-MAIN-MENU.
410
411 0980-END-PROGRAM.                                             00029400
412* * * * * * * * * * * * * * * * * * * * * * * * * * * * * * * 00029500
413*    TERMINATE THE PROGRAM IF OPTION 'X' HAS BEEN SELECTED.   * 00029600
414* * * * * * * * * * * * * * * * * * * * * * * * * * * * * * * 00029700
415        MOVE 'PROCESSING COMPLETE - GOODBYE' TO MESSAGE-AREA.  00029800
416        MOVE +29 TO MESSAGE-LENGTH.                            00029900
Until─────────────────────────────Level=02-Speed=5-Ins-Caps-Num-Scroll
F1=help F2=clear                                                 Escape
```

Figure 10.17. Setting an Until break point.

Unlike a conditional break, the break is not set at a specific line of code.

- Unset—Removes the Until break. Since there is only one, no identification of the break is necessary.
- Examine—The break can be viewed by pressing the E of Examine.

Next-If. Pressing I of the next-If will Zoom through the code until the Animator locates the next If statement. At that point, execution stops and the program code is again displayed on the screen.

The Next-If function looks for the next If statement on any level of code. This is most useful when executing a routine with lots of code in it and the programmer wishes to stop at every If test to validate the data values prior to execution. To invoke this feature from the Animator main menu, press *I* of *next-If.*

Do. The Do feature allows programmers to execute a valid CO-BOL statement. This feature is quite handy as a method to insert a statement to correct the program when code is missing. The code inserted with the Do does not become permanent code in the program. The statement cannot exceed 71 characters, as displayed in Figure 10.18. Once typed in, press Enter. Pressing Enter executes the statement immediately. Do is invoked from the Animator main menu by pressing *D* of *Do.*

The Do feature provides a window for typing in a valid CO-BOL statement, supported by the following functions:

- *F2=Clear*—Used to remove a COBOL statement coded into the Do input area.
- *Escape*—Used to leave the Do submenu without executing the COBOL statement typed in.
- *Enter*—Executes the Do statement immediately.

Querying Data Fields

The Query function allows programmers to view data contained in fields and to alter the value if necessary. As fields are being queried, they can be made to display permanently during the

```
396*    TERMINATE THE PROGRAM IF AN ERROR IS ENCOUNTERED.          * 00028500
397* * * * * * * * * * * * * * * * * * * * * * * * * * * * * * * * 00028600
398        ┌Enter-COBOL-statement-to-be-executed─────────────────┐    00028700
399        │ IF MENSELI = 'I' GO TO 0910-INVALID-SECURITY_        │    00028800
400        │                                                      │    00028900
401        │                                                      │    00029000
402        │ MOVE +20 TO MESSAGE-LENGTH.                          │    00029100
403        │ GO TO 0990-SEND-MESSAGE.                             │    00029200
404        └──────────────────────────────────────────────────────┘    00029300
405 0910-INVALID-SECURITY.
406        MOVE SPACES TO MSG10.
407        MOVE INVALID-SECURITY-MSG TO MSG10.
408        MOVE DFHBMFSE TO MENIDA.
409        GO TO 0100-SEND-MAIN-MENU.
410
411 0980-END-PROGRAM.                                                  00029400
412* * * * * * * * * * * * * * * * * * * * * * * * * * * * * * * * 00029500
413*    TERMINATE THE PROGRAM IF OPTION 'X' HAS BEEN SELECTED.     * 00029600
414* * * * * * * * * * * * * * * * * * * * * * * * * * * * * * * * 00029700
415        MOVE 'PROCESSING COMPLETE - GOODBYE' TO MESSAGE-AREA.       00029800
416        MOVE +29 TO MESSAGE-LENGTH.                                 00029900
Do───────────────────────────────────────────Level=02-Speed=5-Ins-Caps-Num-Scroll
F1=help F2=clear                                                         Escape
```

Figure 10.18. Typing COBOL statements with Do.

animation session. Query, shown in Figure 10.19, is invoked from the Animator main menu by pressing *Q* of *Query*.

The Query submenu provides several useful functions to support a programmer's viewing of data field values:

- Cursor-name—The data field at the current cursor location will be displayed.
- Enter-name—Displays a window for typing in a data field to query (see Figure 10.20). Using one of three methods for identifying a data field: (1) type in the data field name, (2) type in a data field name and an offset, or (3) type in the hexadecimal address from the Data Division.
- Repeat—Displays the value of the last field queried.
- Monitor-off—Stops the constant monitoring of a data field. The monitor will no longer be displayed on the screen.
- Dump-list—Writes the values typed in for a data field to the disk.

```
352     IF  MENSELI = 'R'                                         00024000
353* * * * * * * * * * * * * * * * * * * * * * * * * * * * * * * * 00024100
354*    THE ADD SELECTION WAS MADE - TRANSFER CONTROL TO THE    * 00024200
355*    MEMBER PROCESS                                          * 00024300
356* * * * * * * * * * * * * * * * * * * * * * * * * * * * * * * * 00024400
357         THEN
358             EXEC CICS XCTL                                    00024500
359                 PROGRAM('RPTMEN')                             00024600
360             END-EXEC.                                         00024700
361     IF ┌MENSELI┐= 'X'                                         00027000
362        │        │ TO 0980-END-PROGRAM.                        00027100
363* * * * │        │* * * * * * * * * * * * * * * * * * * * * * * 00027200
364*    AN INVALID SELECTION WAS MADE - REDISPLAY THE MAP WITH AN * 00027300
365*    APPROPRIATE MESSAGE.                                    * 00027400
366* * * * * * * * * * * * * * * * * * * * * * * * * * * * * * * * 00027500
367     MOVE INVALID-SELECTION-MESSAGE TO MSG10.                  00027600
368     MOVE 'N' TO DFHCOMMAREA-SCRN-IND.                         00027700
369     GO TO 0100-SEND-MAIN-MENU.                                00027800
370 0500-EXIT.                                                    00027900
371     EXIT.                                                     00028000
372 0510-SECURITY-CHECK.                                          00023500
Query:    MENSELI────────────────Level=02-Speed=5-Ins-Caps-Num-Scroll
F1=help F2=view F3=align F4=exchange F5=where F6=look-up  F9/F10=word-</> Escape
Cursor-name Enter-name Repeat Monitor-off Dump-list Hide/Org-monitors Watch-off
```

Figure 10.19. Selecting fields to Query or alter.

```
352     IF  MENSELI = 'R'                                         00024000
353* * * * * * * * * * * * * * * * * * * * * * * * * * * * * * * * 00024100
354*    THE ADD SELECTION WAS MADE - TRANSFER CONTROL TO THE    * 00024200
355*    MEMBER PROCESS                                          * 00024300
356* * * * * * * * * * * * * * * * * * * * * * * * * * * * * * * * 00024400
357         THEN
358             EXEC CICS XCTL                                    00024500
359                 PROGRAM('RPTMEN')                             00024600
360             END-EXEC.                                         00024700
361     IF ┌Enter-name-[+-offset]-or-hex-address───────┐         00027000
362        │─                                          │         00027100
363* * * * *│                                          │ * *     00027200
364*    AN IN│                                          │     * 00027300
365*    APPROPRIATE MESSAGE.                            │     * 00027400
366* * * * * * * * * * * * * * * * * * * * * * * * * * * * * * * * 00027500
367     MOVE INVALID-SELECTION-MESSAGE TO MSG10.                  00027600
368     MOVE 'N' TO DFHCOMMAREA-SCRN-IND.                         00027700
369     GO TO 0100-SEND-MAIN-MENU.                                00027800
370 0500-EXIT.                                                    00027900
371     EXIT.                                                     00028000
372 0510-SECURITY-CHECK.                                          00023500
Query-data────────────────────Level=02-Speed=5-Ins-Caps-Num-Scroll
F1=help F2=clear                                               Escape
```

Figure 10.20. Typing in a data field to query.

- Hide-monitors—Hides all monitors until such time as the value changes during execution or until the screen is refreshed.
- Org-monitors—Causes the displayed monitors to be repositioned to the bottom right portion of the screen.
- Watch-off—Stops monitoring of all currently monitored fields.

Query Data-Name Menu. Once a data field has been queried, the Query Data-Name menu appears, which supports either the Hex menu or the ASCII text menu shown in Figure 10.21.

When the Hex menu is selected, the data value will be displayed in the lower left portion of the screen in HEX. The ASCII value appears in the lower right portion of the screen. Data can be altered in either mode.

These features on the Query Data-Name menu appear for both the Hex or ASCII menus:

- *F2=Clear*—Clears out the current data field value to spaces or zeroes, depending on the data field type.

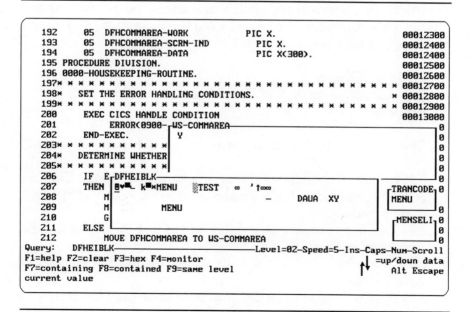

Figure 10.21.   Data-name menu for monitoring.

- *F3=Hex/ASCII*—Switches between Hex or ASCII menus.
- *F4=Monitor*—Permanently monitors a data field while the program is executing.
- *F7=Containing*—Views the contents of a group item.
- *F8=Contained*—Displays the value of the first data item contained in a queried data field.
- *F9=Same-level*—Displays the contents of the next data field on the same level (i.e., "05 sub" and "05 count-lines").
- *F5=Up-table*—Allows a programmer to examine a previous value within a table.
- *F6=Down-table*—Allows a programmer to examine the next value within a table.

Note: The workbench does not allow "scrolling" outside the range of the table.

Query Alt Menu. The query Alt menu allows programmers to create test data for their programs. The programmer can add, change, delete, and view the values. The Alt menu shown in Figure 10.22 displays values on the message line portion of the screen. This submenu is accessed from the Animator main menu by doing the following:

- Press *Q* of *Query*
- Press *C* of *Cursor* or *E* of *Enter* to select a field
- Press *Alt*

The following functions are provided on the Query *Alt* menu:

- *F2=Update-list*—Allows the programmer to change the currently displayed value with the new value typed at the bottom of the screen.
- *F3=Add-list*—Adds a new value to the list of values for the data item queried.
- *F4=Delete-list*—Deletes the displayed value from the list of data values.
- *F5=Up-list*—Allows the programmer to display the previous data value.

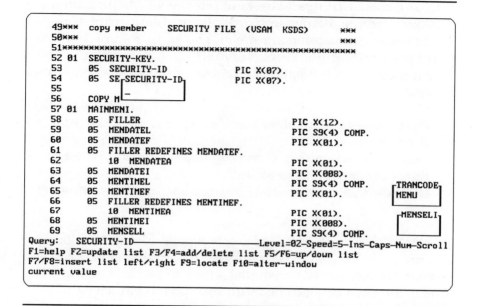

```
49***  copy member    SECURITY FILE (USAM  KSDS)    ***
50***                                              ***
51*************************************************************
52 01  SECURITY-KEY.
53     05  SECURITY-ID          PIC X(07).
54     05  SE┌SECURITY-ID┐      PIC X(07).
55           └─          ┘
56     COPY M┘
57 01  MAINMENI.
58     05  FILLER                   PIC X(12).
59     05  MENDATEL                 PIC S9(4) COMP.
60     05  MENDATEF                 PIC X(01).
61     05  FILLER REDEFINES MENDATEF.
62         10  MENDATEA             PIC X(01).
63     05  MENDATEI                 PIC X(008).
64     05  MENTIMEL                 PIC S9(4) COMP.    ┌TRANCODE┐
65     05  MENTIMEF                 PIC X(01).          MENU
66     05  FILLER REDEFINES MENTIMEF.                 └        ┘
67         10  MENTIMEA             PIC X(01).        ┌MENSELI┐
68     05  MENTIMEI                 PIC X(008).
69     05  MENSELL                  PIC S9(4) COMP.   └       ┘
Query:    SECURITY-ID────────────Level=02-Speed=5-Ins-Caps-Num-Scroll
F1=help F2=update list F3/F4=add/delete list F5/F6=up/down list
F7/F8=insert list left/right F9=locate F10=alter-window
current value
```

Figure 10.22.   The query Alt submenu.

- *F6=Down-list*—Allows the programmer to display the next data value.
- *F7=Insert-list-left*—The value typed at the bottom of the screen is inserted into an existing list of values. The value is inserted into the list in front of the current data value being displayed.
- *F8=Insert-list-right*—The value typed at the bottom of the screen is inserted into an existing list of values. The value is inserted into the list after the current data value being displayed.
- *F9=Locate*—Finds the definition of a field being queried.

While the lists are being created, they are available in memory. They do not exist physically. Lists must be saved or they are lost. To save a list, return to the Query submenu (Escape from the Alt menu) and press the D of the Dump-list function to save as a file. The file will default to "program name.ILS," in the current directory.

Finding Text Strings. The Find feature allows programmers to search for text strings in a program or subprogram. The F of Find on the Animator main menu, shown in Figure 10.23, invokes the find feature. Press *F* of *Find*.

Find supports the following functions in the location of text strings:

- *F2=Clear*—Used to clear out the current value in the Find window.
- *Enter*—Type in a text string (up to 32 characters) and press Enter to search for the string.
- *Escape*—Used to leave the Find menu without searching for a text string.

Once Enter is pressed, Find is only capable of searching forward in a program (i.e., top to bottom) from the current cursor position down. Case sensitivity is required when finding text strings. The Find feature can be controlled with two special characters:

```
189*    DECLARED BY THE PROGRAMMER AS THE FIRST ITEM.           *  00012000
190 LINKAGE SECTION.                                               00012100
191 01  DFHCOMM┌Enter-string-or-string#[Main]─┐                    00012200
192     05  DFH│ MENSELI_                      │                   00012300
193     05  DFH└────────────────────────────── ┘                  00012400
194     05  DFHCOMMAREA-DATA          PIC X(300).                  00012400
195 PROCEDURE DIVISION.                                            00012500
196 0000-HOUSEKEEPING-ROUTINE.                                     00012600
197* * * * * * * * * * * * * * * * * * * * * * * * * * * * * *  *  00012700
198*    SET THE ERROR HANDLING CONDITIONS.                      *  00012800
199* * * * * * * * * * * * * * * * * * * * * * * * * * * * * *  *  00012900
200     EXEC CICS HANDLE CONDITION                                 00013000
201         ERROR(0900-ERROR-DETECTED)                             00013100
202     END-EXEC.                                                  00013200
203* * * * * * * * * * * * * * * * * * * * * * * * * * * * * *  *  00013300
204*    DETERMINE WHETHER TO SEND OR RECEIVE A MAP.           ┌TRANCODE┐ 0
205* * * * * * * * * * * * * * * * * * * * * * * * * * * * * *│MENU    │ 0
206     IF  EIBCALEN EQUAL TO ZEROES                           └         0
207     THEN                                                  ┌MENSELI┐ 0
208         MOVE LOW-VALUES TO MAINMENO                        │       │
209         MOVE 'Y' TO WS-COMM-SCRN-IND                       └        0
Find────────────────────────────────Level=02-Speed=5-Ins-Caps-Num-Scroll
F1=help F2=clear                                                   Escape
```

Figure 10.23. To search for items, use Find.

- # sign—Used to identify the end of a text string. This is particularly good when using spaces as significant characters in a search (i.e., the search string is sub-2 #).
- M—Used in conjunction with the # to restrict the search to the main (current) module.

Locate Program Sections. The Locate feature allows programmers to find the definition of a file name, procedure name, or data item. The L of Locate on the Animator main menu, shown in Figure 10.24, invokes the locate feature. Press *L* of *Locate*.

The Locate feature provides programmers with the following methods of locating fields and labels in a file:

- *Cursor-name*—Finds the definition of the field or paragraph label at the current cursor location.
- *Enter-name*—Once a field or paragraph label is typed in the window, the definition is located.

```
189*    DECLARED BY THE PROGRAMMER AS THE FIRST ITEM.          *  00012000
190 LINKAGE SECTION.                                             00012100
191 01   DFHCOMMAREA.                                            00012200
192        05   DFHCOMMAREA-WORK           PIC X.                00012300
193        05   DFHCOMMAREA-SCRN-IND       PIC X.                00012400
194        05   DFHCOMMAREA-DATA           PIC X(300).           00012400
195 PROCEDURE DIVISION.                                          00012500
196 0000-HOUSEKEEPING-ROUTINE.                                   00012600
197* * * * * * * * * * * * * * * * * * * * * * * * * * * * * *  00012700
198*    SET THE ERROR HANDLING CONDITIONS.                    * 00012800
199* * * * * * * * * * * * * * * * * * * * * * * * * * * * * *  00012900
200        EXEC CICS HANDLE CONDITION                           00013000
201            ERROR(0900-ERROR-DETECTED)                        00013100
202        END-EXEC.                                             00013200
203* * * * * * * * * * * * * * * * * * * * * * * * * * * * * *  00013300
204*    DETERMINE WHETHER TO SEND OR RECEIVE A MAP.     ┌TRANCODE┐ 0
205* * * * * * * * * * * * * * * * * * * * * * * * * * *│MENU     │ 0
206        IF   EIBCALEN EQUAL TO ZEROES                         0
207        THEN                                        ┌MENSELI┐ 0
208            MOVE LOW-VALUES TO MAINMENO                       0
209            MOVE 'Y' TO WS-COMM-SCRN-IND                   └─┘ 0
Locate-declaration─────────────Level=02-Speed=5-Ins-Caps-Num-Scroll
F1=help F2=view F3=align F4=exchange F5=where F6=look-up  F9/F10=word-</> Escape
Cursor-name Enter-name Up-perform-level Down-perform-level
```

Figure 10.24. Locate definitions of fields/label.

- *Up-perform level*—Moves the cursor from the current location to the perform statement that initiated the execution of the current routine.
- *Down-perform level*—Brings the cursor back down to the executing statement where the cursor was located prior to invoking the "up-perform level."

Text Features. The Text feature allows programmers to split and join screens, refresh screens, and switch to the Editor. Text functions are accessed from the Animator main menu by pressing T of Text (see Figure 10.25).

- *Split*—Splits the screen into two windows. At least four lines of code are required to split a window.
- *Join*—Once a window has been split, Join connects the two together into the active window.
- *Refresh*—Redisplays the current screen and any hidden monitors.

```
189*    DECLARED BY THE PROGRAMMER AS THE FIRST ITEM.           * 00012000
190 LINKAGE SECTION.                                              00012100
191 01  DFHCOMMAREA.                                              00012200
192     05  DFHCOMMAREA-WORK            PIC X.                    00012300
193     05  DFHCOMMAREA-SCRN-IND        PIC X.                    00012400
194     05  DFHCOMMAREA-DATA            PIC X(300).               00012400
195 PROCEDURE DIVISION.                                           00012500
196 0000-HOUSEKEEPING-ROUTINE.                                    00012600
197* * * * * * * * * * * * * * * * * * * * * * * * * * * * * * * * 00012700
198*    SET THE ERROR HANDLING CONDITIONS.                      * 00012800

396*    TERMINATE THE PROGRAM IF AN ERROR IS ENCOUNTERED.        * 00028500
397* * * * * * * * * * * * * * * * * * * * * * * * * * * * * * * * 00028600
398     IF  EIBAID = DFHCLEAR                                     00028700
399         THEN MOVE INVALID-SELECTION-MESSAGE TO MSG10          00028800
400             GO TO 0100-SEND-MAIN-MENU.                    ┌TRANCODE┐ 0
401     MOVE 'ENCOUNTERED AN ERROR' TO MESSAGE-AREA.          │MENU     │ 0
402     MOVE +20 TO MESSAGE-LENGTH.                           └─────────┘ 0
403     GO TO 0990-SEND-MESSAGE.                              ┌MENSELI┐ 0
404                                                           │       │ 0
405 0910-INVALID-SECURITY.                                    └───────┘
Text──────────────────────────────Level=02-Speed=5-Ins-Caps-Num-Scroll
F1=help F2=view F3=align F4=exchange F5=where F6=look-up  F9/F10=word-</> Escape
Split Join Refresh Edit
```

Figure 10.25. Animator Text features submenu.

- *Edit*—Fast path to the editor positioned at the current cursor location.

Reset. Reset allows a programmer to control the logic flow in an animation session. The reset function is located on the Animator main menu (see Figure 10.26). Press *R* of *Rst*.

This function does not perform reinitialization of data in Working-Storage or Linkage Section, nor does it close already opened files. In spite of this, it does provide some very useful capabilities.

- *Cursor-position*—Causes the statement at the cursor to be made the next executable statement.
- *Next*—Causes the executable statement following the current statement to become the next executable statement.
- *Start*—Makes the first executable statement in the program the current statement to be executed.
- *Quit-perform*—None of the remaining statements will be executed, and the next executable statement following the perform becomes the current statement to execute.

```
396*    TERMINATE THE PROGRAM IF AN ERROR IS ENCOUNTERED.         *  00028500
397* * * * * * * * * * * * * * * * * * * * * * * * * * * * * * * *  * 00028600
398     IF  EIBAID = DFHCLEAR                                         00028700
399        THEN MOVE INVALID-SELECTION-MESSAGE TO MSG10               00028800
400            GO TO 0100-SEND-MAIN-MENU.                             00028900
401     MOVE 'ENCOUNTERED AN ERROR' TO MESSAGE-AREA.                 00029000
402     MOVE +20 TO MESSAGE-LENGTH.                                  00029100
403     GO TO 0990-SEND-MESSAGE.                                     00029200
404                                                                  00029300
405 0910-INVALID-SECURITY.
406     MOVE SPACES TO MSG10.
407     MOVE INVALID-SECURITY-MSG TO MSG10.
408     MOVE DFHBMFSE TO MENIDA.
409     GO TO 0100-SEND-MAIN-MENU.
410
411 0980-END-PROGRAM.                                          ┌TRANCODE┐ 0
412* * * * * * * * * * * * * * * * * * * * * * * * * * * * * * *│MENU    │ 0
413*    TERMINATE THE PROGRAM IF OPTION 'X' HAS BEEN SELECTED.  └────────┘ 0
414* * * * * * * * * * * * * * * * * * * * * * * * * * * * * * ×┌MENSELI┐ 0
415     MOVE 'PROCESSING COMPLETE - GOODBYE' TO MESSAGE-AREA.  │       │ 0
416     MOVE +29 TO MESSAGE-LENGTH.                            └       ┘ 0
Reset-execution────────────────────────Level=02-Speed=5-Ins-Caps-Num-Scroll
F1=help F2=view F3=align F4=exchange F5=where F6=look-up  F9/F10=word-</> Escape
Cursor-position Next Start Quit-perform
```

Figure 10.26.   Reset logic flow submenu.

EMULATING A BATCH PROGRAM

MCO provides programmers with the capability of running batch programs, source code that contains no CICS commands, from the two emulation functions. Once the [F4] *Emulation with Animator* is selected (Figure 10.27), the programmer selects [F2] *Batch*.

CICS prompts for the name of the batch program to execute via a window. Type in the program name and press Enter to begin execution of the program. Upon completion of the program, any displays to terminal are displayed on the screen (see Figure 10.28).

MCO KEYBOARD MAPPING IN THE ANIMATOR

MCO provides standard mapping of some keys, whether it's an 84 or 101 keyboard, when animating CICS programs:

327x	PC equivalent
Clear	Ctrl + Home
Del	Del
Erase EOF	Ctrl + End
Erase Unprotected	Ctrl + PgDn
ENTER	Ctrl + ENTER or numeric keypad plus sign
Home	Home
Insert	Ins
PA1	Alt + 1
PA2	Alt + 2
PA3	Alt + 3
Reset	Escape
Return	

The standard configuration on a 101 keyboard is

PF1 through *PF12*	equals	*F1*	through *F12*	
PF13 through *PF24*	equals	*Alt + F1*	through *Alt + F12*	

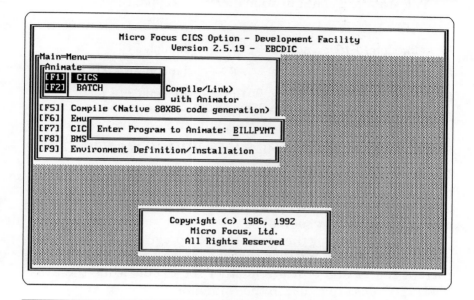

Figure 10.27.   Emulating a batch program.

```
Micro Focus CICS Option - Batch Interface with Micro Focus Animator
Micro Focus COBOL
Version 3.0.22 Copyright (C) 1985,1992 Micro Focus Ltd.
URN AXUPA/ZZ0/08239
  HAWTHORNE            444444444  RI  04456    6848
  MCGRAW              999999999  CT  06296    6848
  KARTOM              333444555  MA  07234    6848
TOTAL BILLS PROCESSED    17



***
```

Figure 10.28.   Output displays of batch program.

The standard configuration on an 84 keyboard is

PF1 through *PF10*	equals	*F1*	through *F10*
PF11 through *PF20*	equals	*Alt + F1*	through *Alt + F10*
PF21 through *PF24*	equals	*Ctrl + F1* through *Ctrl + F4*	

EDIT AND ANIMATE THE SAME PROGRAM USING OS/2

The Micro Focus COBOL Animator does not allow programs to be edited and animated in the same session. Developing applications under OS/2 allows programmers to edit a backup file and animate the current source file.

Prior to beginning the animation of a program, load the source code into the Editor and then save it as a .BAK file. This copies the current source and provides another file to edit while the .CBL/ .INT/.IDY files are in use in the Animator.

Within OS/2, open up a session containing MCO animating the file and another session editing the .BAK file (see Figure 10.29). This method works very well and saves writing any fixes down on paper.

When completed with the animation session, Escape from the Animator and save the .BAK file to .CBL. MCO will prompt that the file already exists and prompt for overriding the file or not. Respond with a yes.

OPEN AND CLOSE DATASETS

VSAM files accessed by a CICS program have to be opened for a program to use the file. When a file is defined to the CICS Resource Definition Tables, programmers can select to have all files opened at the time emulation is started or for files to be manually opened. If the selection is to open files manually, refer to Appendix A to the section covering the CSMT command.

CLOSE THE EMULATOR

When exiting an emulation session (either debugging or in prototype mode), programmers should conclude the session by termi-

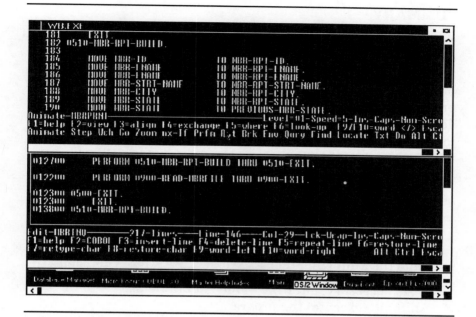

Figure 10.29. OS/2 edit and animate sessions.

nating the CICS emulation function. Refer to Appendix A to the sections covering either CSSF or CSMT commands.

Closing an MCO session by powering down may damage some of the CICS resource files or the data files for the application being tested. Always exit from MCO gracefully by signing off.

ERROR MESSAGES

When animating a program, error messages will be displayed for programmers on the lower left portion of the screen. Messages like this will appear:

```
message text (error nnn)
```

- Message text—Displays the text error message for the programmer.
- nnn—The actual error number that can be examined for more detailed information through the On-Line-Reference facility.

SUMMARY

Emulation and Animation provide programmers with very efficient testing tools. The menus are well laid out for quick and easy access. The Animator is quite robust, and it is unlikely that a programmer could utilize each feature when animating a single program. Over time, each feature might be used for different debugging needs. We have found a very effective method of testing to include at least the following steps:

- Establish break points:
    Establish breaks at key routines within the program.
    Use backtrack if suspected logic flow problem.
    Establish any conditional breaks.
- Query key fields:
    Evaluate program for key fields and set permanent monitors.
    As necessary, alter the value of data fields.
- Animate (execute) the program:
    Go at speeds 3 to 6; this varies for each programmer and machine.
    For close-quarter debugging, try Wch.
    Use the reset feature to restart within the program.
- Additional features—use as needed.

11

Compiling and Running CICS COBOL Programs

After a program has been checked and animated, source code files can be migrated to the mainframe. It might be more prudent to verify a program first by executing it outside of the animation process.

This chapter examines the Compile and Emulation Facility without Animation functions of MCO. Compiling, like checking, is a menu-driven process. JCL is not required; not even a link is required. Programs are compiled to optimize the intermediate (.INT) executable code produced by checking.

Is it really necessary to compile and run? Programs can be migrated to the mainframe without these steps, but these functions ensure that no temporary code placed in the logic during animation is accidentally left out of the source file. Using this function reassures that a program will work in its final state. Compiling programs and a final run test should be required steps of application development.

COMPILE (NATIVE 80X86 CODE GENERATION)

The Compile function is often overlooked as an integral part of an application development life cycle. Yet it should be considered as important a step as animating. The MCO compiler is definitely a powerful tool, allowing for checking during the testing and debugging stages, and compiling during the user and programmer checkout stages.

The Compile function is not used for syntax checking, normally not even for logic problems. This exception to the logic problem is in determining if code inserted in the program during animation has been added to the source file.

Compiles cannot be executed unless a previous error-free check has been performed and an intermediate executable file is created. MCO, via the Micro Focus compiler, uses the generated intermediate (.INT) code to create an optimized (.GNT or .OBJ) file.

Figure 11.1 shows the files used as input and output into the compiler. The compiled output is smaller and faster, and it can be used for prototyping applications (.GNT) or linking PC systems (.OBJ).

MCO DIRECTIVES

Mainframe compiles are controlled by passing parms to the compiler through Job Control Language (JCL). MCO substitutes directives for parms in controlling the compiler process. Directives may be passed to the compiler in several ways.

Micro Focus provides directives with functions similar to those on the mainframe. Others are syntactically different, but they serve the same function (e.g., PMAP—mainframe and ASMLIST—PC). Figure 11.1 shows that there are other methods for passing directives to the compiler:

- Embedded in source file
- From a command line
- In the COBOL.DIR file
- In the directive files WBXXXX.DIR

Groups of directives (directive sets) can be placed in PC files and accessed at compile time. The workbench menu system allows for directives to be keyed into a command line as well. As shown in Figure 11.1, the order of directive acceptance is hierarchical; directives set on a command line override any directives found in the COBOL.DIR file.

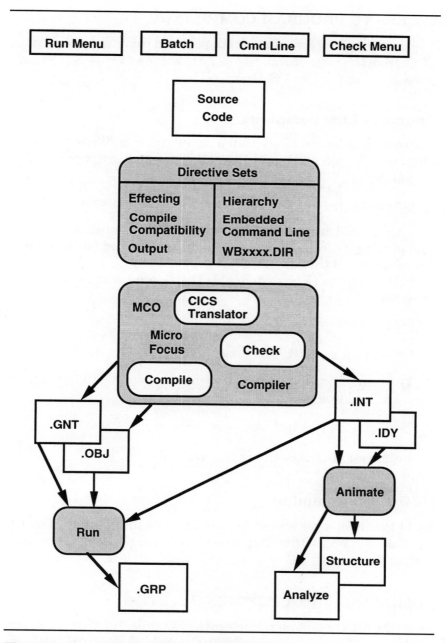

Figure 11.1.   MCO compiler file interfaces.

ACCESS TO PROGRAM COMPILING

Program compiling functions can be accessed from two areas within MCO: from the main menu, select [F5] *Compile (Native 80X86 code generation)*, or from an OS-command line.

Command Line Compiling

Programs can be compiled from a command line. When invoking a function from a command line, all commands are preceded by the following:

```
[XM switches] used for DOS based processing only
```

XM is used to invoke MCO and load the function into extended memory for processing. Switches can be provided to direct XM how to load the function.

Following the [XM switches] is the reference to MCO, keyed as either

```
MFCICS in a DOS environment
                or
PMFCICS in an OS/2 environment
```

The command syntax for executing the Compile function from the command line is

```
[XM switches] MFCICS NCG program
```

* Program: identifies the source code file.

MCO Menu Compiling

MCO provides a compiling function on the main menu. The remaining sections of this chapter will examine the compile process in detail.

COMPILING FROM THE MENU SYSTEM

From the MCO main menu, select the Compile function, as shown in Figure 11.2, by pressing [F5] *Compile (Native 80X86 code generation)*.

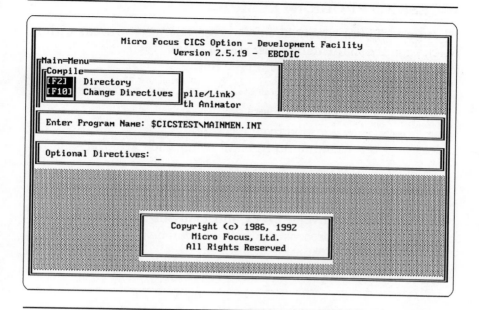

Figure 11.2.   Invoking the Compile process.

When using the Compile feature, it is not necessary to type in the program name and directives. A function key is provided for searching for files:

- *F2=Dir*—Searches directory for all files with an extension of .INT.
- *F10=Optional directives*—Allows entering of directives to be selected and used with the compile.

After typing in any directives, press Enter to accept them. The compile screen redisplays after either (1) pressing Enter from the directives window box, or (2) pressing Escape from the directives window box. Once the directives and source file name are entered, press Enter to initiate the compile of a program. Figure 11.3 displays the results of a successful compile.

If syntax errors do occur, return to the Check feature to debug

```
Micro Focus CICS Option Native 80X86 Code Generation Interface
Micro Focus COBOL
Version 3.0.22 Copyright (C) 1985,1992 Micro Focus Ltd.
URN AXUPA/ZZ0/08239
* Starting code generation
* Micro Focus COBOL Code Generator              Version 3.0.22
* Copyright (C) 1985,1992 Micro Focus Ltd.          URN  AXUPA/ZZ0/08239
* Accepted - OMF(GNT)
* Accepted - GNT"C:\MFCICS\TEST\MAINMEN.GNT"
* Accepted - OMF(GNT)
* Data = 000002296 Code = 000006271




***
```

Figure 11.3. Successfully completed compile.

the syntax errors. When syntax errors are detected, the following message appears:

```
Errors detected during creation of intermediate code
```

PROTOTYPE PROGRAMS

The Emulation Facility without Animator function is suited for two forms of program verification:

- Programmer
- Customer

Programmer Verification. During the animation of a program it is possible to insert temporary code into a program. Code inserted through the Animator main menu feature Do is executed as soon as the Enter key is pressed. This particular type of statement may be very useful in setting values of specific data fields that control the logic flow.

COBOL statements can be inserted into a program's logic during an animation session from within the Break feature. By using the Break and then the Do features, programmers can insert code that can be repetitively executed during a debugging session. This code may need to be inserted into the source CO-BOL file to correct some logic error, for example.

Programmers taking advantage of the Compile and Run features can insure that no code is forgotten from the source file. No one would question the fact that the proper course in this instance would be to do the following:

- Edit and check the source file
- Animate the modified source file

Compile and Run should serve as final verification.

Customer Checkout. During a project's life cycle, requirements can become vague. It is not uncommon for conversations to take place that necessitate program changes. On occasion, documentation to initiate the change never arrives, or the change is just forgotten.

Using the Compile and Emulation Facility without Animation features, the customer can validate that the application meets their requirements. If any design issues arise, they can be resolved prior to migrating the source code file to the mainframe.

EMULATION WITHOUT ANIMATION FROM THE MENU

To execute a program from the MCO main menu, select [F6] *Emulation Facility without Animation* to invoke the process (see Figure 11.4). Once the emulation facility is invoked, programmers can select from the Run submenu to emulate a CICS on-line program or a batch program:

- [F1] *CICS*
- [F2] *Batch*

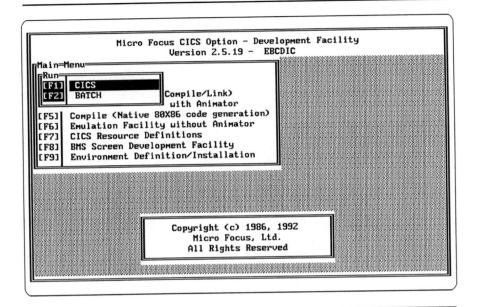

Figure 11.4. Emulation without Animation.

For the purpose of this book, the MCO CICS on-line environment (*F1 CICS—see Figure 11.4*) will be the focus. The batch section of this chapter covers access to emulating a batch program from within MCO.

After the emulation screen is presented, a transaction ID is typed in and Enter (Ctrl + Enter, or use the + [plus] sign on the numeric keypad of a 101-key keyboard) is pressed to begin the execution of a program. As shown in Figure 11.5, the transaction ID can be typed in with or without clearing the screen. To clear the screen and then type in a transaction ID, press Ctrl + Home.

In Emulation using Animation, once the transaction ID is entered and Ctrl + Enter is pressed, MCO positions to the first executable statement of a program. When emulating a program without using the Animator, MCO does not display lines of code in a program. Instead, in an on-line application, the first screen accessed is displayed (see Figure 11.6).

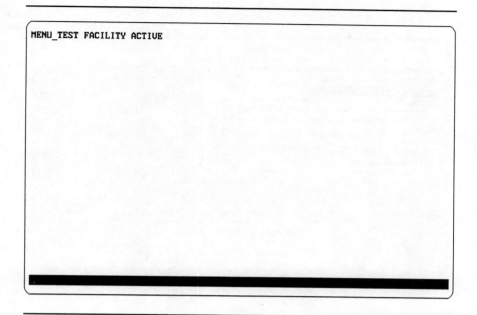

Figure 11.5.   CICS emulation region screen.

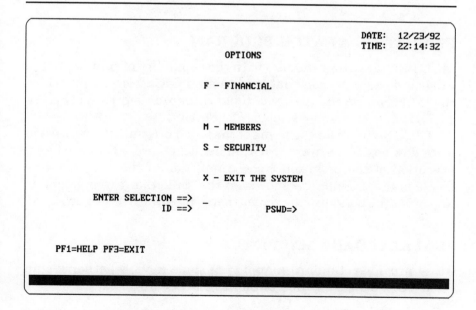

Figure 11.6.   Initial non-animation display.

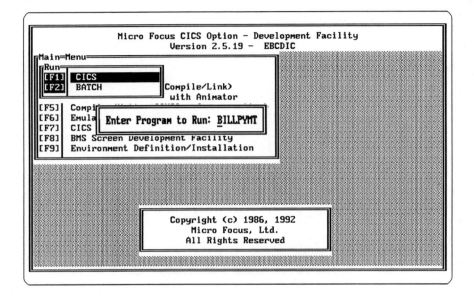

Figure 11.7.   Initiating a batch program.

EMULATING A BATCH PROGRAM

MCO provides programmers with the capability of running batch programs, source code that contains no CICS commands. Once the [F6] *Emulation Facility without Animator* is pressed (Figure 11.7), the programmer selects [F2] *Batch*.

CICS prompts for the name of the batch program to execute via a window box. Type in the program name and press Enter to begin execution of the program. Upon completion of the program, any displays to terminal are shown on the screen, or three asterisks appear at the bottom of the screen (batch program) (see Figure 11.8).

MCO KEYBOARD MAPPING

MCO provides standard mapping of some keys, whether it's an 84 or 101 keyboard, when animating CICS programs:

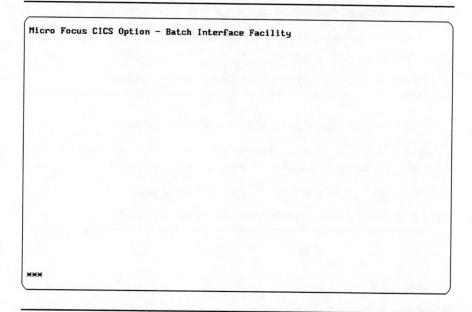

```
Micro Focus CICS Option - Batch Interface Facility




















***
```

Figure 11.8. Batch output results with no animation.

327x	PC equivalent
Clear	Ctrl + Home
Del	Del
Erase EOF	Ctrl + End
Erase Unprotected	Ctrl + PgDn
ENTER	Ctrl + ENTER or numeric keypad plus sign
Home	Home
Insert	Ins
PA1	Alt + 1
PA2	Alt + 2
PA3	Alt + 3
Reset	Escape
Return	↵

The standard configuration on a 101 keyboard is

PF1 through *PF12*	equals	*F1*	through *F12*
PF13 through *PF24*	equals	*Alt* + *F1*	through *Alt* + *F12*

The standard configuration on an 84 keyboard is

PF1 through *PF10*	equals	*F1*	through *F10*
PF11 through *PF20*	equals	*Alt* + *F1*	through *Alt* + *F10*
PF21 through *PF24*	equals	*Ctrl* + *F1* through *Ctrl* + *F4*	

SUMMARY

The Compile and Emulation Facility without Animator features are used for demonstrations of an application's function to the customer community. By using these features in place of Check and Animate, the customer will see exactly what they would see in the production environment.

Mainframe cycles can be reduced if some or all design discrepancies or problems are caught on the PC. With the capability to execute batch files for large numbers of program compiles, a final checkout can be performed fairly quickly. The time spent here is well worth consideration as part of any application development schedule.

12

Using Temporary Storage and Transient Data in MCO

As the complexity of CICS applications grows, and as the inter-connectivity between CICS systems or CICS applications expands, data may need to be stored for future handling. It may only need to be stored for short periods of time, but not indefinitely. This type of data is often a poor candidate for permanent storage files. Temporary files may be the answer.

In the modern menu-driven applications, data is passed between tasks and transactions within CICS environments. This chapter examines various topics relating to alternative methods of storing data in a temporary manner.

CICS DATA

CICS applications process data from three basic file types:

- Permanent data—Data stored on physical devices, available from the time a record is added until it is deleted.
- Temporary data—Data needed for a limited time. The data can be used by other applications as long as the other tasks are in the same CICS region.
- Transient data—Data is temporary in nature, but accessible to applications within or outside the CICS region.

Depending on the need for the temporary data, either a Temporary Storage (TS) or a Transient Data (TD) queue can be used.

DATA STORAGE TECHNIQUES

CICS provides various temporary storage techniques for programmers, so TS and TD queues will be examined more closely in subsequent sections. Often overlooked as a temporary storage area for data is the CICS DFHCOMMAREA.

Unlike TS or TD queues, the DFHCOMMAREA cannot store data for later access by other applications in or out of CICS. The DFHCOMMAREA is useful for passing data between two tasks. The DFHCOMMAREA is managed by CICS, and, other than defining the data fields, no additional code for reads or writes is required in a program.

CICS allocates and deallocates the size of the DFHCOMMAREA from task to task, depending on the receiving program's need. On the mainframe, IBM recommends that the DFHCOMMAREA not exceed 24K. A good rule of thumb is to define a generic DFHCOMMAREA for an application and then have each program code in the DFHCOMMAREA for the amount of data it needs.

TEMPORARY STORAGE QUEUE

Temporary Storage (TS) queues allow data to be stored in the CICS environment until one of two events occurs:

- CICS system programmers "shut down" CICS
- A transaction deletes a TS queue

When processing a TS queue, it helps to think of it as just another file that records are written to and read from. TS queues are managed in a program via the TS queue commands.

TS Queue Commands

TS queues can be managed with three commands:

- WRITEQ TS
- READQ TS
- DELETEQ TS

Each command supports the use of options that further define aspects of the TS queue. Other than where the data is written to or read from, no options are provided for data management. The TS queue is used to store data that has already been edited somewhere else in a program's logic.

The WRITEQ TS command is generally the first coded and logically processed in a program, unless, of course, a program is attempting to access a TS queue that was created by another task. The following are the syntax and options for a WRITEQ TS command:

```
EXEC CICS WRITEQ TS

          QUEUE(ts-name)

          FROM(ts-data-area)

          [LENGTH(data-value)]

          [ITEM(data-value)]

          [REWRITE]

          [MAIN I AUXILIARY]

          [NOSUSPEND]

          [HANDLE I NOHANDLE I [RESP ()]]

END-EXEC.
```

It is used to write a new record to an existing queue, establish a new queue if one does not exist, or write over an existing record. Those options enclosed in brackets [ ] are optional items.

- QUEUE(ts-name)—A data area that identifies the eight-byte name of the TS queue. A good practice is to define the queue name as
  first four characters—Terminal ID, moved from the EIBTRMID data field.
  last four characters—Transaction ID, moved from the EIBTRNID data field.

- FROM(ts-data-area)—Identifies a data area or a literal containing the data. The READQ TS command requires that a data area be used. Because of this, using a data area is preferred.
- LENGTH(data-value)—Defines the length of a record as S9(4) COMP.
- ITEM(data-value)—Identifies a specific record in the TS queue to be written over when used with the REWRITE option. If REWRITE is not supplied, the field is ignored and CICS returns the record number in this field.
- MAIN or AUXILIARY—Identifies how the temporary storage file should be stored.
- NOSUSPEND—Informs CICS that the program should not be suspended when insufficient space is available to write to the TS queue. When TS space is short, CICS returns to the program the error condition NOSPACE.
- HANDLE | NOHANDLE | RESP ()—In the event of error conditions, identifies to CICS what action CICS should take. CICS default action is to HANDLE the error condition.
    HANDLE—Go to the specified routines in the EXEC CICS. HANDLE CONDITION statement and perform the logic found in that routine.
    NOHANDLE—Instructs CICS to ignore the error condition.
    RESP ()—An area defined in a COBOL program where CICS should place the condition code returned. The program can interpret the error condition and make the appropriate response. When using the RESP () option, NOHANDLE should also be coded.

Three potential error conditions can arise when using the WRITEQ TS command. They can be coded in a CICS HANDLE CONDITION or ignored. It is often better to code for them and control the program's actions if these conditions happen:

- ITEMERR—The item number used for a WRITEQ TS is invalid; the CICS abend code is an AEIZ.
- QIDERR—The TS queue named could not be found; the CICS abend code is an AEYH.
- INVREQ—The request is invalid; the CICS abend code is an AEIP.

The READQ TS command is used to read a TS queue by the current task or other tasks. The following are the syntax and options for a READQ TS command:

EXEC CICS READQ TS

        QUEUE(ts-name)

        INTO(ts-data-area) I SET(pointer)

        [LENGTH(data-value)]

        [ITEM(data-value)]

        [NEXT]

        [HANDLE I NOHANDLE I [RESP ()]]

END-EXEC.

The READQ TS is used to read existing records from a TS queue. It can be used to read a specific record or to read an entire TS queue sequentially. Those options enclosed in brackets [ ] are optional items.

- QUEUE(ts-name)—A data area that identifies the eight-byte name of the TS queue. A good practice is to define the queue name as

   first four characters—Terminal ID, moved from the EIBTRMID data field.
   last four characters—Transaction ID, moved from the EIBTRNID data field.
- INTO(ts-data-area)—Identifies a data area that data is read into in a working-storage area.
- SET(pointer)—Identifies a data area that data is read into; specifies the linkage section pointer that points to a TS queue.
- LENGTH(data-value)—Defines the length of a record as S9(4) COMP; contains the length of the record after a record is read.
- ITEM(data-value)—Identifies a specific record in the TS queue to be read; using it identifies that a record can be read, written, or updated.

- NEXT—Set up the read of a TS queue in a sequential manner.
- HANDLE | NOHANDLE | RESP ()—In the event of error conditions, identifies to CICS what action CICS should take. CICS default action is to HANDLE the error condition.

> HANDLE—Go to the specified routines in the EXEC CICS. HANDLE CONDITION statement and perform the logic found in that routine.
> NOHANDLE—Instructs CICS to ignore the error condition.
> RESP ()—An area defined in a COBOL program where CICS should place the condition code returned. The program can interpret the error condition and make the appropriate response. When using the RESP () option, NOHANDLE should also be coded.

Three potential error conditions can arise when using the READQ TS command. Each can be coded in a CICS HANDLE CONDITION or ignored. It is often better to code for them and control the program's actions if these conditions happen:

- ITEMERR—The item number used for a READQ TS does not exist in the TS queue; the CICS abend code is an AEIZ.
- QIDERR—The TS queue named could not be found; the CICS abend code is an AEYH.
- LENGERR—The record read is larger than the specified LENGTH option; the CICS abend code is an AEIV.

The DELETEQ TS command is coded to delete an entire TS queue. Individual records cannot be deleted from a TS queue, but they can be marked with a delete indicator if such a field is defined on the TS queue record. The following are the syntax and options for a DELETEQ TS:

```
EXEC CICS DELETEQ TS
          QUEUE(ts-name)
          [HANDLE | NOHANDLE | [RESP ()]]
END-EXEC.
```

Deleting a TS queue is frequently done in programs just prior to writing a TS queue. Those options enclosed in brackets [] are optional items.

- QUEUE(ts-name)—A data area that identifies the eight-byte name of the TS queue. A good practice is to define the queue name as

   first four characters—Terminal ID, moved from the EIBTRMID data field.
   last four characters—Transaction ID, moved from the EIBTRNID data field.
- HANDLE | NOHANDLE | RESP ()—In the event of error conditions, identifies to CICS what action CICS should take. CICS default action is to HANDLE the error condition.

   HANDLE—Go to the specified routines in the EXEC CICS. HANDLE CONDITION statement and perform the logic found in that routine.
   NOHANDLE—Instructs CICS to ignore the error condition.
   RESP ()—An area defined in a COBOL program where CICS should place the condition code returned. The program can interpret the error condition and make the appropriate response. When using the RESP () option, NOHANDLE should also be coded.

One potential error condition can arise when using the DELETEQ TS command. It can be coded in a CICS HANDLE CONDITION or ignored. It is often better to code for it and control the program's actions if this condition happens:

- QIDERR—The TS queue named could not be found; the CICS abend code is an AEYH.

Main vs. Auxiliary Storage

Using temporary storage can cause performance problems and even some deadlock-type conditions with high-volume transactions or when heavily using temporary storage.

Two types of temporary storage are available in CICS applications:

- MAIN—Data stored is accessible without physical I/O when reading or writing the data. Data stored in MAIN is not recoverable in the event of a system crash.
- AUXILIARY—Data is usually stored as a VSAM ESDS file and is recoverable in the event of a system crash.

Generally, MAIN should be used when the data being stored is only a few hundred bytes. AUXILIARY is best selected when the data cannot be lost in the event of a crash. CICS and MCO search both MAIN and AUXILIARY storage if the READQ TS does not specify either.

One or Many Records in the Queue

Temporary storage queues can contain one or more records in a queue. TS queues storing only a single record can be accessed by just identifying the queue name. TS queues storing multiple records require access to the queue using either the NEXT or ITEM(data value). Multiple records are stored in a queue by a relative position. In this manner, the storage of fixed or variable records has no bearing on the data in a queue.

TS Queue Uses

TS queues provide application programmers with four useful reasons to use temporary storage:

- Scratch Pad Area—Temporary storage queues are used frequently for intermediate work file areas.
- Program-to-Program Data Transfer—Application programs often build data to pass between programs. The data is available until the queue is deleted or CICS comes down.
- Pseudoconversation—Temporary storage can be used to transmit a pseudoconversational operation. A task initiates and stores data in a queue and then ends. Later the task is reinitiated and the data is still available for use.

- Page Storing—Temporary storage queues are often used to store consecutive pages of data generated from BMS to allow operators to page through the data on a terminal.

Using a TS Queue to Fill a MAP

As noted earlier, TS queues are often used to read records from a file, store the data in memory, and then read to build BMS MAP images for display on a terminal. With the data in a queue, the task can end and display data in a formatted manner to the terminal. Operators can press [F8] (scroll down) or [F7] (scroll up) to view more data.

To begin the process, the TS queue must be defined in working storage (see Figure 12.1). TS queues can be defined in the linkage section using some of the older languages. For demo purposes, the language selected is VS COBOL II, release 3.

Areas of note in the definition of a TS queue are the queue

```
┌─MBRINQ.CBL─────────────────────────────────────────────────────────────┐
│         01   TSQ-WORK-AREAS.                                            │
│              05   TSQ-FILE-NAME.                                        │
│                   07   TSQ-NAME-TERMINAL        PIC X(4).               │
│                   07   TSQ-NAME-TRANSID         PIC X(4).               │
│              05   TSQ-LENGTH                     PIC S9(4) COMP VALUE +80.│
│              05   TSQ-ITEM                       PIC S9(4) COMP VALUE +0. │
│         01   TSQ-MEMBER-RECORD.                                         │
│              05   TSQ-MBR-ID          PIC X(04).                        │
│              05   FILLER              PIC X(03).                        │
│              05   TSQ-NAME.                                             │
│                   10   TSQ-LNAME       PIC X(15).                       │
│                   10   FILLER          PIC X(06).                       │
│                   10   TSQ-FNAME       PIC X(12).                       │
│                   10   FILLER          PIC X(06).                       │
│              05   TSQ-ADDR.                                             │
│                   10   TSQ-STRT-NAME   PIC X(14).                       │
│                   10   TSQ-CITY        PIC X(12).                       │
│                   10   TSQ-STATE       PIC X(02).                       │
│         _    05   TSQ-SPECIAL-NOTES    PIC X(01).                       │
│ Edit─MBRINQ────────459─lines────Line─81────Col─8────────Wrap─Ins─Caps─Num─Scroll│
│ F1=help F2=library F3=load-file F4=save-file F5=split-line F6=join-line F7=print│
│ F8=calculate F9=untype-word-left F10=delete-word-right                  │
└─────────────────────────────────────────────────────────────────────────┘
```

Figure 12.1.   Temporary storage queue definition.

```
┌─MBRINQ.CBL────────────────────────────────────────────────────────────────◆
│       0500-LOAD-TSQ.
│           MOVE EIBTRMID TO TSQ-NAME-TERMINAL.
│           MOVE EIBTRNID TO TSQ-NAME-TRANSID.
│
│           EXEC CICS DELETEQ TS
│               QUEUE(TSQ-FILE-NAME)
│               NOHANDLE
│           END-EXEC.
│
│           IF WS-COMM-MBR-ID IS EQUAL TO LOW-VALUES OR SPACES
│           THEN
│                  MOVE ZEROES TO MBR-ID
│           ELSE
│                  MOVE WS-COMM-MBR-ID TO MBR-ID.
│
│           EXEC CICS STARTBR
│               DATASET('MBRFILE')
│               RIDFLD(MBR-ID)
│           END-EXEC.
│
├────────────────────────────────────────────────────────────────────────────
│Edit-MBRINQ────────458-lines────Line-227────Col-8────────Wrap-Ins-Caps-Num-Scroll
│F1=help F2=library F3=load-file F4=save-file F5=split-line F6=join-line F7=print
│F8=calculate F9=untype-word-left F10=delete-word-right
└────────────────────────────────────────────────────────────────────────────
```

Figure 12.2. Delete existing queue before read.

name, queue length, and queue item. The specific names are un-important, but the fields need to be defined as indicated in the display.

Once the TS queue is defined, various procedure division routines need to utilize a TS queue. The following example is based on reading data from a physical VSAM KSDS file and storing it in a TS queue for later processing in the program. The use of VSAM can easily be replaced with a DL/I or DB2 file.

Although not a requirement, prior to writing a new queue it is a good idea to delete first any existing queue that this specific task might have created. As shown in Figure 12.2, this program (MBRINQ—member inquiry program) executes a DELETEQ TS prior to initiating a browse (STARTBR) against a physical file.

After a file is opened to browse, data can be read (READNEXT) and subsequently written (WRITEQ TS) to the TS queue (see Figure 12.3). Once the data is read, usually in a loop routine, the data is then written to a TS queue via another loop routine.

```
┌─MBRINQ.CBL────────────────────────────────────────────────────────────────┐
│              EXEC CICS READNEXT                                             │
│                    DATASET('MBRFILE')                                       │
│                    RIDFLD(MBR-ID)                                           │
│                    INTO(MEMBER-MASTER-RECORD)                               │
│              END-EXEC.                                                      │
│              IF BROWSE-COUNT < 45                                           │
│              THEN                                                           │
│                  NEXT SENTENCE                                              │
│              ELSE                                                           │
│                  GO TO 0600-EXIT.                                           │
│              MOVE MBR-ID                TO TSQ-MBR-ID.                       │
│              MOVE MBR-LNAME             TO TSQ-LNAME.                        │
│              MOVE MBR-ADDR              TO TSQ-ADDR.                         │
│              ADD +1 TO TSQ-ITEM.                                            │
│              EXEC CICS WRITEQ TS                                            │
│                    QUEUE(TSQ-FILE-NAME)                                     │
│                    FROM(TSQ-MEMBER-RECORD)                                  │
│                    LENGTH(TSQ-LENGTH)                                       │
│          _   END-EXEC.                                                      │
├────────────────────────────────────────────────────────────────────────────┤
│ Edit─MBRINQ────────452-lines────Line-287────Col-8────────Wrap-Ins-Caps-Num-Scroll │
│ F1=help F2=library F3=load-file F4=save-file F5=split-line F6=join-line F7=print   │
│ F8=calculate F9=untype-word-left F10=delete-word-right                      │
└────────────────────────────────────────────────────────────────────────────┘
```

Figure 12.3.   Reading data and storing in TS.

After all the data is read, the file or cursor should be closed. For this example (Figure 12.4) use the ENDBR command to close the VSAM file.

At this point data is stored in a temporary storage queue for use later in this program (see Figure 12.5). As a TS queue is read, data can be formatted and moved to the MAP display area and displayed to a terminal, as shown in Figure 12.6.

TRANSIENT DATA QUEUE

Transient Data (TD) queues are often a confusing item because of the similarity to TS queues. Each function stores data in a temporary manner using the same basic commands. TD queues store data for subsequent program use, but the program can be an on-line CICS program or a batch program. When building storage areas for a TD queue, data can be stored for two distinct purposes:

```
┌─MBRINQ.CBL────────────────────────────────────────────────────◆
│       0998-END-OF-FILE.
│
│           EXEC CICS ENDBR
│                   DATASET('MBRFILE')
│           END-EXEC.
│
│           MOVE +0 TO TSQ-ITEM.
│           MOVE  1 TO BROWSE-COUNT.
│           PERFORM 0700-BUILD-MAP THRU 0700-EXIT
│               UNTIL BROWSE-COUNT IS GREATER THAN 14.
│
│           MOVE 'Y' TO WS-COMM-SCRN-IND.
│           GO TO 0100-SEND-INQUIRY-SCREEN.
│
│       0998-EXIT.
│           EXIT.
│
│       0999-END-PROGRAM.
│           IF  EIBAID = DFHCLEAR
Edit-MBRINQ────────449-lines────Line-414────Col-8────────Wrap-Ins-Caps-Num-Scroll
F1=help F2=library F3=load-file F4=save-file F5=split-line F6=join-line F7=print
F8=calculate F9=untype-word-left F10=delete-word-right
```

Figure 12.4. Closing the VSAM KSDS file.

```
┌─MBRINQ.CBL────────────────────────────────────────────────────◆
│           EXEC CICS READQ TS
│                   QUEUE(TSQ-FILE-NAME)
│                   LENGTH(TSQ-LENGTH)
│                   INTO(MEMBER-MASTER-RECORD)
│                   ITEM(TSQ-ITEM)
│           END-EXEC.
│           IF BROWSE-COUNT < 15
│           THEN
│               NEXT SENTENCE
│           ELSE
│               GO TO 0700-EXIT.
│           MOVE SPACE          TO BROWSE-SEL-IND.
│           MOVE MBR-ID         TO BROWSE-EMPNO.
│           MOVE MBR-LNAME      TO BROWSE-LNAME.
│           MOVE MBR-ADDR       TO BROWSE-ADDR.
│           IF BROWSE-COUNT IS EQUAL TO 01
│           THEN
│               MOVE BROWSE-LINE TO LINE010
Edit-MBRINQ────────449-lines────Line-311────Col-8────────Wrap-Ins-Caps-Num-Scroll
F1=help F2=library F3=load-file F4=save-file F5=split-line F6=join-line F7=print
F8=calculate F9=untype-word-left F10=delete-word-right
```

Figure 12.5. Reading the previously stored queue.

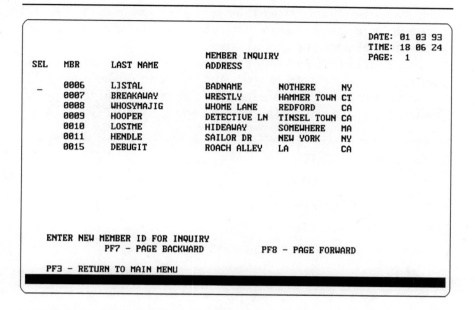

```
                                                          DATE: 01 03 93
                                                          TIME: 18 06 24
                                  MEMBER INQUIRY          PAGE:  1
  SEL   MBR      LAST NAME        ADDRESS

   _    0006     LISTAL           BADNAME       NOTHERE      NY
        0007     BREAKAWAY        WRESTLY       HAMMER TOWN  CT
        0008     WHOSYMAJIG       WHOME LANE    REDFORD      CA
        0009     HOOPER           DETECTIVE LN  TINSEL TOWN  CA
        0010     LOSTME           HIDEAWAY      SOMEWHERE    MA
        0011     HENDLE           SAILOR DR     NEW YORK     NY
        0015     DEBUGIT          ROACH ALLEY   LA           CA




      ENTER NEW MEMBER ID FOR INQUIRY
              PF7 - PAGE BACKWARD            PF8 - PAGE FORWARD

      PF3 - RETURN TO MAIN MENU
```

Figure 12.6.   Screen built from TS queue data.

- Intrapartition access—Data is collected and allocated within the CICS region. Data can only be stored as Direct Access Datasets on DASD.
- Extrapartition access—Data is collected on-line but stored for external access to the data. Data can be stored on any sequential device managed by QSAM.

TD Queue Commands

TD queue commands are similar to those of a TS queue, but not all of the options are supported. The three commands used to manage TD queues are the following:

- WRITEQ TD
- READQ TD
- DELETEQ TD

Each command supports the use of options to further define aspects of the TD queue. Other than where the data is written to or read from, no options are provided for data management. The TD queue is being used to store data that has already been edited somewhere else in a program's logic.

The WRITEQ TD command is used to write records to the queue. Each new record is written to the end of the queue. TD queue data is not rewritten; only new data is added to a queue. The following are the syntax and options for a WRITEQ TD:

```
EXEC CICS WRITEQ TD
          QUEUE('TD-name')
          FROM(TD-data-area)
          [LENGTH(data-value)]
          [HANDLE I NOHANDLE I [RESP ()]]
END-EXEC.
```

Those options enclosed in brackets [] are optional items.

- QUEUE(TD-name)—The four-character name of the transient data queue.
- FROM(TD-data-area)—Identifies a data area or a literal containing the data.
- LENGTH(data-value)—Defines the length of the record as S9(4) COMP.
- HANDLE I NOHANDLE I RESP ()—In the event of error conditions, identifies to CICS what action CICS should take. CICS default action is to HANDLE the error condition.
    HANDLE—Go to the specified routines in the EXEC CICS. HANDLE CONDITION statement and perform the logic found in that routine.
    NOHANDLE—Instructs CICS to ignore the error condition.
    RESP()—An area defined in a COBOL program where CICS should place the condition code returned. The program can interpret the error condition and make the appropriate response. When using the RESP() option, NOHANDLE should also be coded.

Two potential error conditions can happen when using the WRITEQ TD command. They can be coded for in a CICS HANDLE CONDITION or ignored. It is often better to code for them and control the program's actions when the conditions happen:

- QIDERR—The TD queue named could not be found; the CICS abend code is an AEYH.
- INVREQ—The request is invalid; the CICS abend code is an AEIP.

The READQ TD command is coded to read a TD queue by the current task or other tasks including batch programs. The following are the syntax and options for a READQ TD command:

```
EXEC CICS READQ TD
          QUEUE('TD-name')
          INTO(TD-data-area) I SET(pointer)
          [LENGTH(data-value)]
          [NOSUSPEND]
          [HANDLE I NOHANDLE I [RESP ()]]
END-EXEC.
```

The READQ TD is used to read records sequentially from a TD queue. As records are read, the next sequential record becomes the first record in the TD queue (read destructive). If the TD queue has been defined as reusable, the space released during a READQ TD can be reused. Those options within the brackets [] are optional items.

- QUEUE(TD-name)—The four-character name of the transient data queue.
- INTO(TD-data-area)—Identifies a working-storage data area that data is read into.
- SET(pointer)—Identifies a data area that data is read into; specifies the linkage section pointer that points to a TD queue.

- LENGTH(data-value)—Defines the length of the record as S9(4) COMP; contains the length of the record after the record that is read.
- NOSUSPEND—Informs CICS that the program does not wish to be suspended when insufficient space is available to write to the TD queue. When TD space is short, CICS returns to the program with the error condition (NOSPACE).
- HANDLE | NOHANDLE | RESP ()—In the event of error conditions, identifies to CICS what action CICS should take. CICS default action is to HANDLE the error condition.
  HANDLE—Go to the specified routines in the EXEC CICS. HANDLE CONDITION statement and perform the logic found in that routine.
  NOHANDLE—Instructs CICS to ignore the error condition.
  RESP()—An area defined in a COBOL program where CICS should place the condition code returned. The program can interpret the error condition and make the appropriate response. When using the RESP() option, NOHANDLE should also be coded.

Two potential error conditions can happen when using the READQ TD command and can be coded for in a CICS HANDLE CONDITION or ignored. It is often better to code for them and control the program's actions when the conditions happen:

- QIDERR—The TD queue named could not be found; the CICS abend code is an AEYH.
- LENGERR—The record read is larger than the specified LENGTH option; the CICS abend code is an AEIV.

The DELETEQ TD command is coded to delete an entire TD queue. The following are the syntax and options for a DELETEQ TD command:

```
EXEC CICS DELETEQ TD
          QUEUE(TD-name)
          [HANDLE | NOHANDLE | [RESP ()]]
END-EXEC.
```

Deleting a TD queue is frequently done in programs just prior to writing a TD queue. Those options enclosed in brackets [] are optional items.

- QUEUE(TD-name)—The four-character name of the transient data queue.
- HANDLE | NOHANDLE | RESP ()—In the event of error conditions, identifies to CICS what action CICS should take. CICS default action is to HANDLE the error condition.
    HANDLE—Go to the specified routines in the EXEC CICS. HANDLE CONDITION statement and perform the logic found in that routine.
    NOHANDLE—Instructs CICS to ignore the error condition.
    RESP()—An area defined in a COBOL program where CICS should place the condition code returned. The program can interpret the error condition and make the appropriate response. When using the RESP() option, NOHANDLE should also be coded.

One potential error condition can happen when using the DELETEQ TD command, which can be coded for in a CICS HANDLE CONDITION or ignored. It is often better to code for them and control the program's actions when the conditions happen:

- QIDERR—The TD queue named could not be found; the CICS abend code is an AEYH.

Destination Control Table (DCT)

Transient Data queues must be defined in the CICS resource table DCT. Separate entry is made for each TD queue in use. The four-character TD queue name is similar to a batch JCL DD name. A specific transaction can be triggered from the DCT table and the trans ID must be defined in the Program Control Table (PCT). Two types of TD queues can be defined:

- INTRA—Intrapartition (Figure 12.7) dataset used to store data for passing within a CICS region.
- EXTRA—Extrapartition (Figure 12.8) dataset used to store data for access by programs outside of the CICS region.

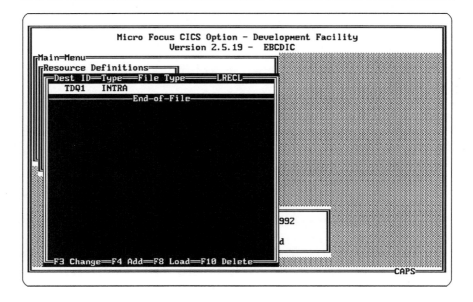

Figure 12.7.   Defining a Temporary Storage queue.

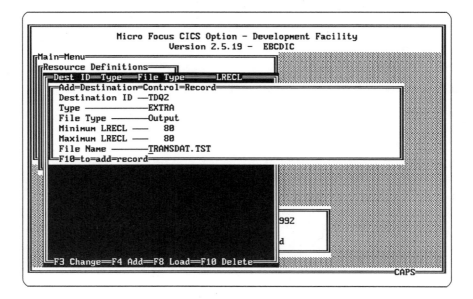

Figure 12.8.   Defining a Transient Data queue.

TD Uses

TD queues provide application programmers with three useful reasons to use Transient Data:

- Collecting data from other terminals—Collect data on an on-line terminal and then use the data in a batch program to update the master file.
- Store terminal output—Using intrapartition datasets to store reports that will be viewed later within the CICS region.
- Transferring data between two CICS regions or between a CICS region and a batch application.

Using a TD Queue to Fill a MAP

The following sample demonstrates using a Transient Data queue to pass a key search field from one program to another. The MBR-ID field value is stored in a TD queue (TDQ1), as shown in Figure 12.9.

```
654
655
656        IF MBRIDI = ZEROES                                    00024600
657        THEN                                                   00024600
658            MOVE ZEROES              TO MBR-SKILL-ID           00024600
659            MOVE SPACES TO MSG10
660            MOVE MEMBER-ID-NOT-ENTERED        TO MSG10
661            MOVE DFHBMFSE TO MBRIDA
662            GO TO 0100-SEND-MAIN-MENU
663        ELSE
664            NEXT SENTENCE.                                     00024600
665
666        MOVE MBRIDI        TO WS-COMM-MBR-ID.                  00024600
667        MOVE MBRLNMEI      TO WS-COMM-MBR-LNAME.               00024600
668        MOVE MBRFNMEI      TO WS-COMM-MBR-FNAME.               00024600
669        MOVE MBRSKILI      TO WS-COMM-MBR-SKILL.               00024600
670
671        EXEC CICS WRITEQ TD
672             QUEUE('TDQ1')                                    ┌MBRIDI┐
673             FROM(MBRIDI)                                      │0006  │
674             LENGTH(4)                                         └──────┘
Options-MBRMEN────────────────────────────Level=04-Speed=5-Ins-Caps-Num-Scroll
F1=help F2=analyzer on/off F3=structure/code F4=save-analysis F5=save-structure
F6=display F7=print
```

Figure 12.9.   Writing a record to the TD queue.

```
478            EXEC CICS XCTL
479                PROGRAM('MAINMEN')
480            END-EXEC.
481
482     PERFORM 0300-RECEIVE-MAP THRU 0300-EXIT.
483     EXEC CICS RECEIVE
484         MAP('MBRINQ')
485         INTO(MBRINQI)
486     END-EXEC.
487     PERFORM 0050-TDQ-READ THRU 0050-EXIT.
488
489
490 0050-TDQ-READ.
491     EXEC CICS READQ TD
492         QUEUE('TDQ1')
493         INTO(WS-COMM-MBR-ID)
494         LENGTH(TDQ-LENGTH)
495     END-EXEC.
496                                      ┌WS-COMM-MBR-ID┐
497 0050-EXIT.                           │0006          │
498     EXIT.                            └              ┘
Options-MBRINQ─────────────────────────Level=01-Speed=5-Ins-Caps-Num-Scroll
F1=help F2=analyzer on/off F3=structure/code F4=save-analysis F5=save-structure
F6=display F7=print
```

Figure 12.10. Data returned from the TD queue.

Once this program is complete, the TD queue can be used by the next program in the demonstration. Normally the second program might be invoked by another program, but in this case the program has been started directly by the trans ID. Once started, the first logic performed is examining a TD queue (TDQ1) for any stored data values. If the TD queue contains a value, it is used as the search point for prefilling the display screen. Figure 12.10 shows the read of the TD queue with a value returned.

After the data value is read into the work area, it can be used as part of the normal logic found in the program for prefilling the screen. Once the physical file is read, the MAP is displayed with the data beginning from the key value found in the TD queue (see Figure 12.11).

SUMMARY

Temporary Storage queues are quite useful for low volumes of data and can even help performance in low-volume transactions.

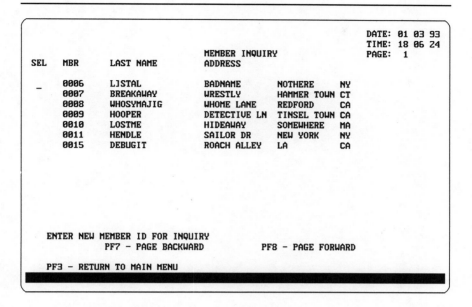

```
                                                          DATE: 01 03 93
                                                          TIME: 18 06 24
                                      MEMBER INQUIRY       PAGE:  1
  SEL   MBR      LAST NAME           ADDRESS

   _    0006     LISTAL              BADNAME        NOTHERE      NY
        0007     BREAKAWAY           WRESTLY        HAMMER TOWN  CT
        0008     WHOSYMAJIG          WHOME LANE     REDFORD      CA
        0009     HOOPER              DETECTIVE LN   TINSEL TOWN  CA
        0010     LOSTME              HIDEAWAY       SOMEWHERE    MA
        0011     HENDLE              SAILOR DR      NEW YORK     NY
        0015     DEBUGIT             ROACH ALLEY    LA           CA




        ENTER NEW MEMBER ID FOR INQUIRY
                 PF7 - PAGE BACKWARD              PF8 - PAGE FORWARD

        PF3 - RETURN TO MAIN MENU
```

Figure 12.11.   Display screen after TD queue read.

High-volume data or transaction activity and using a TS queue can have an adverse impact on performance.

Transient Data queues are often confused with Temporary Storage queues. The intended use is usually quite different. TD queues are read-destructive verses a TS queue that retains data until the queue is deleted.

13

Establishing Databases for Use in CICS Programs

CICS applications interface with various Database Management Systems (DBMS). This chapter examines how databases are established for use in CICS programs:

- VSAM
- DL/I
- DB2

The chapter covers an overview of functions supported by other products. It is not intended to answer all questions regarding these tools. The tools to be covered include those used to establish the following:

- VSAM files using Mirco Focus COBOL's Workbench File Loader (WFL)
- DL/I files accessed through IMSVS86
- DB2 tables supported by XDB or Database Manager

While this topic is not MCO CICS-related, the subject of this chapter is critical to application development using MCO.

VSAM FILES

MCO supports VSAM (Virtual Storage Access Method) file types found on the mainframe, as shown in Figure 13.1.

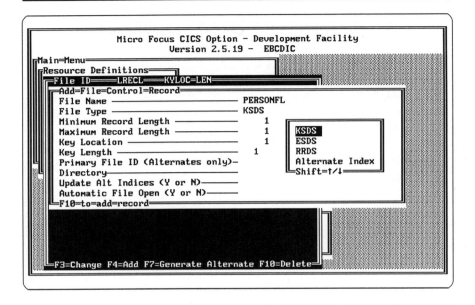

Figure 13.1.   Display of valid VSAM files.

- KSDS (Keyed-Sequenced Datasets): access to the data is by a key for each record on the file or the relative byte address.
- RRDS (Relative Record Data Set): access to fixed-length records via the relative record number.
- ESDS (Entry-Sequenced Dataset): stores data in the order in which it was entered; data cannot be deleted from an ESDS file. Data is retrieved in the same order in which it was entered via the relative byte address.
- Alternate Indexes for ESDS and KSDS files.

MCO stores VSAM data as two physical files on the PC: the data file (file name.DAT) and the primary index (file name.IDX).

ESDS files are stored as indexed files, with the Relative Byte Address (RBA) stored as a four-byte key (9(8) COMP-X). ESDS files processing within the MCO environment function like standard mainframe ESDS files, although one exception is that the RBA values may be different.

WFL

MCO does not have the capability to generate VSAM files. The following steps are presented to demonstrate one method of establishing VSAM files.

Micro Focus COBOL provides a File Utility–Workbench File Loader (WFL) that can generate VSAM files from sequential files. The logical first step is to transfer a sequential file from the mainframe to the PC and then convert the file.

The File Utility submenu is accessed from the Micro Focus COBOL MDE menu by selecting *F2=Files*. The utility for converting data files is invoked by pressing *F5=WFL*. Once in WFL, the programmer defines both the input and output files (see Figure 13.2).

The following file information must be supplied by programmers:

- File name
- File type

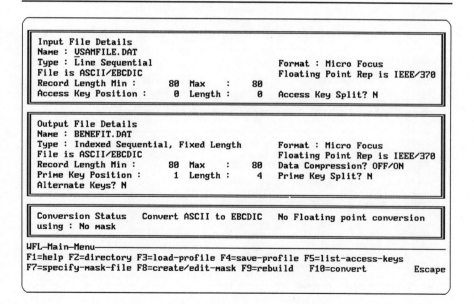

Figure 13.2.   Define files for conversion in WFL.

- Minimum and maximum record lengths
- ASCII or EBCDIC
- Key information

After typing in all necessary information, press *F10=Convert* to convert the file from a record sequential to an indexed sequential fixed-length (KSDS) file in this example (see Figure 13.3).

DL/I FILES

MCO does not provide direct support of IMS databases, but it interfaces with IMSVS86. This section will provide a brief look at what is required in the IMSVS86 product to allow a CICS application to use an IMS database. They can be accessed by pressing [*F9*] *Environment Definition/Configuration* from the MCO main menu and pressing [*F9*] *DLI Options Menu*. After the DL/I Options menu is displayed, programmers select the appropriate function (see Figure 13.4).

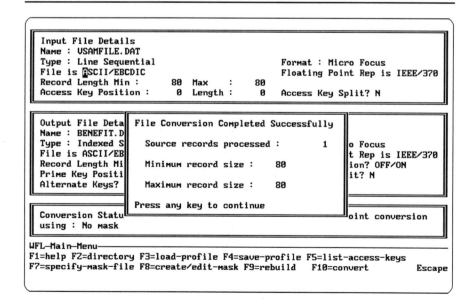

Figure 13.3. Successful conversion to VSAM KSDS.

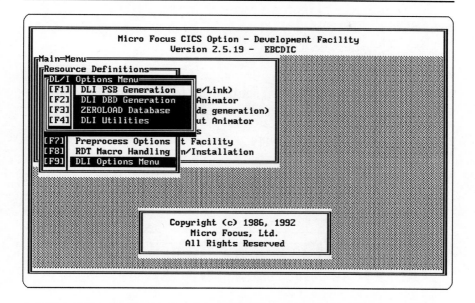

Figure 13.4.   IMS functions accessible to CICS.

DBDGEN

A Database Descriptor (DBD) input file is required (see Figure 13.5). The DBD file defines the physical definition of the database. To generate a DBD in CICS, programmers select [*F7*] *CICS Resource Definitions* from the CICS main menu. From the Resource Definitions submenu, select [*F9*] *DLI Options Menu* to access IMSVS86 functions. To invoke the DBD generation function from the DL/I Options submenu, as shown in Figure 13.6, press [*F2*] *DLI DBD Generation* and type in the name of the DBD input file. Verify the results of the DBD generation to insure that the database is ready for use (see Figure 13.7).

ZEROLOAD

To prime the database, select [*F7*] *CICS Resource Definitions* from the CICS main menu, and from the Resource Definitions submenu select [*F9*] *DLI Options Menu*. To invoke the ZEROLOAD function from the DL/I Options submenu (Figure 13.8), press [*F3*]

```
┌─SALARY.DBD──────────────────────────────────────────────────────────────◆
│          DBD     NAME=USALARY,                                      X
│─                 ACCESS=(HDAM,OSAM),                                X
│                  RMNAME=(DFSHDC40,5,00047)
│DSGROUP0 DATASET DD1=USALTESD,                                       X
│                  DEVICE=3380,                                       X
│                  BLOCK=(4072)
│          SEGM    NAME=USALRSEG,                                     X
│                  PARENT=0,                                          X
│                  BYTES=80,                                          X
│                  PTR=(T)
│          FIELD   NAME=(USALRKEY,SEQ,U),                             X
│                  BYTES=04,                                          X
│                  START=1,                                           X
│                  TYPE=C
│          SEGM    NAME=UPAYRSEG,                                     X
│                  PARENT=((USALRSEG,SNGL)),                          X
│                  BYTES=38,                                          X
│                  PTR=(T)
│          FIELD   NAME=(URAT1KEY,SEQ,U),                             X
│
├─Edit─SALARY─────────49─lines───────Line─1───────Col─1───────Wrap─Ins─Caps─Num─Scroll
│ F1=help F2=library F3=load-file F4=save-file F5=split-line F6=join-line F7=print
│ F8=calculate F9=untype-word-left F10=delete-word-right
└
```

Figure 13.5.   Sample Datebase Descriptor (DBD).

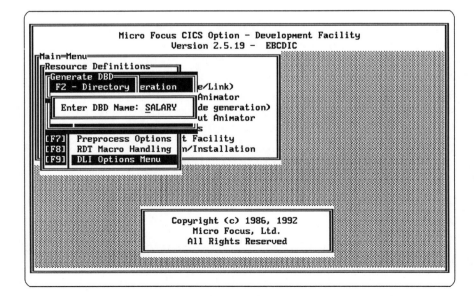

Figure 13.6.   Invoking the DBD generation in IMS.

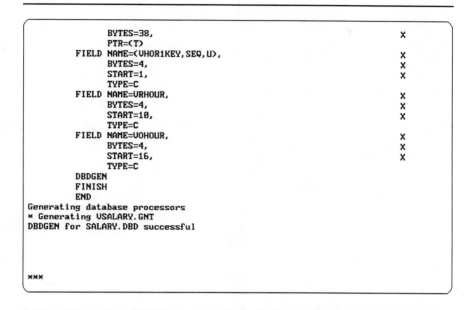

```
                    BYTES=38,                                    X
                    PTR=(T)
           FIELD NAME=(VHOR1KEY,SEQ,U),                          X
                    BYTES=4,                                     X
                    START=1,                                     X
                    TYPE=C
           FIELD NAME=VRHOUR,                                    X
                    BYTES=4,                                     X
                    START=10,                                    X
                    TYPE=C
           FIELD NAME=VOHOUR,                                    X
                    BYTES=4,                                     X
                    START=16,                                    X
                    TYPE=C
           DBDGEN
           FINISH
           END
Generating database processors
* Generating VSALARY.GNT
DBDGEN for SALARY.DBD successful


***
```

Figure 13.7.   Successful generation of a database.

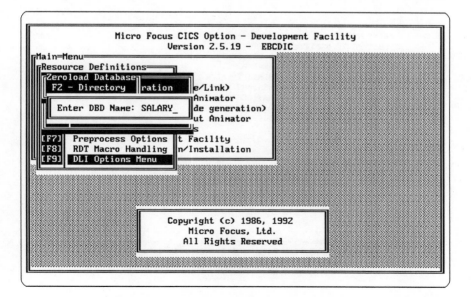

```
            Micro Focus CICS Option - Development Facility
                    Version 2.5.19 -  EBCDIC
┌Main=Menu
 ┌Resource Definitions
  ┌Zeroload Database
   F2 - Directory   ration    e/Link)
                              Animator
     Enter DBD Name: SALARY_  de generation)
                              ut Animator
                             s
   [F7]  Preprocess Options  t Facility
   [F8]  RDT Macro Handling  n/Installation
   [F9]  DLI Options Menu




                   Copyright (c) 1986, 1992
                     Micro Focus, Ltd.
                     All Rights Reserved
```

Figure 13.8.   Invoking the IMS ZEROLOAD function.

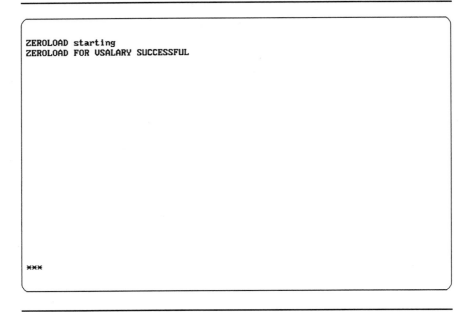

Figure 13.9. Successfully primed IMS database.

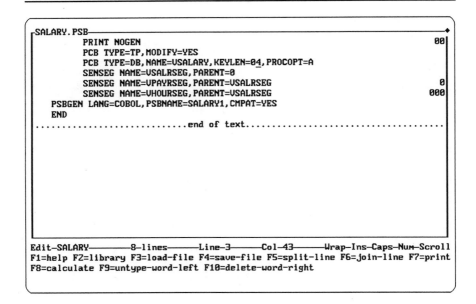

Figure 13.10. Program Specification Block (PSB).

ZEROLOAD Database. Verify the results of the ZEROLOAD to insure that the database is primed (see Figure 13.9.)

PSBGEN

A Program Specification Block (PSB) file is required (see Figure 13.10). The PSB file defines the logical view of a database. To define the logical view of a database, select *[F7] CICS Resource Definitions* from the CICS main menu. From the Resource Definitions submenu, select *[F9] DLI Options Menu* for access to IMSVS86 functions. To invoke the PSBGEN function from the DL/ I Options submenu (Figure 13.11), press *[F1] DLI PSB Generation.* Verify the results of the PSB generation to insure that the logical view of the database is ready for use (see Figure 13.12).

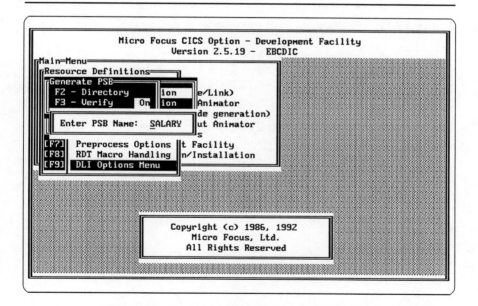

Figure 13.11.   Invoking the IMS PSB function.

```
PSBGEN starting
PSBGEN - Searching for PSBGEN macro
PSBGEN - Processing PSB
        PRINT NOGEN
        PCB TYPE=TP,MODIFY=YES
        PCB TYPE=DB,NAME=USALARY,KEYLEN=04,PROCOPT=A
        SENSEG NAME=USALRSEG,PARENT=0
        SENSEG NAME=UPAYRSEG,PARENT=USALRSEG
        SENSEG NAME=UHOURSEG,PARENT=USALRSEG
   PSBGEN LANG=COBOL,PSBNAME=SALARY1,CMPAT=YES
   END
PSBGEN for SALARY.PSB successful



***
```

Figure 13.12.   Successful PSB generation in IMS.

IMSGEN

MCO can access the previously defined database, but not until it is defined in IMS (see Figure 13.13). From the IMSVS86 main menu press *F10=IMSGEN*, and then select function one (1) to add transactions. The following items need to be defined to IMS for the database to be used:

- Program type
- Trancode name
- PSB name
- Program name
- SPA size
- Process limit cnt
- Max segno

```
╔══════════════════════════════════════════════════════════════╗
║          I M S U S 8 6   Define Transaction Codes             ║
║  Copyright 1986,1990 - Stingray Software Company Inc.          ║
╚══════════════════════════════════════════════════════════════╝

OPT  PROGRAM   TRANCODE  PSB NAME  PROGRAM  SPA SIZE  PROCESS    MAX
     TYPE      NAME                NAME               LIMIT CNT  SEGNO
     BMP                 SALARY1   DBUTIL   00000        00       000
  _  MPP       SAL1      SALARY1   EMPINQ   00000        99       999
     MPP       VB99005   VB99005   VB99005  00000        99       999
     MPP       VB99006   VB99006   VB99006  00000        99       999











Press Enter to process changes, F3/Esc to cancel
Z_■
```

Figure 13.13. Generating transactions to IMSVS86.

DBUTIL

Once the database is defined to IMS, it can be loaded from a batch file. The DBUTIL function can be accessed from either *F4=Animate-IMS* or *F6=Run-IMS* from the IMSVS86 main menu and then executing a BMP process linked via IMSGEN to the program DBUTIL.

DB2 Files

MCO does not provide direct support of DB2 databases, but it interfaces with the following:

- GUPTA SQLbase
- OS/2 Data Manager (Database Manager)
- XDB

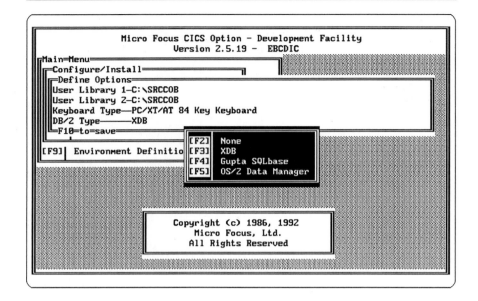

Figure 13.14. Define to CICS DB2 support.

To emulate the mainframe environment, OS/2 Database Manager or XDB are the frontrunners. Of these two, XDB provides a more compatible emulation of the EBCDIC database environment.

OS/2 does not emulate an EBCDIC environment, but Micro Focus COBOL markets an additional product, Host Compatibility Option (HCO), which allows EBCDIC emulation of SQL databases in an OS/2 environment.

This section will provide an overview of what is required to establish data files in OS/2 and XDB. MCO does not perform DB2 database functions. As shown in Figure 13.14, DB2 products are selected by pressing [F9] *Environment Definition/Configuration* from the MCO main menu and selecting [F2] *Define Configuration*.

From this submenu programmers select the appropriate DB2 emulator by pressing one of the following:

- [F3] *XDB*
- [F4] *GUPTA SQLbase*
- [F5] *OS/2 Data Manager*

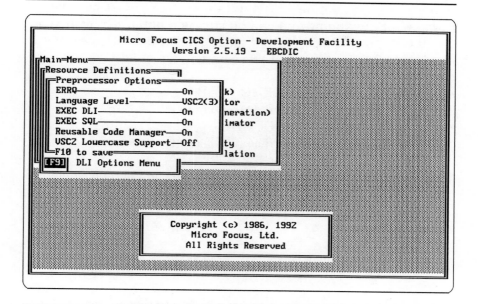

Figure 13.15. Toggle on the DB2 preprocessor.

Once DB2 has been defined to CICS, Check and Animate require that directives to utilize the DB2 preprocessor be selected. To accomplish this from the MCO main menu, select [F7] *CICS Resources* (Figure 13.15) and then press [F7] *Preprocess Options*. Position the cursor on the EXEC SQL option and press Enter to toggle "on" a DB2 preprocessor.

OS/2 Database

OS/2 Database Manager only supports the creation of ASCII-based databases. Programmers looking to emulate the EBCDIC mainframe environment should consider Host Compatibility Option (HCO) to emulate EBCDIC collating sequence of mainframe databases. This section provides only a brief overview of the DB2 environment with HCO.

Database Definition. To create a database from within Database Manager (DBM), programmers can invoke the Query function of OS/2 and define ASCII database. HCO must be invoked from an OS/2 window and can be run as a batch job or interactively (GUI or GUI emulation mode). The interactive screen is invoked by executing one of two commands:

- RUNPM $HCODIR\ MFHCOCDB
  Graphical User Interface (GUI) mode
- RUN $HCODIR\ MFHCOCDB
  Graphical User Interface (GUI) emulation mode

Once executed, the EBCDIC database creation screen opens up (see Figure 13.16).

The creation of a database can be run as a batch job by keying in the following at an OS/2 window prompt:

```
RUN $HCODIR\MFHCOCDB CREATE DATABASE
dbname ON drive letter IN code-page WITH "comments"
```

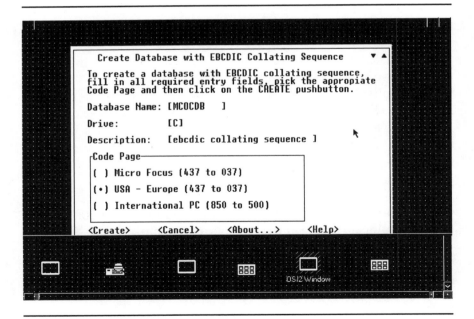

Figure 13.16. Creating EBCDIC collating sequence.

The lower-case items are defined as follows:

- db name—Up to an eight-character name of the database that must start with a letter or $ or # or @.
- drive letter—The drive that the database will be created on.
- code-page—Identifies the type of pages used (037 if USA/Europe, or 500 for international).
- comments—Up to a 30-character text string describing the database (optional).

As on the mainframe, the database must be defined prior to creating any DB2 tables for data storage.

Define and Load Tables. Relational tables can be defined via the OS/2 Database Manager screens and stored in ASCII or HCO as EBCDIC format. HCO provides a batch set of programs to create and load DB2 tables on the PC. This utility will execute most SQL statements. The syntax is

```
RUN $HCODIR\MFHCODDL [database] [inputdsn] [options]
```

The values of the "directives" are as follows:

- database—The database name that the SQL statements will be executed against. Replacing a database with a question mark displays syntax and options.
- inputdsn—Identifies the input file containing SQL statements.
- options—List optional parameters for the utility; at least one space must be before each parameter.
  /L listname—Identify the list file dataset; the default file name is MFHCODDL.LST.
  /NL—Specifies that no LST file should be created.
  /N value—DBM does not support NOT NULL WITH DEFAULT; this option converts these fields to NOT NULL or NULLABLE. If left blank, the fields become NULLABLE.

Once the database and table have been defined with HCO, programmers can key in data directly through DBM panels.

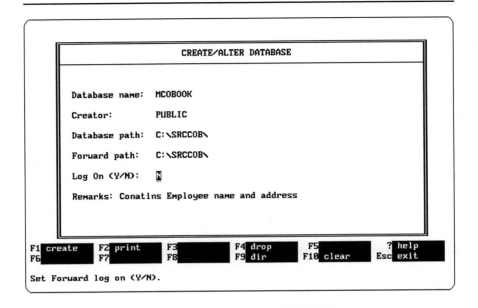

Figure 13.17. Define a DB2 database using XDB.

XDB Database

XDB supports the creation of both ASCII- or EBCDIC-based databases. Programmers looking to emulate the EBCDIC mainframe environment should consider XDB as a valuable resource. This section provides an overview of defining DB2 objects with XDB.

Define Database. To create a database in XDB, see Figure 13.17. Programmers invoke the *F1-Create/Alter* function from the XDB main menu and then press *d=database*. After all database information has been typed in, press [*F1*] *Create* and the database is established.

Define Table. To create a table in XDB, see Figure 13.18. Programmers can invoke the [*F1*] *Create/Alter* function from the XDB main menu and then press *t=table*. They then define the table's

```
                               CREATE/ALTER TABLE
        TABLE NAME :        EMPL_FILE

        NO    FIELD NAME          DATA TYPE              LENGTH   NULL PERMITTED?

        1     EMP_NO              Smallint                 2      No
        2     EMP_LNAME           Char                    14      No
        3     EMP_FNAME           Char                    12      No
        4     EMP_DOB             Date                     6      Yes
        5     EMP_PHONE           Char                    12      No w/default
        6     ████████████████

       F1 create    F2 print    F3           F4              F5          ? help
       F6 move      F7 add      F8 delete    F9 directory  F10 clear   Esc exit

       Enter a field name.
```

Figure 13.18.   Defining a DB2 table using XDB.

columns, data type, column lengths, and whether nulls are allowed for each data field. After all columns are defined, press [*F1*]
Create to establish a table.

Load Table. There are two methods to load a DB2 table in XDB:
Data entry and Interactive SQL functions. To use the *F2=Data
entry* function to load a table, type in values for data fields, as
shown in Figure 13.19. Enter all values for data fields on the
table and then press [*F1*] *Insert*.

XDB does provide a method of executing files containing previously coded INSERT statements by running command files within
F3=Interactive SQL from the XDB main menu (see Figure 13.20).
Press *F5=CMD file*. Programmers select the option USE from the
list window and then press Enter to execute the SQL statements
found in the file.

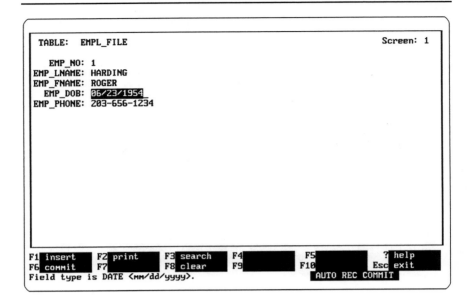

```
   TABLE:  EMPL_FILE                                        Screen: 1

     EMP_NO: 1
 EMP_LNAME: HARDING
 EMP_FNAME: ROGER
   EMP_DOB: 06/23/1954
 EMP_PHONE: 203-656-1234
```

```
F1 insert    F2 print    F3 search   F4        F5                ? help
F6 commit    F7          F8 clear    F9        F10             Esc exit
Field type is DATE <mm/dd/yyyy>.                   AUTO REC COMMIT
```

Figure 13.19. Load a table using XDB data entry.

```
                        B A T C H   S Q L

 CREATE TABLE EMPL
 (
     NBR                     CHAR(2),
     LNAME                   CHAR(10),
     FNAME                   CHAR(8),
     DOB                     INT,
     HIREDTE                 INT,
     PERF                    SMALLINT,
     JOB                     CHAR(4),
     DEPT                    CHAR(3),
     PROJ                    CHAR(2)
 );



 Executing
```

Figure 13.20. Loading a table with interactive SQL.

SUMMARY

MCO can interface with various databases within an application. This flexibility allows MCO to mirror mainframe development needs closely. This chapter presented only the barest overview of defining databases.

14

Accessing Databases from MCO CICS Programs

Making the switch from the mainframe to the PC is essential to being competitive. Applications need to be delivered in a shorter time frame and with as near zero defects as possible. The sets of tools necessary to assist programmers in this area exist now for the PC environment.

This chapter examines various topics concerning migration to the PC, evolution of PC technology, and reasons to migrate to the PC:

- VSAM
- DB2
- DL/I
- Combining DBMS data files

DEFINING THE DATABASE

In the last chapter, defining databases was examined with respect to the following:

- DL/I
- VSAM
- DB2

From a compatibility point of view there are few show-stoppers to prevent application development and testing on the PC. IMS considerations are for the GSAM file differences. VSAM processes the same, but the initial offset address is 1, not 0. DB2 compatibility spans a range.

XDB provides the ability to be 100 percent mainframe DB2 compatible. With Database Manager you may get test results different from the mainframe. Database Manager databases are ASCII based, but using Host Compatibility Option (HCO) the data can be retrieved in EBCDIC-collating sequence and thus give results more similar to those of the mainframe. As long as you are aware of this, test results can be predicted.

Each section of this chapter will take a single program, MBRINQ.CBL, and highlight a different DBMS by displaying return codes and/or the data returned.

Using VSAM Databases

VSAM is the default database type supported within the CICS environment on the PC or mainframe. As a reminder, the first step within CICS is to define the VSAM file to CICS (see Figure 14.1). FCT entries are not defined for TS or TD queues. Once the entry is defined and a file with data exists, the program can read the file. MBRINQ actually demonstrates accessing three different VSAM files:

- Temporary Storage queue (Figure 14.2)
- Transient Data queue (Figure 14.3)
- VSAM KSDS—membership data file (Figure 14.4)

MCO fully supports access to the following:

- KSDS files
- ESDS files
- RRDS files
- Alternate Indexes

VSAM datasets are straightforward from an application development perspective. Using VSAM does not require any additional directives when compiling or animating programs. Batch pro-

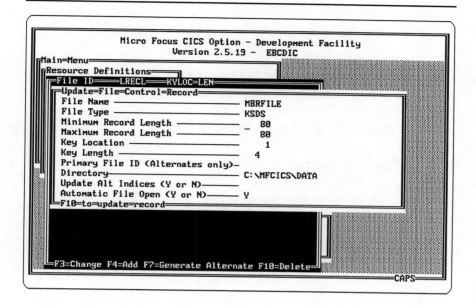

Figure 14.1. VSAM file defined on the FCT file.

```
┌MBRINQ.CBL──────────────────────────────────────────────────────────────────
│
│          EXEC CICS READQ TS
│                QUEUE(TSQ-FILE-NAME)
│                LENGTH(TSQ-LENGTH)
│                INTO(MEMBER-MASTER-RECORD)
│                ITEM(TSQ-ITEM)
│          END-EXEC.
│          IF BROWSE-COUNT < 15
│          THEN
│                NEXT SENTENCE
│          ELSE
│                GO TO 0700-EXIT.
│          MOVE SPACE              TO BROWSE-SEL-IND.
│          MOVE MBR-ID             TO BROWSE-EMPNO.
│          MOVE MBR-LNAME          TO BROWSE-LNAME.
│          MOVE MBR-ADDR           TO BROWSE-ADDR.
│     _    IF BROWSE-COUNT IS EQUAL TO 01
│          THEN
│                MOVE BROWSE-LINE TO LINE010
│
├─────────────────────────────────────────────────────────────────────────────
Edit─MBRINQ────────449-lines──────Line-311──────Col-8────────Wrap-Ins-Caps-Num-Scroll
F1=help F2=library F3=load-file F4=save-file F5=split-line F6=join-line F7=print
F8=calculate F9=untype-word-left F10=delete-word-right
```

Figure 14.2. Reading a Temporary Storage queue.

```
478              EXEC CICS XCTL
479                  PROGRAM('MAINMEN')
480              END-EXEC.
481
482     PERFORM 0300-RECEIVE-MAP THRU 0300-EXIT.
483     EXEC CICS RECEIVE
484          MAP('MBRINQ')
485          INTO(MBRINQI)
486     END-EXEC.
487     PERFORM 0050-TDQ-READ THRU 0050-EXIT.
488
489
490 0050-TDQ-READ.
491     EXEC CICS READQ TD
492          QUEUE('TDQ1')
493          INTO(WS-COMM-MBR-ID)
494          LENGTH(TDQ-LENGTH)
495     END-EXEC.
496                                              WS-COMM-MBR-ID
497 0050-EXIT.                                   0006
498     EXIT.
Options-MBRINQ───────────────────────Level=01-Speed=5-Ins-Caps-Num-Scroll
F1=help F2=analyzer on/off F3=structure/code F4=save-analysis F5=save-structure
F6=display F7=print
```

Figure 14.3.   Reading a Transient Data queue.

```
596 0600-BROWSE-MF.
597
598     ADD 1 TO BROWSE-COUNT.
599
600     EXEC CICS READNEXT
601          DATASET('MBRFILE')
602          RIDFLD(MBR-ID)
603          INTO(MEMBER-MASTER-RECORD)
604     END-EXEC.
605
606     IF BROWSE-COUNT < 45
607     THEN
608          NEXT SENTENCE
609     ELSE
610          GO TO 0600-EXIT.
611
612     MOVE MBR-ID              TO TSQ-MBR-ID.
613     MOVE MBR-LNAME    MEMBER-MASTER-RECORD
614     MOVE MBR-ADDR     0001  SANFORD          SANDY        LONG
615                       BEACH  MOHAVE      CT
616     ADD +1 TO TSQ-IT
Options-MBRINQ───────────────────────Level=02-Speed=5-Ins-Caps-Num-Scroll
F1=help F2=analyzer on/off F3=structure/code F4=save-analysis F5=save-structure
F6=display F7=print
```

Figure 14.4.   Reading a VSAM KSDS data file.

grams accessing VSAM should be compiled and animated from within MCO.

Using Relational Databases

Whether the access to relational DMBS is via Database Manager or XDB, the code in the CICS program is coded exactly as on the mainframe. Programs must define the following:

- SQLCA
- DCLGENs
- DML statements
  SELECT
  INSERT
  UPDATE
  DELETE

Figure 14.5 demonstrates a CICS program reading (SELECT) a record from the SELECT security file. In the display, both the

```
655*    END-EXEC.
656
657    EXEC SQL
658        SELECT *
659            INTO :WS-SEC-ID, :WS-SEC-PSWD
660        FROM SECFILE
661            WHERE SECURITY_ID   = :WS-COMM-SEC-ID AND
662                  SECURITY_PSWD = :WS-COMM-SEC-PSWD
663    END-EXEC.
664
665    IF SQLCODE = TO +000
666    THEN
667        NEXT SENTENCE                         WS-SEC-ID
668    ELSE                                      1111111
669        GO TO 0910-INVALID-SECURITY.
670                                              WS-SEC-PSWD
671                                              SEC01
672 0510-EXIT.                                              0
673    EXIT.                                     SQLCODE      0
674                                              +0000000000
675 0600-BROWSE-MF.
Options-MBRINQ                          Level=02-Speed=5-Ins-Caps-Num-Scroll
F1=help F2=analyzer on/off F3=structure/code F4=save-analysis F5=save-structure
F6=display F7=print
```

Figure 14.5.   Reading a relational table.

data and the SQLCODE (return code) are displayed for a successful find of the data. When interfacing with SQL files, several directives may have to be added to the directive files:

- SQL—Invoke the SQL precompiler using Micro Focus COBOL.
- SQL "IBMES1DBM"—Link to Database Manager.
- NOSQLINIT—Used by program (CICS and IMS) containing SQL code or programs calling other programs using SQL.
- SQLDB2—Handle working storage variables and include copy files like mainframe DB2.

Additional directives can be used for various purposes. I am not attempting to document all directives, as this is a CICS book, not a relational book. Batch programs accessing DB2 can be compiled and animated from within MCO or from Micro Focus COBOL.

Using DL/I Databases

Access to DL/I files is via Micro Focus IMS Option (IMSVS86). The components of DL/I used by IMS and MCO are the same. DBDGENs and PSBGENs can be shared by an IMS and a CICS application. When connecting CICS application logic to a DL/I database, an additional 3 MB of memory should be available for the interface.

The IMS DL/I interface runs with any version of CICSVS86 or MCO. MCO provides a menu for performing normal IMS functions:

- DBD Generation
- PSB Generation
- ZEROLOAD
- Utilities

One notable exception from the MCO menus is the ability to use the DBUTIL process to load a database. For this processing, invoke the IMS product from the Micro Focus MDE menu.

Two environment settings are available only from the CICSVS86 or MCO products directing locations of source for the DBDs and PSBs. When DBDs or PSBs are not defined to the cur-

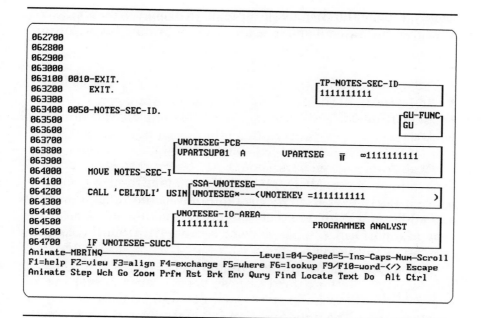

Figure 14.6.   Reading a DL/I database.

rent directory, key the following into AUTOEXEC.BAT (DOS) or CONFIG.SYS (OS/2):

```
SET DLIDBD=C:\DBDSOURCE
SET DLIPSB=C:\PSBSOURCE
```

MCO use of DL/I functions is no different than if the program calling the IMS database were being run as an IMS program. Figure 14.6 displays the read of a DL/I file.

SUMMARY

MCO is a product that will deliver the capability of developing CICS applications on the PC. In my examination of the product, I found no areas that greatly concerned me. This tool should be used as an application developer.

The interconnectivity of database products is handled fairly simply within the MCO environment. Through this program I have demonstrated a single source file containing the following:

- VSAM
- TS queue
- TD queue
- Relational DBMS Table
- DL/I

Mainframe developers should not be concerned with database support using MCO. MCO delivers mainframe compatibility in a fairly user-friendly presentation of the functions. This and additional PC-based tools can provide mainframe host planning and performance people with some relief from the congestion found on the mainframe.

The 1990s and beyond belong to the PC as the most logical development platform for business needs. MCO is just one of many tools that is here. It works quite well and it can deliver great returns. The only question left unanswered in this book relates to your company: Is your company in the driver's seat, or is it just a passenger?

MCO-Provided CICS Transactions

Mainframe CICS provides programmers and CICS operators with many CICS commands. MCO provides several transactions as part of the load disks. This appendix looks at which transactions are provided and their purpose:

- CSMT
- CSSF
- CMAP

CSMT

The CSMT transaction is used either to (1) open or close datasets, or (2) shut down the emulation facility. CSMT is used to open or close files defined on the FCT.

Open All Files

As files are processed in MCO, they can be opened automatically from the FCT file or at emulation time. This command is used to open all files processed during an emulation session:

```
CSMT OPEN ALL
```

Open an Individual File

Select specific files to open during an emulation session:

```
CSMT OPEN dataset
```

Shutdown CICS Emulation Facility

Used to close down the emulation facility and all files opened during the session:

```
CSMT SHUTDOWN
CSMT SHUT
```

CSSF

The CSSF transaction is used to close down the CICS emulation facility. Once executed, three asterisks are displayed at the bottom of the screen. Press the PC Enter key to return to the MCO menus. To close down CICS, type in

```
CSSF
CSSF LOGOFF
```

CMAP

The CMAP transaction is used to display an assembled BMS macro file on the terminal. This is useful when the BMS code is ready, but the COBOL program has to be coded. Why wait until the COBOL program is coded and checked to view how the screen will be presented to a customer? Use the CMAP transaction to request the display of a MAPSET/MAP, as shown in Figure A.1. Invoke the emulation facility by typing in

```
CMAP
```

The CMAP transaction prompts for the name of the MAPSET and MAP that is to be displayed. To view the screen, press Enter and the screen is displayed. See Figure A.2.

To select another MAPSET/MAP to view, press *PA1 (Alt + 1* in MCO). To exit out of the view facility, press the Ctrl + Home (clear screen) and type in CSSF.

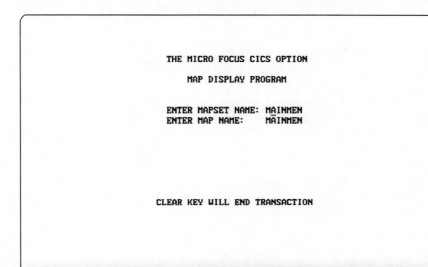

Figure A.1.   MAP display facility provided in MCO.

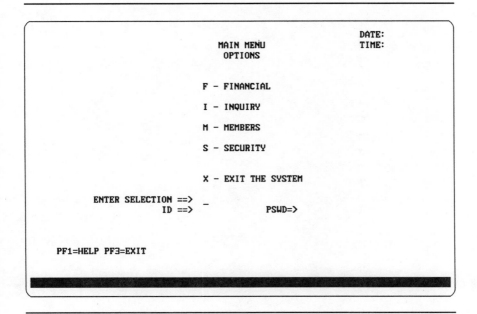

Figure A.2.   Displayed results after using CMAP.

Appendix **B**

CICS BMS Macro Options

Mainframe CICS provides programmers with many BMS options supporting screen development. MCO provides support for these options as well. This appendix is provided to assist MCO developers with a reference source in developing BMS on the PC. The following BMS macros are covered:

- DFHMSD—Found twice in a MAPSET, defining the beginning and end of a MAPSET.
- DFHMDI—One for each MAP defined in a MAPSET.
- DFHMDF—Definition of each data field or literal.

DFHMSD

MAPSET macros (DFHMSD) are used to define the global information applicable to each MAP in a MAPSET. Most companies have standard options used when defining a MAPSET. DFHMSD macros define the beginning and end of a MAPSET that contains one or more MAPs. The following sample has been extracted from an actual production application.

MAPSET macros have two different formats:

```
LABEL   MACRO   OPTIONS                         CONTINUATION
1-7     10      17 (16 on continued lines)      72
```

```
MAINMEN DFHMSD
TYPE=&SYSPARM,LANG=COBOL, X
   MODE=INOUT,TIOAPFX=YES
   .
   .
   DFHMSD TYPE=FINAL
   END
```

Syntax requires a comma between each option, and continuations are identified by a nonblank character in column 72. All MAPSETs must have a name of one to seven characters that is defined in the PPT file on the mainframe. MCO does not currently support a PPT file.

The MAPSET name forms a link between execution and COBOL in a CICS environment. In an MVS environment, the MAPSET name is the same as linked to the executable load library. It also identifies the copybook file of the symbolic MAP contained in a MAPSET.

The last consideration for the name is that COBOL programs support up to eight characters in a name. MAPSET names are up to seven characters. This difference in size makes it difficult to support common names between COBOL and BMS source code.

DFHMSD Options

Many options are available when defining a MAPSET. Only the most commonly used are covered here:

- BASE—Specifies that the same storage base will be used for symbolic MAPs of a MAPSET containing more than one MAP. This operand cannot be used in conjunction with STORAGE=AUTO.
- CTRL=(FREEKB,ALARM,FRSET,PRINT,LENGTH):
    FREEKB—Unlock the keyboard after a SEND command.
    ALARM—Sound the terminal alarm when a MAP is sent.
    FRSET—Prior to SEND MAP commands, the Modified Data Tag (MDT) attribute flags are reset.
    PRINT—Required when using the SEND command to route data to a printer.
    LENGTH—Used in conjunction with the PRINT option, identifying the length of a printer's page.

- EXTATT=YES | NO | MAPONLY—Specifies whether extended attributes are used, left over from earlier releases.
- HILIGHT=OFF | BLINK | REVERSE | UNDERLINE—Identify the default highlighting used for data fields.
- LANG=COBOL | ASM | PLI | C—What language the symbolic MAP is created for.
- MODE=INOUT | IN | OUT—Identifies whether the MAP is to be used for input, output, or both.
- OBFMT—Specifies if outboard formatting is to be used; available for 3650 logical units or 8100 series running DPS Release 2.
- PS—Identifies that the programmed symbols are to be used; this operand is overridden by the same operand on the DFHMDI and also the DFHMDF statements.
- STORAGE=AUTO | BASE=dataname—Identifies how much memory the symbolic MAP will need.

  STORAGE=AUTO—If more than one MAP is part of the MAPSET, they are contiguously allocated in memory. The option is ignored if there is only one MAP. If STORAGE= AUTO is not used, subsequent MAPs in a MAPSET overlay the first in memory.

  BASE=dataname—Useful when there is more than one MAP per MAPSET, but only one MAP will be used during an execution (at the point the program gains control from CICS until a RETURN command is executed).
- TERM=3270-2—Identifies the terminal type to interface with; this option assists in making the data interface more efficient.
- TIOAPFX=YES—Always code this as yes.
- TYPE=&SYSPARM | DSECT | MAP | FINAL—Defines to assembler the type of MAP being created.

  DSECT—A symbolic MAP.

  MAP—Identifies that a MAP should be generated.

  FINAL—Identifies the end of a MAPSET.

  &SYSPARM—The MAP type will be identified in JCL.
- VALIDN=MUSTFILL | MUSTENTER | MUSTFIL, MUSTENTER—Identifies that validation is to be used on an 8775 terminal; this operand is overridden by the same operand on the DFHMDI and also the DFHMDF statements.

  MUSTFILL—A data field must be completely filled with data.

MUSTENTER—A data field must be entered but does not have to be completely filled with data.

- COLOR—Indicates a color default for the MAPSET; this operand is overridden by the same operand on the DFHMDI and also the DFHMDF statements.

DFHMDI

When defining attributes of single MAP, the DFHMDI macro is used. Follow company standards for options selected in defining MAPs. MAP macros apply to a single MAP contained in a MAPSET.

MAP macros have one format:

```
LABEL   MACRO   OPTIONS                      CONTINUATION
1-7     10      17 (16 on continued lines)   72

MAINMEN DFHMDI SIZE=(24,80)
```

Syntax requires a comma between each option, and continuations are identified by a nonblank character in column 72. All MAPs must have a name of one to seven characters. The MAP name is not used outside of a COBOL program.

Many of the keywords used on the DFHMDI statement are the same as those found on the DFHMSD statement (COLOR, CTRL, DATA, HILIGHT, OBFMT, PS, TIOAPFX, VALIDN). These additional keywords are used:

- COLUMN= number—Identifies what column the MAP will be mapped to at the receiving terminal; the default is 1.
- HEADER—Allows the MAP to be used during page building without stopping overflow.
- JUSTIFY=LEFT | FIRST | RIGHT | LAST—Identifies the position of the MAP on a page.
- LINE= number—Identifies what line the MAP will be mapped to at the receiving terminal; the default is 1.
- SIZE=(line, column)—Identifies the screen area to be used by the MAP; typically, (24 × 80) is used for application screens.
- TRAILER—Allows the MAP to be used during page building without stopping overflow.

DFHMDF

When defining the attributes of data fields on a MAP, DFHMDF macros are used. Use company standards for options used in defining data fields. Data field macros apply to a single MAP contained in a MAPSET.

Data field macros have one format:

```
LABEL   MACRO   OPTIONS                        CONTINUATION
1-7     10      17 (16 on continued lines)     72

        DFHMDF POS=(01,63),ATTRB=(PROT,BRT),   X
        LENGTH=06,INITIAL='DATE:'
MENDATE DFHMDF
POS=(01,70),ATTRB=(PROT,FSET),   X
        LENGTH=08,
```

Syntax requires a comma between each option, and continuations are identified by a nonblank character in column 72. Names are optional on literals but necessary on data fields. Data field names are up to seven characters. The name supplied will be generated in the symbolic MAP. Each data field will have five different field names:

- field nameL   —L for the length of the field
- field nameF   —F for the flag
- field nameA   —A for the attribute byte
- field nameI   —I for the input data value
- field nameO   —O for the output value

Fields ending in I and O are redefines of each other. Fields ending in F and A redefine each other. As data fields are defined, attribute bytes are generated for each field. A standard screen (24 × 80) has the capability to store 1,920 positions on a screen. There are two reasons for not attempting to utilize all screen positions:

- Attribute bytes
- Cluttered screens

When designing a MAP, literals usually have one attribute defined prior to it, usually set to ASKIP or PROT. Data fields are defined with two attributes: one prior to the field to UNPROT and allow data entry, and the second at the end to PROT or ASKIP, preventing continued keying of data.

Many options on a data field (DFHMDF) are also found on the DFHMDI or DFHMSD statements (COLOR, OCCURS, PS, VALIDN, JUSTIFY). The following options are the most used when coding DFHMDF statements:

- ATTRB=([ASKIP | PROT | UNPROT] [,BRT | DRK | NORM] [,NUM] [,FSET] [,IC]) All of the values within the parentheses are optional. Within the brackets only one value can be selected.

    ASKIP—Identifies the field as protected from data entry and causes the cursor to jump to the next field.

    BRT—Displays the field in high-intensity fashion.

    DRK—The field will not be displayed on a screen or a printer.

    FSET—Identifies that the Modified Data Tag (MDT) should be set on when the field is sent to the terminal.

    IC—Identifies that the field should have the cursor placed in the first position of the data field.

    NORM—Causes fields to be displayed in normal brightness; this is the default.

    NUM—Allows only numeric values in the field; causes fields to be right-justified (high order positions filled with zeros).

    PROT—Protects a field from data entry.

    UNPROT—Allows the entry of data values into fields.
- COBOL NAME—Allows programmers to define a COBOL data field name to be used in the generation of copybook files.
- INITIAL='literal'—Identifies a value that should be displayed in the field on first display of the screen. If no initial value, the field will contain low values.
- GRPNAME—A one- to seven-character name used to generate the symbolic storage definitions and to combine fields under a group.
- JUSTIFY=(LEFT | RIGHT | [,BLANK | ZERO])—Used with the NUM option to control how fields are received into a program; the default is left-justified.
- LENGTH=number—Defines the size of the data field and does

not include the attribute byte. This option is not required when the PICIN and PICOUT options are used.

- PICIN='COBOL PIC value'—BMS does not use this option to format data; only application programs can use it.
- PICOUT='COBOL PIC value'—BMS does not use this option to format data; only application programs can use it.
- POS=(line, column)—Defines at what point on the screen the attribute byte for a field is located; the data begins in the next position.

Screen Sample

BMS MAPSETs are relatively easy to code once you have a basic understanding of assembler. This is a fully created set of macros:

```
MAINMEN DFHMSD TYPE=&&SYSPARM,LANG=COBOL,              X
               MODE=INOUT,TIOAPFX=YES
MAINMEN DFHMDI SIZE=(24,80)
        DFHMDF POS=(01,63),ATTRB=(PROT,BRT),          X
               LENGTH=06,INITIAL='DATE: '
MENDATE DFHMDF POS=(01,70),ATTRB=(PROT,FSET),         X
               LENGTH=08,PICOUT='X(8)'
        DFHMDF POS=(02,36),ATTRB=(PROT,BRT),          X
               LENGTH=09,INITIAL='MAIN MENU'
        DFHMDF POS=(02,63),ATTRB=(PROT,BRT),          X
               LENGTH=06,INITIAL='TIME: '
MENTIME DFHMDF POS=(02,70),ATTRB=(PROT,FSET),         X
               LENGTH=08,PICOUT='X(8)'
        DFHMDF POS=(03,37),ATTRB=(PROT,BRT),          X
               LENGTH=07,INITIAL='OPTIONS'
        DFHMDF POS=(06,33),ATTRB=(PROT),LENGTH=20,    X
               INITIAL='F—FINANCIAL '
        DFHMDF POS=(08,33),ATTRB=(PROT),LENGTH=20,    X
               INITIAL='I—INQUIRY '
        DFHMDF POS=(10,33),ATTRB=(PROT),LENGTH=20,    X
               INITIAL='M—MEMBERS '
        DFHMDF POS=(12,33),ATTRB=(PROT),LENGTH=20,    X
               INITIAL='S—SECURITY '
        DFHMDF POS=(15,33),ATTRB=(PROT),LENGTH=20,    X
               INITIAL='X—EXIT THE SYSTEM'
        DFHMDF POS=(17,12),ATTRB=(PROT,BRT),          X
               LENGTH=19,INITIAL='ENTER SELECTION =='
MENSEL  DFHMDF POS=(17,33),ATTRB=(UNPROT,IC),LENGTH=01
```

```
           DFHMDF POS=(17,35),ATTRB=(PROT),LENGTH=01
           DFHMDF POS=(18,25),ATTRB=(PROT,BRT),               X
               LENGTH=06,INITIAL='ID =='
   MENID DFHMDF POS=(18,33),ATTRB=(UNPROT),LENGTH=07
           DFHMDF POS=(18,41),ATTRB=(PROT),LENGTH=01
           DFHMDF POS=(18,45),ATTRB=(PROT,BRT),               X
               LENGTH=06,INITIAL='PSWD='
 MENPSWD DFHMDF POS=(18,52),ATTRB=(UNPROT),LENGTH=07
           DFHMDF POS=(18,60),ATTRB=(PROT),LENGTH=01
           DFHMDF POS=(22,05),ATTRB=(PROT,BRT),               X
               LENGTH=20,INITIAL='PF1=HELP PF3=EXIT '
   MSG1    DFHMDF POS=(23,05),ATTRB=(PROT,BRT),LENGTH=62
   MSG2    DFHMDF POS=(24,05),ATTRB=(PROT,BRT),LENGTH=62
           DFHMSD TYPE=FINAL
           END
```

COBOL Copybook Sample

As part of the symbolic MAP generation, a copybook is created for use in COBOL programs. These copybooks are specified in MCO from within the Generate/Conversion submenu.

```
01 MAINMENI.
   05 FILLER       PIC X(12).
   05 MENDATEL     PIC S9(4) COMP.
   05 MENDATEF     PIC X(01).
   05 FILLER REDEFINES MENDATEF.
      10 MENDATEA  PIC X(01).
   05 MENDATEI     PIC X(008).
   05 MENTIMEL     PIC S9(4) COMP.
   05 MENTIMEF     PIC X(01).
   05 FILLER REDEFINES MENTIMEF.
      10 MENTIMEA  PIC X(01).
   05 MENTIMEI     PIC X(008).
   05 MENSELL      PIC S9(4) COMP.
   05 MENSELF      PIC X(01).
   05 FILLER REDEFINES MENSELF.
      10 MENSELA   PIC X(01).
   05 MENSELI      PIC X(001).
   05 MENIDL       PIC S9(4) COMP.
   05 MENIDF       PIC X(01).
   05 FILLER REDEFINES MENIDF.
      10 MENIDA    PIC X(01).
   05 MENIDI       PIC X(007).
   05 MENPSWDL     PIC S9(4) COMP.
```

```
  05 MENPSWDF        PIC X(01).
  05 FILLER REDEFINES MENPSWDF.
    10 MENPSWDA      PIC X(01).
  05 MENPSWDI        PIC X(007).
  05 MSG1L           PIC S9(4) COMP.
  05 MSG1F           PIC X(01).
  05 FILLER REDEFINES MSG1F.
    10 MSG1A         PIC X(01).
  05 MSG1I           PIC X(062).
  05 MSG2L           PIC S9(4) COMP.
  05 MSG2F           PIC X(01).
  05 FILLER REDEFINES MSG2F.
    10 MSG2A         PIC X(01).
  05 MSG2I           PIC X(062).
01 MAINMENO REDEFINES MAINMENI.
  05 FILLER          PIC X(12).
  05 FILLER          PIC X(03).
  05 MENDATEO        PIC X(8).
  05 FILLER          PIC X(03).
  05 MENTIMEO        PIC X(8).
  05 FILLER          PIC X(03).
  05 MENSELO         PIC X(001).
  05 FILLER          PIC X(03).
  05 MENIDO          PIC X(007).
  05 FILLER          PIC X(03).
  05 MENPSWDO        PIC X(007).
  05 FILLER          PIC X(03).
  05 MSG1O           PIC X(062).
  05 FILLER          PIC X(03).
  05 MSG2O           PIC X(062).
```

SUMMARY

BMS MAPs are coded as assembler macros or within the BMS screen painter of the MCO product. Only the surface of understanding BMS screen development was covered here. The assumption made is that programmers using this tool will already have skills in maintaining MAPs.

BMS Command Line Edit Function

MCO provides programmers with a BMS editing tool that is not accessed from the menu system. The menu systems for editing BMS macros are more often selected as the edit tool primarily because of the menu-driven accessibility.

INVOKING BMS EDITOR

The BMS edit tool, shown in Figure C.1, is invoked from an OS prompt by typing in:

```
RUN BMSSCRNS
```

Access to the BMS editor process can be selected from the main menu . The functions supported from the main menu are:

- [F2] *edit-map*—Position the cursor on a BMS file in the window and press *Enter* to invoke the edit process for the selected file.
- [F3] *load-set*—Invokes the load submenu, used to load BMS files from current or other directories.
- [F4] *save-set*—Invokes the save submenu, for saving the changes made in memory to a physical file.

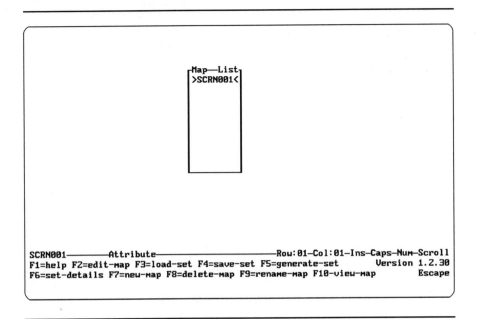

```
                        ┌Map──List┐
                        │>SCRN001<│
                        │         │
                        │         │
                        │         │
                        │         │
                        │         │
                        │         │
                        └─────────┘




SCRN001────────Attribute──────────────Row:01-Col:01-Ins-Caps-Num-Scroll
F1=help F2=edit-map F3=load-set F4=save-set F5=generate-set    Version 1.2.30
F6=set-details F7=new-map F8=delete-map F9=rename-map F10=view-map   Escape
```

Figure C.1.   Command line BMS screen editor main menu.

- [*F5*] *generate-set*—Validates the current image of the screen and invokes the generation menu.
- [*F6*] *set-details*—Allows the setting of MAPSET detail information.
- [*F7*] *new-map*—Creates a new MAP using the default name of SCRN9999.
- [*F8*] *delete-map*—Select a MAP and delete the file.
- [*F9*] *rename-map*—Used to rename the selected MAP to another MAP name.
- [*F10*] *view-map*—Display the executable image on the terminal.

Loading Files

This function invokes a submenu shown in Figure C.2 where files are identified to load.

The load process supports loading:

```
List files :   C:\mfcics\bms\*.bms
Date          Time       Size  Name

 6-Mar-93     1:10pm     6948  MBRMEN.BMS
20-Jan-93     8:34pm     8590  MBRINQ.BMS
29-Dec-92     6:05pm     1926  MBRADD.BMS
28-May-91    10:05am     6311  BADD400.BMS
 5-Aug-92     6:49pm     2199  MAINMEN.BMS
28-May-91    10:05am     4921  BDLT400.BMS
28-May-91    10:05am     4314  BMEN400.BMS
21-Jan-93     7:37pm     1787  MBRPAG.BMS
27-Feb-92     5:19am     2805  DFH0CMP.BMS
 1-Jan-93     6:11pm     1787  BPAG400.BMS
                        ═══════end of directory═══════




Default───C:\────────────────────────Asc-unsorted-Ins-Caps-Num-Scroll
F1=help
F5=sort-size F6=sort-ext          F8=browse-file
total size= 63,700,992 available space=  1,949,696    listed files=    41,588
```

Figure C.2.   Loading a BMS file directory search function.

- Forms or Forms-2 files, Forms-2 files must use an extension of .S00
- BMS macro files with an extension of .BMS

Once the file is identified and after pressing *Enter,* the BMS file is loaded into memory (see Figure C.3).

BMS Editor

Once the file is loaded, pressing *F2=edit* invokes the actual edit function (see Figure C.4).

The BMS edit main menu provides various functions for altering the BMS code, plus two additional submenus—*Alt* and *Ctrl*:

- [F2] *mark / unmark*—Used to mark code as part of a block of code to be edited further.

```
                                                              DATE: ^^^^^^^^
                                                              TIME: ^^^^^^^^
                                    ┌Map──List┐BERS
                                    │ >MBRADD <│
      MEMBER NUMBER: ^^^^           │          │
                                    │          │
      LAST NAME: ^^^^^^^^^^^^^^^    │          │
                                    │          │
      FIRST NAME: ^^^^^^^^^^^^      │          │
                                    │          │
      STREET: ^^^^^^^^^^^^^^^       │          │
                                    │          │
      CITY: ^^^^^^^^^^^^            │          │
      NOTES:  ^^^^^^^^^^^^^^^^^^^^^^^^^^^^^^^^^^^^^^^^^^^^^^^^^^^^^^^^^^^^^^^^^^



  MBRADD──────────Attribute─────────────────Row:01─Col:01─Ins─Caps─Num─Scroll
  F1=help F2=edit-map F3=load-set F4=save-set F5=generate-set    Version 1.2.30
  F6=set-details F7=new-map F8=delete-map F9=rename-map F10-view-map    Escape
  Error Trail File Created (.TRL)
```

Figure C.3.   BMS file loaded into memory.

```
                                                              DATE: ^^^^^^^^
                                                              TIME: ^^^^^^^^
                             ADD MEMBERS
      MEMBER NUMBER: ^^^^  _

      LAST NAME: ^^^^^^^^^^^^^^^

      FIRST NAME: ^^^^^^^^^^^^

      STREET: ^^^^^^^^^^^^^^^

      CITY: ^^^^^^^^^^^^       STATE: ^^
      NOTES:  ^^^^^^^^^^^^^^^^^^^^^^^^^^^^^^^^^^^^^^^^^^^^^^^^^^^^^^^^^^^^^^^^^



  MBRADD──────────Attribute─────────────────Row:06─Col:26─Ins─Caps─Num─Scroll
  F1=help F2=unused F3=unused F4=unused F5=select-char (0/064/40h) F6=draw
  F7=read-char F8=read-attr F9=delete-field-def'n F10=delete-occurs-def'n
```

Figure C.4.   BMS edit main menu.

- [F3] *field*—Defines a group of ^ as characters and invokes the field menu.
- [F4] *occurs*—Used to duplicate a marked field horizontally across the screen.
- [F5] *paint-attribute*—Paints the current attribute to the current area. An area is:
   A field
   The current cursor position
   A defined block
- [F6] *attribute-roll*—Scrolls through the five default attributes.
- [F7] *cut-to-block*—Once a block of code is marked (*F2*) it can be cut or moved from the current location to another portion of the screen using the *Block* submenu (see Figure C.5).
- [F8] *copy-to-block*—Once a block of code is marked (*F2*) it can be copied from the current location to another portion of the screen using the *Block* submenu (see Figure C.5).
- [F9] *restore-block*—Once a block of code is marked (*F2*) and

```
                                                      DATE: ^^^^^^^
                                                      TIME: ^^^^^^^
                              ADD MEMBERS

    MEMBER NUMBER: ^^^^                      ^^^^

    LAST NAME: ^^^^^^^^^^^^^^^^

    FIRST NAME: ^^^^^^^^^^^^^

    STREET: ^^^^^^^^^^^^^^^^^

    CITY: ^^^^^^^^^^^^      STATE: ^^
    NOTES:   ^^^^^^^^^^^^^^^^^^^^^^^^^^^^^^^^^^^^^^^^^^^^^^^^^^^^^^^^^^^^



    Block————————Attribute———————————————————Row:06-Col:45-Ins-Caps-Num-Scroll
    F1=help F2=paste-block F3=copy-from-block F4=store-block
    cursor-keys=move-block                                            Escape
```

Figure C.5.   BMS edit block submenu.

previously cut from its current location it can be restored back to the current location of the cursor using the *Block* submenu (see Figure C5).

- [*F10*] *field-order*—Displays the current order of fields on the screen and allows the field to be moved to a different order on the screen.

BMS Field Submenu

The BMS field submenu allows programmers to identify a field's (clause) characteristics (see Figure C.6).

- [*F2*] *select/unselect-clause*—Position to a field and press *F2* to identify the field options for later processing.
- [*F3*] *edit-clause*—Use the previously selected clause and edit it further.
- [*F4*] *toggle-prot/unprot*—Toggles on and off the use of protection for a field.

```
                                      <Field  name>         DATE: ^^^^^^^^
                                      BLANK fill            TIME: ^^^^^^^^
                                      ZERO fill
                                      RIGHT justified
      MEMBER NUMBER: ^^^^      XXXX    LEFT justified
                              _        MUSTENTER
      LAST NAME: ^^^^^^^^^^^^^^^       MUSTFILL
                                      >DRK (no echo)    <
      FIRST NAME: ^^^^^^^^^^^^         FSET
                                       IC
      STREET: ^^^^^^^^^^^^^^^          NUM

      CITY: ^^^^^^^^^^^^      STA|    PICIN
      NOTES:   ^^^^^^^^^^^^^^^^^^^^|  PICOUT          ^^^^^^^^^^^^^^^^^^^^


 Field————————Attribute——————————Field————Row:06—Col:29—Ins—Caps—Num—Scroll
 F1=help F2=select/unselect-clause F3=edit-clause F4=toggle-prot/unprot    Escape
```

Figure C.6.   BMS field setting submenu.

```
                                                    DATE: ^^^^^^^^
                                                    TIME: ^^^^^^^^
                            ADD MEMBERS

   MEMBER NUMBER: ^^^^
                  _
   LAST NAME: ^^^^^^^^^^^^^^^^

   FIRST NAME: ^^^^^^^^^^^^

   STREET: ^^^^^^^^^^^^^^^^

   CITY: ^^^^^^^^^^^^      STATE: ^^
   NOTES:   ^^^^^^^^^^^^^^^^^^^^^^^^^^^^^^^^^^^^^^^^^^^^^^^^^^^^^^^^^^^^^^^^




Occurs————————Attribute—AMBRID————————Ocr01————————Row:06—Col:20—Ins—Caps—Num—Scroll
F1=help F2=unused F3=repeat-horizontally F4=unused
F5=delete-horizontally F6=unused
                                                                        Escape
```

Figure C.7.   BMS submenu for establishing occurs fields.

BMS Occurs Submenu

The BMS occurs submenu allows programmers to identify and repeat a field across a screen horizontally (see Figure C.7).

- [F2] *unused*
- [F3] *repeat-horizontally*—Repeats the marked field to the right of the current field as long as space is available on the screen.
- [F4] *unused*
- [F3] *delete-horizontally*—Deletes the marked field from the right of the screen to the original field.
- [F6] *unused*

BMS Alt Submenu

The BMS main edit menu provides an additional submenu accessed by pressing the *Alt key* (see Figure C.8).

```
 _____
(                                                                  )
 -                                                DATE: ^^^^^^^^
                                                  TIME: ^^^^^^^^
                           ADD MEMBERS

    MEMBER NUMBER: ^^^^

    LAST NAME: ^^^^^^^^^^^^^^^

    FIRST NAME: ^^^^^^^^^^^^

    STREET: ^^^^^^^^^^^^^^^^

    CITY: ^^^^^^^^^^^^     STATE: ^^
    NOTES:   ^^^^^^^^^^^^^^^^^^^^^^^^^^^^^^^^^^^^^^^^^^^^^^^^^^^^^^^^^^^




    MBRADD————————Attribute—————————————————Row:01-Col:01-Ins-Caps-Num-Scroll
    F1=help F2=attribute-on/off F3=map-definition F4=unused F5=unused F6=clear
    F7=delete-line F8=insert-line F9=attribute-palette
(                                                                  )
 ‾‾‾‾‾‾‾‾‾‾‾‾‾‾‾‾‾‾‾‾‾‾‾‾‾‾‾‾‾‾‾‾‾‾‾‾‾‾‾‾‾‾‾‾‾‾‾‾‾‾‾‾‾‾‾‾‾‾‾‾‾‾‾‾‾‾
```

Figure C.8.   BMS Alternate edit submenu.

This menu supports functions to modify attributes of a screen:

- [F2] *attribute-on-off*—Toggles on or off the use of attributes.
- [F3] *map-definition*—Used to define MAP data, invokes the field definition submenu.
- [F4] *unused*
- [F5] *unused*
- [F6] *clear*—Clear out existing changes.
- [F7] *delete-line*—Delete the line that the cursor is currently located on.
- [F8] *insert-line*—Inserts a blank line onto the screen at the current cursor position. Cannot insert:
    Into a group
    A line on the screen that forces an existing data line to roll off the bottom of the screen.
- [F9] *attribute-palette*—Provides a list of attributes to select from.

BMS Ctrl Submenu

The BMS main edit menu provides an additional submenu accessed by pressing the *Ctrl key* (see Figure C.9).

This menu supports function to modify characters and attributes of a screen:

- [*F2*] *unused*
- [*F3*] *unused*
- [*F4*] *unused*
- [*F5*] *select-char (@/064/40H)*—Select one of the characters and display it at the current cursor location.
- [*F6*] *draw*—Access to the DRAW submenu for drawing informational pictures inside the source file for program clarity.
- [*F7*] *read-char*—Select a character at the current cursor location and move to the prompt line.
- [*F8*] *read-attr*—Select the attribute where the cursor is cur-

```
 —                                                         DATE: ^^^^^^^^
                                                           TIME: ^^^^^^^^
                              ADD MEMBERS

      MEMBER NUMBER: ^^^^

      LAST NAME: ^^^^^^^^^^^^^^^^

      FIRST NAME: ^^^^^^^^^^^^^

      STREET: ^^^^^^^^^^^^^^^^^

      CITY: ^^^^^^^^^^^^        STATE: ^^
      NOTES:  ^^^^^^^^^^^^^^^^^^^^^^^^^^^^^^^^^^^^^^^^^^^^^^^^^^^^^^^^^^^^^



 MBRADD————————Attribute————————————————Row: 01-Col: 01-Ins-Caps-Num-Scroll
 F1=help F2=unused F3=unused F4=unused F5=select-char (@/064/40h) F6=draw
 F7=read-char F8=read-attr F9=delete-field-defn F10=delete-occurs-defn
```

Figure C.9.   BMS Ctrl edit submenu.

rently located and the attribute will be displayed on the status line.

- [*F9*] *delete-field-defn*—Delete the field that the cursor is currently located on.
- [*F10*] *delete-occurs-defn*—Deletes the definition of the occurs field that the cursor is currently located on; field reverts back to the original field (one entry).

SUMMARY

The command line driven BMS editor is available for programmers as an alternative edit path. Quite often, the screen painter is the simpler route to select for editing BMS files.

Index